IMPROVING
IN-SERVICE EDUCATION

EDITED BY **louis j. rubin**

DEAN, NOVA UNIVERSITY

IMPROVING
IN-SERVICE EDUCATION:
Proposals and procedures for change

ALLYN AND BACON, INC.

BOSTON, MASSACHUSETTS

Theodore Lownik Library
Illinois Benedictine College
Lisle, Illinois 60532

Copyright © 1971
by Allyn and Bacon, Inc.,
470 Atlantic Avenue, Boston.
All rights reserved. No part of the material
protected by this copyright notice may be reproduced
or utilized in any form or by any means, electronic or mechanical,
including photocopying, recording, or by any informational
storage and retrieval system, without written
permission from the copyright owner.

Library of Congress Catalog Card Number: 77–143253

Printed in the United States of America

Second printing . . . August, 1972

*Much of the work reported in these essays
was made possible by a grant from the Ford Foundation.
The Foundation's support is gratefully acknowledged.*

371
.146
R896i

CONTRIBUTORS

DWIGHT W. ALLEN
The University of Massachusetts

ROBERT N. BUSH
Stanford University

MARIO FANTINI
The Ford Foundation

LOUIS FISCHER
The University of Massachusetts

ABRAHAM S. FISCHLER
Nova University

ROBERT FOX
The University of Michigan

PHILIP W. JACKSON
The University of Chicago

RONALD LIPPITT
The University of Michigan

EDWARD J. MEADE, JR.
The Ford Foundation

LOUIS J. RUBIN
Nova University

HERBERT A. THELEN
The University of Chicago

RALPH W. TYLER
Director Emeritus, Center for Advanced Study in the Behavioral Sciences

CONTENTS

PREFACE

This book is about the continuing education of teachers. It was written with several specific audiences in mind. First, it offers all those who supervise teachers—whether in the college and university or the public school—an overview of the problems of teacher professional growth. Second, it provides the school principal, the designated instructional leader, with an understanding of the organizational conditions that are prerequisite to the professional development of his staff. Third, it gives curriculum workers a deeper insight into the connections between a course of study or a program of instruction and the human teacher who translates their ideas into reality.

The heart of the volume is embodied in a series of eleven chapters written by some of the most distinguished minds in American education. Each of these chapters treats a different facet of teacher professional growth. Each, in its own way, describes the margin between what now is and what could be. Beyond this, however, an effort has been made to give the book a utility that goes beyond the usual collection of disjointed essays. In the commentary after each chapter, the reader will find a series of practical implications for educational workers in the field. The theoretical ideas that constitute the heart have been extended into the bone and muscle of practical application.

As in so many other aspects of the educational process, our knowledge of the subject is incomplete. As a consequence there are places in which the writers disagree. Here, the accompanying recommendations are set forth as potential options. There are many other points, however, on which there is relatively strong agreement. As a result, the consequent recommendations are treated somewhat more dogmatically. But in either instance the message of the writing is clear: the on-going professional growth of the teaching profession is of crucial importance. Historically, the matter has been treated either cavalierly or not at all. The need for experimentation, therefore, and for a rigorous effort to learn from trial and error is very great. If the volume does no more than inspire its readers to seek a better way, it will have served its purpose.

L. J. R

IMPROVING
IN-SERVICE EDUCATION

part I

THE CHANGING TIMES

Much has been written in the recent past about the need for a new approach to schooling. It is not just the radicals who are concerned; even conservative observers—scholars who have followed the evolution of the schools for two and three decades—are aware of the alterations made necessary by the age that is dawning.

In the four chapters that follow, Tyler, Jackson, Bush, and Thelen discuss what may be the most significant of the required readjustments: the need to overcome whatever is defective and obsolete in teaching. There are, of course, many facets to the reform: educational technology will soon come into its own; the irrelevance of subject matter is being countered by extending the classroom outward into the real world; we are beginning to acknowledge that since children learn in different ways and at different rates, there must be alternative programs of instruction; and, importantly, major renovations in the curriculum are underway. In the last analysis, however, the value of each of these disparate efforts to improve education will depend upon the quality of the teaching that takes place.

3

What is crucial, therefore, is that we anticipate what lies ahead and begin now to make the necessary preparations. The professional development of the teacher now in service seems to be a central element in this preparation. While, admittedly, much remains to be done in the way of bettering the pre-service training of teachers, it is the teacher already in the school who must serve as the agent of reform. Since practitioners rarely adapt instantly to an innovation, the evolution of teaching must go hand in hand with new developments in the process of education.

Thus, the need for continual professional growth represents a common thread that unifies the fabric of the first section. The major themes are easily recognizable: we must devise a workable system for improving teaching practice; the system must allow for the vast range of individuality among teachers; it must increase rather than decrease the instructional options available; and, above all, it must assist the teacher to clarify long-standing personal perceptions of self, school, and society.

As Jackson points out, the roads to salvation are many, and there is no universal solution. A mounting stockpile of research evidence suggests that all teachers cannot use the same techniques with equal success. In addition, the assets and liabilities of individual teachers vary greatly. It is for this reason, if for no other, that teachers must become self-evolving. In teaching, as in other human endeavors, understanding, desire, and persistence of effort usually are rooted more strongly in the person than in the organization.

ralph w. tyler

CHAPTER ONE

IN-SERVICE EDUCATION
OF TEACHERS:
A look at the past and future

The world changes so rapidly that we are likely to think of the
past as totally different. Hence, it is useful from time to time to
examine the development over the years of institutions, issues,
and problems, to perceive again that they do not spring from
nowhere but have been emerging and progressing for some time.
The task of this paper is to furnish a reminder of how in-service
education of teachers has developed and to make somewhat
hazardous projections regarding the future.

Where to begin? How to make this rapid review?

Perhaps a period 120 to 130 years ago will serve as a bench
mark. At that time, in our commitment to universal elementary
education, we employed thousands of teachers who had little or
no preparation. Indeed, many of them had not even the benefit
of high school education. For example, my grandfather came to
Fort Wayne, Indiana, from New England in 1857 and assumed

the principalship of an elementary school. Neither he nor any of
the teachers in the school had any training specifically related to
teaching or to elementary education. They were given much
advice by influential laymen in the community about how to
maintain order in the school, how to develop obedience, and how
to administer corporal punishment so that a whipping would
bring pain but not injury to the child. Most laymen in those days,
however, did not consider themselves sufficiently competent to
advise on how to teach children reading, writing, and "ciphering,"
as arithmetic was then referred to. These matters teachers had to
learn in other ways. Typically in the 1850s and '60s and '70s, they
depended upon institutes of two or three days' duration and short
courses in the evening to furnish in-service education.

The purpose of these institutes was primarily to enable
teachers to bridge the gap between what they were expected to
know and do and what were in fact their level of knowledge and
their teaching competencies; that is, in-service education of that
time was largely remedial. The institutes usually included a
review of the "common branches," arithmetic, spelling, geography, and history, with comments on points of difficulty, a
statement of principles of discipline, and recommended approaches to the teaching of reading, writing, and numbers. In
that period, school singing had become popular both with pupils
and with adults. The program of school "box suppers" that
brought the community close to the school included a good deal
of singing in which all in attendance, young and old, were
expected to join. Evening singing schools were established in
many frontier communities to teach adults generally and
teachers, in particular, the rudiments of singing.

CONCEPT OF CONTINUOUS DEVELOPMENT

In the midperiod of the nineteenth century, the idea that the
curriculum and teaching procedures should be in continuous
development was not commonly accepted. The technological and
social changes in those days were proceeding less rapidly than
now, and school learning was considered desirable but not neces-

sary for an individual's survival. Some pupils, it was thought, had little capacity for book learning and after a brief exposure would leave school to go to work. How to educate those who dropped out was not perceived as a meaningful question. Problems of this sort, now major concerns of current in-service education programs, serve to illustrate the contemporary outlook that teaching is a changing and developing task.

Although a century ago the curriculum and teaching were viewed as relatively stable, this did not mean that in-service education was offered only to those beginning their teaching careers. The ideal teacher at that time was thought to be one who was always gaining new understanding of the old content, and new skills in carrying on his work. Like a master artisan in the jeweler's shop, the ideal teacher would continue to study and learn so that every day he was becoming a greater master of the art of teaching. From the reports of the teachers' institutes of that period, veteran teachers showed greater interest in learning a new approach to a task like teaching decimal fractions than did beginners.

The Land Grant College Act of 1862, although given no significant attention at that time by leaders of elementary and secondary education, was the forerunner of the idea that American educational institutions should be expected to respond to the realities of social change. By 1860 the "agricultural and mechanical classes" had become an important and influential part of the American community. Their children rarely were enrolled in the colleges of the day, which required training in Latin and Greek for admission and which offered no programs of instructions that would have been relevant to the needs of students from this lower middle class background. The failure of the existing colleges to give attention to the needs of these new members of the middle class led to pressure on the Congress that eventually resulted in the Morrill Act. This act offered each state United States public land to help support the establishment of a college to serve the agricultural and mechanical classes.

The problems these new land grant colleges faced in meeting their mandate were difficult, but their undoubted success gave powerful support to the development of the doctrine that education must and can change to meet the changing needs of a modern society. New students can be served, new knowledge can be developed into meaningful and useful educational content, new means of learning can be devised, and new uses for learning can be developed. These views are in sharp contrast to the earlier philosophy about education for teachers in service.

SUMMER—THE SEASON FOR LEARNING

From 1880 until the First World War, the summer courses in the normal schools were strategically the most important agencies of in-service education in America. For example, my father had been teaching for several years in the rural schools of Nebraska. He had attended the various teachers' institutes held in the county, but his great goal was to save enough money to go to the Fort Scott Kansas Normal School for a summer term. This he did in 1888, and he reported how exciting an experience it was to be hundreds of miles from home, to hear great experts on teaching, and to talk far into the night with other teachers about their problems, their views, and their special insights and skills. When talking to me about this summer session thirty years later, he still recalled the excitement of recognizing new moral ideas in some of the selections in the upper grade readers, of getting a new approach to teaching poetry, of learning simple ways to analyze grammatically and diagram a complex sentence, and of discovering how to make the method of extracting square root sensible to a farm boy or girl. The summer programs in the normal schools were more cosmopolitan than the county teachers' institutes, and they brought a wider range of specialists with more training, but they still gave primary emphasis to the acquisition of knowledge and skills thought to be important in teaching. The traditional notion of content persisted, as did the view that only certain students are proper candidates for public education.

The very heavy immigration into the United States from Europe from 1870 until the First World War brought to attention new problems for the American schools. Children enrolled who spoke no English in the home or in the local community. Children came to school with attitudes, habits, and values different from those which had been taken for granted by the schools in the past. I went to a school in Nebraska in which only one-fourth of the children spoke English in the home. The majority of my classmates were themselves born in Eastern Europe, or their parents had been born there. Almost every day I found that things I took for granted were challenged by most of my classmates: for example, knowing certain proverbs and folk tales, believing that drinking alcoholic beverages was evil, and treating girls with the same or more consideration than boys. This change forced many teachers to re-examine the assumptions upon which their practices had been based, and it stimulated the addition of new topics for consideration in in-service training programs.

In this period, too, the ideas of Darwin and of other modern scientists were influencing some educators to look more carefully at the teaching-learning situation and to try new ideas in the classroom. John Dewey was profoundly influenced by the spirit and contributions of science. His *School and Society* made a great impression upon the more venturesome writers and speakers at institutes and in summer schools. Francis W. Parker, first in Quincy, Massachusetts, and then in Chicago, developed a large following as he sought to change the schools from institutions that "imprison man in the cells of custom" to those that "free the human spirit" and aid man in developing his own potential. The enrollment in summer sessions at the Cook County Normal reached its peak during the short time Colonel Parker was there.

Frederick Burke at the San Francisco Normal not only lectured on the extent of individual differences among pupils but also developed a plan in the demonstration school, including a curriculum and a set of procedures for individualizing instruction. Through his work in in-service programs there, he stimulated Carleton Washburne, Helen Parkhurst, and Willard Beaty to develop programs of individualized instruction in Winnetka and in the Dalton schools.

These are only a few illustrations of the wave of new ideas being presented in in-service programs in the normal schools at the turn of the century. Sheldon at Oswego was influential in spreading Herbart's views and in developing a United States modification that guided many teachers in their planning. Montessori's methods were being presented in more than a score of institutions. The Sloyd conception of manual training as an integrated part of cognitive learning was imported from Sweden, and its exposition and demonstration in summer schools led to the adoption of manual training as a required course in several states. This was a period of questioning, promotion of new ideas, recognition of new educational problems, and introduction of new subjects into the curriculum, such as hygiene, civics, and vocational education. The in-service education programs of institutes and summer sessions were the chief means for helping teachers to deal with the changes that were proposed.

EMERGENCE OF QUANTITATIVE STANDARDS

After the First World War and until the Great Depression of the 1930s, in-service education was greatly affected by the establishment of quantitative standards for teaching certificates. At that time educators believed that major improvement in the quality of teaching in the American public schools could be brought about by requiring all teachers to have a bachelor's degree. When the drive to implement this view began, over half of the teachers could show on their credentials only the equivalent of two years of college. Hence, to attain the goal of a bachelor's degree for all required a tremendous investment in in-service courses that would count on the credentials toward the bachelor's degree. Hence, from 1918 until fifteen or twenty years later, in-service programs were not aimed primarily at helping teachers meet new problems but rather at filling gaps in college degree requirements. This had a deleterious effect both on the institutions and on the teachers enrolled. Instead of planning for summer courses that were new and exciting to the professors who offered them, colleges and universities sought to identify and offer old courses that teachers had not taken previously. The teachers came, not with the purpose of getting new insight, understanding, and competence, but rather with the purpose of getting certificates renewed by patching up their backgrounds.

The Great Depression brought new problems to the schools

and added new tasks for in-service education. With a sharp re-
duction in economic activity came a high level of unemployment.
Young people could no longer drop out of school and get jobs.
The proportion of youth enrolled in American high schools rose
to more than eighty per cent and included a considerable fraction
who did not plan to attend college and who found the high school
curriculum irrelevant to their purposes and out of touch with
contemporary society. The lack of interest in school, the low
morale, and the negative motivation toward school achievement
on the part of a considerable proportion of high school students
stimulated educational leaders to re-examine the high school
curriculum and procedures and to try out new ideas.

The Eight-Year Study begun in 1933 involved thirty school
systems which, under an agreement with the colleges and universities, were made responsible for developing and implementing
new educational programs designed to reach all high school
students. Shortly thereafter, a similar arrangement was established for selected southern high schools, and this was followed
by a state-wide program of secondary school curriculum development in Michigan. By 1939, colleges of teacher education became
involved in pre-service and in-service education focused on the
new educational programs of the schools. The American Council
on Education established the Commission on Teacher Education
and aided a selected group of colleges and universities to develop
new programs of teacher education and new ways of working
with schools and teachers.

The differentiating characteristics of in-service education
during the period arose from the primary concern of developing
curricula and educational procedures that would better serve
youth under the conditions of the day. This involved new
approaches to curriculum building, the identification of new content, the development of new instructional materials, the discovery of new teaching-learning procedures, and the education of
teachers to understand and to conduct new programs effectively.
In connection with the Eight-Year Study, a commission on the
curriculum was established, which in turn set up (1) a committee on the study of adolescents, to gain understanding of the
needs of youth, (2) committees on language, literature, mathe-

matics, science, social science, and the arts, to identify in these subjects content of potential significance to adolescence, and (3) a group concerned particularly with the formulation of educational theory and construction of materials relevant to the adolescent's development in his human relations.

These activities were exciting and afforded new insights into the role of education in the development of youth and in the maintenance and improvement of modern society. However, the initial efforts of the schools to implement some of the proposals showed clearly that it is impossible to do new things in schools when teachers do not understand the needs for new things, or the bases of the new proposals, or the ways in which new ideas can be effectively employed. I was Director of the Evaluation Staff of the Eight-Year Study and was able to arrange with Ohio State University, where I was a faculty member, to bring four teachers from each of the thirty schools to the campus of the university to spend six weeks in the summer of 1936. Here the teachers actually worked on the development of instructional resource units and the devices to evaluate these curriculum elements. This period of intensive work proved very helpful in putting new ideas into practice in the schools and in affording a means for the education of teachers. This was the first workshop. Thereafter, until the end of the project, several workshops were held by the Eight-Year Study each summer. The other major curriculum projects also established workshops as a primary instrument for the in-service education of teachers. Mention of the names of a few of the teachers involved in the workshops of the Eight-Year Study provides some indication of the effects of these workshops. Names that readily come to mind are Hilda Taba, Lavone Hanna, Lee Cronbach, Herbert Thelen, Chester Harris, and William Menge.

CONSTRUCTIVE INVOLVEMENT OF TEACHERS

At that time, most of us viewed the teacher education activities of these curriculum studies as necessary ancillary tasks, and we thought that the chief contributions were the new curricula developed, the new ideas such as the core curriculum, the new approaches to the subject fields, and the new achievement-testing theories. We were wrong. When ideas and materials are reified, they are likely to become the ends rather than the means. Every institution is subject to an ossification that arises when it becomes enamored with its program and finds itself seeking clients to fit the program rather than continually focusing on its clientele and their needs. Thus, in the Eight-Year Study many saw its contribution to be the core curriculum, or some course or set of materials developed in the project. They were deeply disappointed when these were no longer widely used. We now see that the most significant contribution of the Eight-Year Study was the education it provided in problem-solving, in developing attitudes and skills of educational inquiry. We learned something of great importance to in-service education of teachers: that the constructive involvement of teachers in attacking real educational problems that they face is a powerful instrument of continuing education.

The Second World War, followed by a sharp increase in the birth rate, created conditions in which there was an acute shortage of teachers. In-service education during this period largely offered courses that would enable teachers to fill the gaps in meeting certification requirements. For the past ten years, the national curriculum projects like the PSSC and BSSC, the problems of school desegregation, and the efforts to educate disadvantaged children have again focused in-service teacher education on the development of understanding and skills required to implement these national efforts.

THE PAST IS PROLOGUE

As we look at the present against the background of 125 years of in-service education, we can make a few generalizations. Much less attention is given today than in earlier times to remedying gross deficiencies in the pre-service preparation of teachers. In-service education is still viewed by many teachers as a means of increasing communication and reducing the sense of loneliness and isolation that is prevalent in an occupation in which contact with other adults is limited. In-service education is still a major way of achieving social mobility in the educational profession, not only by acquiring paper credentials that are necessary for more responsible positions and higher salaries, but also by gaining wider visibility in the professional world. In-service education continues to be one avenue by which an individual teacher's personal interests and needs can be served. Actually, the only new major purpose of in-service education since 1930 is to aid the school in implementing new educational programs by helping teachers acquire understanding, skills, and attitudes essential to the roles they are to play in the new programs.

Most of my discussion has referred to the past, yet I am asked also to take a look at the future. I can only venture a few comments about what may lie ahead. From the changes that have recently taken place, I predict that in-service education of tomorrow will place great emphasis upon helping teachers acquire what is perceived by school leaders to be essential to the implementation of the plans of the school system. The in-service education program will also be expected to help gain wide participation in evolving and revising these plans.

In-service training of the future will deal with real problems in the system both directly and by simulation. The training program will build in feedback as teachers work on problems, so that a basis for correction and revision is available. To illustrate real problems that will represent content for these in-service programs, I suggest the following: the education of disadvantaged children, new curricula for high school and college that better reflect the changing problems of society and are more relevant to the interests and abilities of students, the adaptation of work experience to school education, content and structures to involve older and younger pupils together in significant learning activities, and utilization of new technologies to aid effective learning. New tasks for the school will generate new problems to be dealt with in in-service programs. The acceptance of new tasks will generally result from pressures from without the system rather than from reforms instituted internally. This has been true in the past as with the land grant colleges, the high school curriculum revisions of the depression years, and the concern with the disadvantaged.

In-service training of the future will not be limited to college and university campuses or to school buildings but will be carried on in a variety of settings related to the problems and the resources to be dealt with. For example, some will be carried on in welfare agencies and other slum settings, some in factories or other work environments, some in laboratories, some in camps, parks, or other recreation spots, some in communication centers, and some will be quasi internships in political and social organizations.

In-service education of the future will not be seen as "shaping" teachers but rather will be viewed as aiding, supporting, and encouraging each teacher's development of teaching capabilities that he values and seeks to enhance. The guiding and pervasive spirit will be one in which learning itself is of primary importance. The learning experiences in these programs will furnish ample illustrations of role models to guide teachers as they are involved in studying problems and resources, setting goals for group and individual efforts, developing plans for attaining goals, appraising progress toward the goals, and re-examining and replanning when the appraisal indicates inadequacies.

These are tremendously dynamic possibilities for future developments in in-service education of teachers. They are not wildly utopian but are reasonable projections of past experience.

■ CLUES TO ACTION

Fittingly, at the very outset Tyler poses a central issue—who shall determine the substance of activities that contribute to the continuing education of teachers in service? The issue will arise repeatedly throughout the volume. Moreover, as the reader will perceive, it appears to be one on which wise men disagree. Jackson and Thelen, for example, in the chapters that follow, lean toward teacher self-determinism. Allen and Meade, on the other hand, favor a good deal more external direction. Tyler does not see the issue as paradoxical, suggesting that both the individual and the organization must play a part in determining needed professional growth.

In the period ahead we are likely to see a host of changes in the sum and substance of schooling: new kinds of instructional programs for disadvantaged children, a renewed emphasis upon education that occurs both in the classroom and in the world of work, greater individualization of the curriculum, and the introduction of a variety of technological apparatus with which to carry on instruction. Each will entail new requirements for the teacher. We therefore must anticipate these requirements and plan efficient procedures through which they can be met. Here the onus is on management and administration. For one thing, leadership is in the best position to anticipate these changes, and, for another, the organizational reform that improved opportunities for professional growth will require can be initiated only by school administrators.

But Tyler also believes it imperative to establish machinery through which the personal needs and interests of teachers can be satisfied. Assuming that the teacher has a strong desire to become as adept as possible in assisting the children to learn, it may be that in many instances his own estimate of his professional needs is more reliable than any other which can be made. Moreover, we have long known that a worker's morale is directly linked to his control over his own actions. Insofar as a teacher is likely to behave in accordance with his own perception of his role, we would do well, as Tyler implies, to respect his opinions. The critical task, obviously, is to assist the individual teacher to enhance the shrewdness of his judgments regarding his professional needs. It is in this connection that the supervising agent who works with the teacher must—in the fashion of a therapist—assist the teacher to clarify his own insights and perceptions. In Tyler's phrase: "In-service education of the future will not be seen as 'shaping' teachers but rather will be viewed as aiding, supporting, and encouraging."

Finally, Tyler distinguishes between professional growth based upon exposure to new ideas and materials and professional growth that is based upon the acquisition of new understandings and skills. If, indeed, we are to go beyond the walls of the classroom into the larger environment, if we are to go beyond books and pencils as the tools of learning, the need for teachers to form new points of view, to reach new understandings regarding the process of education, and to acquire new skills is inescapable.

■ OPERATIONAL IMPLICATIONS

1. In the period ahead we will see the introduction of new technological devices, the extension of the classroom to the resources of the community-at-large, and the emergence of new instructional materials and

methods. Each of these will demand special teaching skills. **We must capitalize upon the lead time remaining, identify these skills as soon as possible, and institute programs of professional growth which guarantee skill mastery.**

2. The improvement of teaching performance must be attacked with reasonable precision. **Principals, supervisors, and others who work with teachers in the area of skill development must acquire systematic procedures through which the diagnosis of teaching strengths and weaknesses can be accomplished.**

3. The teacher must participate in the governance of his own professional growth. **Those who serve as facilitating agents must themselves acquire the skills of collaborative interaction which permit them to work effectively with teachers.**

4. The improvement of teaching skills must become a routine aspect of professional life. **Teachers must be given time and other resources with which to assess their professional needs and to carry on improvement activities.**

philip w. jackson

CHAPTER TWO

OLD DOGS AND NEW TRICKS:
Observations on the
continuing education of
teachers

Any discussion of a topic as broad and amorphous as what to do with or for practicing teachers ought to begin, in my judgment, with a confession of ignorance. In addition to being good for the soul, such an admission clears the air of false expectations and thus helps to reduce the sense of disappointment so often aroused by our search for answers to educational questions. It is also in keeping, as you will see, with one of the ideas to be developed in my remarks.

I confess, therefore, at the outset that I do not know what should be done for teachers, in the way of further training, once they have completed an adequate program of professional preparation. Moreover, I am not even sure how much importance we should attach to the whole business of in-service training, at least as it has been conventionally defined. Any proposal aimed at improving the quality of teaching is naturally appealing to all who are interested in education; yet there is nothing self-evident about the relative superiority of plans for improving teaching through programs of in-service training. With the same goal in mind we might argue with equal fervor for upgrading the quality of pre-service education, for attracting more talented people into teaching, for weeding out the incompetent from among those who are already working in classrooms, for improving the materials of instruction, and so on. In-service training, in other words, is only one of many schemes to make teaching better. Whether it is the one on which we should pin our highest hopes and expend our major energies is a question I am not prepared to answer. For purposes of the present discussion, however, my ignorance, which I take to be shared by others, is not a great hindrance. All we need assume is that in-service training, as a strategy for improving education, is of sufficient merit to warrant further thought. Whether the money spent on such activities would have been better spent on a new rug for the teachers' lounge no one knows, nor can we wait to find out before trying to move ahead toward a fuller understanding of the various shapes and forms in-service programs might take.

The burden of my comments rests on a distinction between two ways of looking at what might be done to help teachers improve in their work. Each of these points of view is complex. Each comprises a set of assumptions about why anyone would want to get involved in in-service work, what methodological and administrative strategies hold the most promise, where the control of in-service activity should rest, and so on. These two perspectives arise, fundamentally, from differing conceptions of what teaching is all about. When describing them now I shall undoubtedly err in the direction of oversimplification and I shall also likely exaggerate the differences between them. As we all know, the black and white dichotomies that serve us so well in our discussions and debates have a way of becoming various shades of gray when we search for them in the real world. I offer, therefore, a caricature of reality, a quickly drawn sketch in which some features are deliberately made bigger than life and others smaller.

Finally, before plunging ahead I must state that I do not feel

equally sympathetic toward the two points of view I shall describe. In fact, I have a definite preference, which soon will be
obvious, thus adding yet another source of distortion to those
created by brevity and the exaggerations of caricature. I am not
apologizing for taking sides, but since I intend to do so, it seemed
fair to warn the reader.

THE "DEFECT" POINT OF VIEW

The first of the two perspectives from which the business of
in-service training might be viewed is found in the notions of
repair and remediation. For this reason I have chosen to call it
the "defect" point of view. It begins with the assumption that
something is wrong with the way practicing teachers now operate
and the purpose of in-service training is to set them straight—to
repair their defects, so to speak.

And what exactly are these defects? The most common one,
it seems, is ignorance, arising from a lack of exposure to the latest
developments of instructional techniques. Many teachers, so the
proponents of this point of view would have us believe, have
simply not kept up with what is going on in education. They do
not know CIA from CAI or i.t.a. from IPI. They don't know what
behavioral objectives are, much less how to write them. The
mention of micro-teaching in their presence receives a blank look,
as does interaction analysis. They associate discovery learning
with John Dewey rather than with Jerome Bruner. In short, they
are not "with it." They suffer from one of the most feared conditions in our society: premature obsolescence.

This condition is usually thought to have one of two causes.
Either the teacher has been away from formal training for a long
time (he is, in effect, an old dog who has not yet been taught the
new tricks of the trade), or, if his training has been more recent
and he still seems to be out-of-date, he obviously must have gone
to the wrong school. Those who are in the old dog category and
who have not kept up with recent developments on their own are
also vulnerable to the charge of being professionally lazy. But
whatever the explanation of the condition, its status as a defect

remains. Moreover, it is a defect of which the affected person is assumed to be unaware (otherwise, the question arises as to why he hasn't done something about it). It is, further, a defect that is not shared by everyone else, particularly not by the person who identifies it and suggests a remedy.

At the heart of the defect conception of in-service training is the belief that education is a rapidly developing field in which old ways of doing things are constantly being replaced by new and better ways. This belief is reflected in the salience and high prestige accorded the research worker in education. Teachers and administrators, at their annual conventions and in their trade journals, are constantly being informed of what research *now* says about how to teach reading or how to manage classroom discipline or how to group for maximum achievement, as if today's answers to these questions are likely to be quite different from yesterday's. This belief is flattering to all of us who work in education because it implies that we are members of a wide-awake profession that is constantly on its toes trying to do its job better, and also because it implies that our work is an exciting affair in which change and discovery are commonplace. Rapid progress, as we all know, is a mark of some of the most prestigious branches of science. Small wonder, therefore, that we educators look on with slight envy at the happy plight of our friends in medicine and biochemistry, and are somewhat slow to correct the impression that our educational know-how is growing by leaps and bounds.

Yet, if we want to think sensibly about the alternative forms our in-service programs might take, it is necessary to ask whether the progress of knowledge in our field is real or apparent. Would a teacher's skills really become obsolete quickly if he allowed his subscriptions to professional journals to expire, or failed to attend the summer workshop at his state university? In other words, is the necessity of keeping up-to-date the strongest argument that can be made in support of in-service training? I believe not. Even though our dignity as professionals may suffer a bit by the admission, I believe we, as educators, must face the fact that we are not overwhelmed by new discoveries calling for instant communication to workers in the field. Indeed, except for the teachers of subjects that are themselves undergoing rapid change, such as some of the sciences, the goal of keeping up-to-date in education is about as important as wearing a skirt of the proper length or correctly flared bell-bottom trousers—fun to do, perhaps, but of no great consequence. This is not a popular opinion, I know, and therefore I feel compelled to say more about my reasons for holding it.

Consider the following hypothetical situation. Suppose you are the principal of an elementary school in the suburbs and you are seeking to hire a fourth grade teacher to replace a member of your staff who is retiring. Among the applicants is a forty-four-year-old man who had four years of teaching experience in the fourth grade prior to service in the Korean War, after which he decided to become an insurance salesman, a job at which he has worked for the past fifteen years. Although he was moderately successful in the insurance business (earning more than you are prepared to pay him as a teacher), he has come to realize, he tells you, that teaching is a more challenging and rewarding occupation than selling family insurance to suburban home owners and now, at forty-four, he would like to return to the classroom. He goes on to explain that although he has not tried to keep up with developments in education, he is an avid reader of the *New York Review of Books* and the *Saturday Review*. In this way he claims to have remained aware of some of the names and ideas that have sparked educational controversy in recent years.

An examination of his academic and employment records reveals that he graduated with a B+ average from a college of education at a nearby state university. His supervisor and critic teacher wrote glowing accounts of his practice teaching; the principal under whom he worked for four years was equally generous in his praise. His former principal also indicated a willingness to keep a place for the applicant upon his return from military service. Assuming that all the information I have given you is correct and that further investigation reveals nothing contradictory, would you be tempted to hire this man? I suspect you would.

Now what about the fact that he has had no formal contact with teaching for at least fifteen years? How far behind his freshly trained colleagues will that lapse of contact with the world of education place him? The answer, I fear, is: "not far." His out-of-date-ness will probably not be noticeable. In fact, if he really has kept up with the *New York Review of Books* and the *Saturday Review,* he may even be more *au courant* about the latest developments in education than are most of the people with whom he will share the teachers' lounge.

If this hypothetical case does not strike you as too far-fetched, and I have tried to keep it within the bounds of belief, it should help to explain my contention that keeping up-to-date is not of paramount importance for most teachers. Although the old-timer may feel ill at ease when his student teacher talks about the new "romantic critics of education," or some other topic that is the latest rage back on the campus, he need not worry that his way of working with children has suddenly become passé without his knowing it.

The most dramatic educational change in this century, at least insofar as teaching methodology is concerned, has doubtlessly been occasioned by the rise and decline (perhaps *temporary* decline) of the progressive movement. It is this change that has accounted for what historian Lawrence Cremin has aptly called "the transformation of the American schools." No one passing through a teacher training program during the past forty years in this country could possibly have avoided being exposed to the tenets and practices associated with the progressive movement. Indeed, the teacher has hardly been exposed to much else, for nothing of great consequence seems to have happened since the heyday of progressivism. If we accept this judgment, and I think it would be difficult to disprove, educators seeking a justification for the establishment of in-service programs would do well to give up basing their appeal on the teacher's need to keep in style. This year's model may look shinier than last year's, but strip away the chrome fixtures, turn off the ad man's banter, and the difference is insignificant.

Closely associated with the defect approach to in-service

training, though not logically necessitated by it, is the tendency to focus on the behavioral aspects of teaching—its skill components —with a consequent neglect of understanding and belief. The practice of limiting one's conception of teaching to what happens when teacher and students are confronting each other is also a part of this same tendency. The ability to plan ahead, to make decisions about the choice of materials and activities, to ponder the consequences of alternative actions, is not usually introduced into the discussion by scholars focusing on the interactional aspects of the teacher's work. A videotaped record of a teacher absorbed in thought after the kids have gone home is hardly the thing on which to try out the latest observational scheme.

Thus, for reasons that are not immediately obvious, persons who espouse the defect view of in-service education typically, though not always, are behaviorally oriented and tend to emphasize the more molecular aspects of the teacher's work. Their goal seems to be that of equipping teachers with specific skills—teaching them how-to-do-it.

Perhaps this brief description is sufficient to convey an impression of what is meant by the defect approach to in-service training. It begins with a judgment of weakness, usually diagnosed by an outsider, and proceeds to suggest a remedy for correcting that weakness, usually through a training program designed to change specific aspects of the teacher's behavior in the classroom. Because of its prescriptive emphasis, it commonly reduces the range of a teacher's choice and de-emphasizes the rationality behind his actions. He is exhorted to behave in accordance with the model presented to him because that is what research or the experts or some other vaguely identified authority says should be done. Permeating this view is the notion that someone knows more about how the teacher should behave in his classroom than he does himself. In many ways the defect position partakes of one of the most enduring of all conceptions of the educational process. It is the one in which the student is seen as essentially helpless and the teacher as omniscient; only in this case the teacher himself is in the role of the student and his all-knowing guide is the designer of the in-service program.

THE "GROWTH" APPROACH: A CONTRAST

The point of view I now would like to contrast with the one just described begins with the assumption that teaching is a complex and multifaceted activity about which there is more to know than can ever be known by any one person. From this point of view the motive for learning more about teaching is not to repair a personal inadequacy as a teacher but to seek greater fulfillment as a practitioner of the art. Consequently, I have chosen to call this point of view the "growth" approach to in-service training. I realize that *growth* is a "good" word and *defect* a "bad" one, the first implying health, and the second sickness. Doubtlessly it would probably have been better to have avoided this word bias by choosing descriptive labels that did not have such highly evaluative overtones. Yet if we remember that proponents of the defect point of view are really out to do good, as they see it, the negative connotations of the word itself can be partially overcome. Actually, there is also some value in keeping the concepts of health and sickness in mind as we think about in-service training, for at the heart of the topic is the question of whether the majority of teachers are really suffering from an ailment requiring emergency treatment or whether, like the children with whom they work, they simply have a lot more growing to do. Our choice of either the health or the sickness metaphor has profound implications for the way in which we, the outside "experts" and consultants, might function in in-service work. If, on the one hand, the patient is really sick, the need for professional help is obvious. If, on the other hand, the task is to facilitate normal development, the role of the outside expert becomes much more ambiguous.

If we think seriously about how professional growth might take place during in-service training, we soon become aware of the arbitrariness of our common definition of teacher. Obviously, when we pause to consider it, there is no specific time at which a person stops being a nonteacher and becomes a teacher, any more than there is a specific time at which he stops being a child and becomes an adult. Both distinctions are purely legalistic. More-over, if we really took an honest look, I think we would have to admit that there is no defensible rationale for our certification procedures except on economic grounds and as a crude protection against putting our classrooms in the charge of grossly incompetent people. Why should pre-service training take four years on the average? Why not ten years or so, as in the case of surgeons? Why can't we train people to be teachers in three months, the way we prepared ninety-day wonders in our officer training units during World War II? The answer to these questions, strangely enough, has very little to do with what one has to know in order to teach, for there is no consensus on what those prerequisites should be. I am not trying to criticize present certification re-quirements and pre-service practices (though I think there is much about them that needs criticism), but only to point out that we have no meaningful definition of what a person must know or be able to do in order to be a teacher.

Not only is there no specific time at which a person becomes a teacher, but there is also no definable time at which a teacher stops becoming one. This is simply another way of saying that there is no such thing as the "complete" teacher. Though some people obviously know more about pedagogy than do others, those who know the most conform to no single model of perfection. In teaching, as in life, the roads to wisdom are many.

Before examining the implications of this point of view for the design of in-service programs, it is necessary to consider the possible sources of a teacher's knowledge about his work. I be-lieve anyone who thinks about it will have to admit that the single most important source is the act of teaching itself. Indeed, the acceptance of this fact is clearly reflected in the salary schedules of most school systems. The services of a teacher who has taught for two years are worth more, in cold cash, than are those of his colleague down the hall who has had only one year of experience and his services will continue to increase in worth during a large portion of his career. A teacher who did nothing but teach presumably would grow in his professional ability even if he never read a professional journal or attended a professional convention. Thus, from one point of view, the greatest contribution to in-service training is the experience of teaching itself.

Yet, as we all know, experience, though it may be the best teacher, is often insufficient to stimulate continued growth. To achieve that end we must not just *have* experience; we must *benefit* from it. This means we must reflect on what happens to us, ponder it, and make sense of it—a process that in turn requires a certain distancing from the immediate press of reality. As everyone who has been in charge of a classroom knows, it is very difficult to teach and to think about teaching at the same time. What is needed, therefore, is both the time and the tools for the teacher to conceptualize his experience, to imbue it with personal meaning in a way that alters his way of looking at his world and acting on it.

SOME IMPLICATIONS OF THE GROWTH APPROACH

These, then, are the central goals of in-service training from a growth perspective: to help the teacher become progressively more sensitive to what is happening in his classroom and to support his efforts to improve on what he is doing. Unfortunately for those of us who would like to know exactly how to proceed, there are many routes to these goals, and our choice from among these must be determined by the specific situation in which we and our teachers find ourselves. Thus, within two adjacent schools at any particular time the in-service activities might look quite different. In one school the staff might be engaged in almost as many separate activities as there are teachers; in the other they might have banded together to employ the services of an outside consultant in order to master a specific skill in which the majority are interested. One school may be launched on a program of several years' duration; the staff of the other may have to decide each month what to do next. The question of which school has the better in-service program is likely unanswerable. At best, the answer would require a careful examination of the specifics of each institution. Even then, given the situational complexities of each setting, it would probably be impossible to make a meaningful comparison.

But if the ways in which teachers might choose to grow are really as numerous as is here implied, what hope is there for those of us who hold to the growth perspective and who wish to make some statements about the future or the reform of in-service education? The answer, I believe, is twofold.

First, we can work to give teachers at all levels more time to think about what they are doing, and, second, we can try to alter the power structure in education so that teachers have more control over their own professional destinies and administrators have less. The establishment of these facilitating conditions is sure to create alarm and resistance from segments of both the lay and the professional public. Unfortunately, I see no way of avoiding this kind of discomfort. The planned improvement of teaching, if it is ever to occur (and I am not sure we are yet ready for it), is bound to cost great sums of money and is certain to weaken the power of entrenched authorities. I cannot see either happening without a struggle.

Anyone who has ever taught knows that teaching is a demanding task. People who measure the difficulty of a job by the amount of sweat on the worker's brow may find this fact hard to accept, but those of us who have been in charge of twenty-five or thirty children from 8:45 in the morning until 3:15 in the afternoon know how comforting it can be to see the last yellow bus pull out of the school driveway. The idea of then turning our attention to the serious business of trying to understand what happened to the students that day or of trying to prepare for tomorrow's classes is ridiculous; yet, at present, that is exactly what almost a million and a half classroom teachers are expected to do every day of the week.

I see absolutely no hope for the future of in-service education unless we are willing to pay for what we want. If we are going to pay more than lip service to the goal of helping teachers make sense of what they are doing, we must be prepared to face the fact that the costs of education could well double in the process. Teachers who now have twenty or thirty contact hours a week with their students should probably have half that many. In addition to cutting down—hopefully, cutting in half—the number of teaching hours per week, we also need to supply teachers with assistance to relieve them of many of the mundane and clerical duties associated with their work. If these goals, or ones close to them, are too unrealistic to contemplate, then I think we should stop kidding ourselves by holding conferences on the reform of in-service education and turn, instead, to the more manageable task of redesigning the cumulative folder or enlarging the hot lunch service.

Notice that I am not arguing that teachers should teach less because they are overworked. If anything, they are *underworked*. They are forced to do their job without putting their minds to it, without devoting the amount of hard thought to it that the task requires. As a result, they have no choice but to rely on ritualized and routine actions to carry them through the day. Whether they want to or not, they are forced to make heavy use of prepackaged and ready-made materials, as contrasted with ones specially designed for the students with whom they are working. It is much simpler, in many ways, to behave thoughtlessly than to ponder one's actions and make conscious decisions, simpler to be carried along by the press of reality than to pause and consider what to do next. Thinking, clear thinking, is by no means easy. In fact, it is probably just as difficult, if not more so, to spend an afternoon thinking about how we might do a better job of teaching as it is to make it through the same afternoon with a roomful of third graders. Therefore, if teachers were really given sufficient time to think about what they were doing, the overall severity of the demands made upon them likely would *in*crease, not *de*crease.

MAKING ROOM FOR CHANGE

If teachers are to grow in their jobs, they need more than time off from their regular classroom duties. They require an institutional climate that supports and encourages their efforts to learn more about what they are doing. And even this may not be enough, given the conservative and bureaucratic ethos that has come to dominate so many of our schools. The kind of professional inquiry we are talking about here has been absent for so long in most school systems that the seeds of it no longer exist, even in a dormant state, in the soil. It needs to be planted again, protected and nurtured again during the early phases of its growth, and made room for when it is healthy and robust enough to continue growing on its own. In short, thousands of teachers all over the country are badly in need of leadership, not just leadership of the kind that helps them get higher salaries or better janitorial services (although those things are needed, too), but the kind that will excite their intellectual curiosity, that will inspire—yes, I'm forced to use that old-fashioned word inspire—them to want to do their work better.

Each fall, across America, most teachers engage in an activity that has become as widespread an educational ritual in this country as the annual Thanksgiving Day football game. It goes under different names—orientation day, teacher's institute, or whatever—and is often described as part of the in-service training program. On the day in question, all the teachers in a school district file into the local high school auditorium to hear a few words of welcome from their superintendent and an "inspiring message" delivered by a visiting fireman from a nearby university. The speech is followed by the usual list of announcements, after which the teachers disperse to their separate schools to begin the messy but exciting business of unpacking books and chalk for the big event that is only a few hours off.

Usually there are several things wrong with these autumnal rites, beginning with the lamentable fact that the speaker is uncommonly dull and uninspiring and ending with the equally lamentable fact that in many school systems this is it, so far as in-service training is concerned. But the saddest fact of all, at least the one that always strikes me as saddest as I do my stint each fall, is that my hosts, the administrators of the system, had to import a stranger to add the inspirational note, to remind the teachers of the importance of the work ahead. Why, I wonder, don't the administrators themselves do the inspiring, if it has to be done? Are they incapable as public speakers? Would it embarrass them to speak words that are genuinely stirring? Or, worst thought of all, is it because they themselves are no longer animated by a spirit of intellectual curiosity about educational matters and, therefore, are unable to awaken that same spirit in others?

In educational circles we talk a lot—too much, I sometimes think—about the virtues of innovation, experimentation, creativity, and other processes that have the general effect of shaking things up. But I often wonder whether we are talking simply to make ourselves and our listeners feel good (like that September morning speaker in the high school auditorium) or whether we really mean it. I suspect we do not. As I travel about the country and as I look about the school in which I work, I am not at all impressed by the amount of genuine experimentation and serious thought about teaching that comes to my attention. Oh, there are isolated pockets of excitement and change, to be sure—a school here, a handful of teachers there—but these are by far the exceptions rather than the rule. This state of affairs, I contend, is due at least in part to the fact that we do not really mean what we say. We are like early adolescents who like to talk a lot about sex, but who are still a little too afraid of what might happen to really try it.

In-service education that derives its direction from the kind of problems teachers encounter in their classrooms—our so-called growth perspective—must allow for the possibility, even the likelihood, of dramatic change in the way our schools are run, or else it will degenerate into an uninspired tinkering to keep alive the illusion of an intellectual ferment whose bubbling has long ago stopped.

Remember our Korean veteran, the forty-four-year-old insurance salesman who decided to return to teaching? Remember we said that he probably wouldn't look much different from his freshly trained colleagues, despite his absence from teaching for fifteen years? The point being made at that time was that not very much has happened during that fifteen-year period for our returning teacher to catch up with. We concluded, therefore, that the defect view of in-service training, at least insofar as it is directed to the goal of keeping teachers up-to-date with the latest developments, is pretty much a waste of time. Now, how about the growth view of in-service training? How might our returnee have fared if he had had fifteen years in which to broaden and deepen his insights into teaching? The interesting and frustrating fact is that we might not be able to tell what that experience or lack of it had done to him. This absence of visible evidence generally drives practical-minded people, such as most school board members, mad. How can we afford the luxury of investing in programs that lack tangible evidence of their efficacy? This is the kind of question that people who are interested in cost benefit analysis keep bringing up, and I think we are going to have to confront it directly, sooner or later, whether we want to or not.

The answer, I believe, is that in education, as in many other domains of human endeavor, we must act on the basis of belief rather than knowledge. We must do what we believe is right rather than what we know will pay off. Those who feel uncomfortable about proceeding on such shaky grounds should consider the basis of most of our actions in education (and life in general, for that matter). Why, for example, should spelling or mathematics have the place it has in our present curriculum? Who says that school should be in session six hours a day, one hundred and eighty days a year? How do we know that the discovery method will produce a better crop of scientists than will the old-fashioned recitation method? The answer, of course, is that no one knows, nor is anyone likely to find out in the foreseeable future. Yet act we must; so we move ahead on the basis of what seems to be most reasonable, given our present state of ignorance. I do not see how we can insist that our in-service program rest on a firmer foundation of fact than is available for comparable programs in other spheres of educational activity.

Returning to our newly rehired teacher, we have no guarantee that he would be better off today, as a teacher, if he had acquired fifteen years of teaching experience coupled with a good in-service program; yet it is hard to believe that he would not be. Moreover, the question is not merely whether or not he would be a better teacher today but also how he might have affected the educational experience of the children who would have been his students. Our objective, in other words, is not to produce teachers who reach the peak of pedagogical wisdom on the eve of their retirement, but teachers whose actions at every stage of their development are as wise as possible. These will be people whose teaching style will change with the years not simply because their skills have become more polished, nor because they have kept in touch with what the latest research says about how to teach (though they may have done that, too), but because they have changed as people, because they see their world and themselves and their students and their subject matter differently than they did at other points in their career . . . because they have grown, not necessarily up, or out, or sideways, but in all directions.

These are heady words, I know, and I have no illusions about the extent to which they match present reality. Today many teachers, perhaps most, live out their careers in a most desultory manner, with one eye on the troublemaker in the back of the room and the other on the clock. This condition is not likely to change very rapidly. Yet, even though I lean toward a pessimistic view of the future, I find myself agreeing with Robert Schaefer, who, in his fascinating book *The School as a Center of Inquiry*, reminds us:

Given the deficiencies and omissions in training and the lack of support and assistance to be found in the schools, what is remarkable is not that so many teachers forget the excitement of learning, but that a heartening few somehow maintain vigorous scholarship and positive attitudes toward their pupils. This stubborn corps of those who retain a live curiosity and who continue to respond zestfully to the inherent fascinations of teaching provide a reassuring reminder of what the school might potentially be for other teachers and other students.[1]

It is what schools and teachers *might* be, rather than what they are, that helps us to preserve the small kernel of hope without which our efforts would be meaningless. Part of that vision of the possible includes, as Schaefer points out, a school whose teachers "retain a live curiosity and who continue to

[1] Robert J. Schaefer, *The School as a Center of Inquiry* (New York: Harper & Row, Publishers, 1967), p. 44.

respond zestfully to the inherent fascinations of teaching." Such an ideal staff, if it ever could be assembled, would hardly fit the description, even if made jocularly, of a bunch of old dogs who, periodically, had been taught new tricks. Nor would those teachers in turn be likely to conceptualize their own task as that of teaching old tricks to *new* dogs. Dogs and their training, it turns out, bear little resemblance to what goes on in the classroom. Thank goodness.

▪ CLUES TO ACTION

It has been said that the difference between training and education is that the former reduces the individual's range of alternatives and the latter increases it. We must have, Jackson warns, a complete teacher. If we try to reach this goal by identifying and correcting defects, or by updating the teacher's supply of information, or by merely substituting something new for something old, we shall fail. He argues that experience is not enough, for only those experiences which generate new meaning will make any real difference. "What is needed," he says, "is both the time and the tools for the teacher to conceptualize his experience, to imbue it with personal meaning in a way that alters his way of looking at his world and acting on it."

Significantly, Jackson joins with Tyler and Bush in arguing for individual autonomy in the means and ends of professional growth. Pointing out that the best clues to a teacher's needs lie in the teaching itself, he believes that continuing education activities should assist the teacher to understand the deeper subtleties of the events that go on in his classroom. New teaching methods are not necessarily better than old ones, and what is most advantageous can be determined only by a rational analysis of the particular conditions that exist. Put another way, the thoughtless acceptance of current fashion or the automatic rejection of any practice that is dated would constitute high irrationality.

Like Tyler, Jackson wants teachers to learn as their students should learn: through a self-directed encounter with meaningful problems. If we persist in designing in-service activities that are based upon our own notions of what is good for teachers, we shall defile the very principles that are at the core of the educational process. The teacher is not a helpless learner, and his own perception of what will enable him to function more effectively may serve as our most intelligent point of departure. Apart from its psychological validity, such an approach will circumvent the individual's resistance to external direction, and it will make him an active rather than a passive participant in the shaping of his own growth.

"The motive for learning more about teaching," Jackson writes, "is not to repair a personal inadequacy as a teacher but to seek greater fulfillment as a practitioner of the art." This statement gives rise to several clues regarding the direction in-service education must take. It suggests, for example, that successful teaching stems from the teacher's desire for self-fulfillment rather than from his mastery of a collection of techniques. Further, it suggests that we would do better to help a teacher accomplish his aims more effectively than to focus on the correction of what we presume to be his weaknesses. And, above all, it suggests that professional growth has no end, that no teacher will ever reach the point where his growth is complete.

"In teaching, as in life," he states, "the roads to wisdom are many." With Bush, he fears the loss that will come from searching for the one best way. He is not opposed, obviously, to helping a teacher replace an inferior method with a superior one. Nor is he opposed to asking teachers to devote more of the energy of mind and body to their task. However, he wants teacher learning to occur in a different climate—a climate that nurtures mind and spirit as well as technique, and one that provides the psychological freedom to grow. In sum, facilitating the learning of teachers—as in facilitating the learning of children—is a matter of openness rather than one of closedness.

■ OPERATIONAL IMPLICATIONS

1. Effective teaching is characterized by the ability to make rational choices through which means are adapted to ends. **Programs of continuing teacher education should increase the number of instructional options.**

2. To grow, a teacher must have knowledge of the consequences of his own work. **Programs of professional growth must provide the teacher with the time and tools necessary to conceptualize his experience, to reach insights that alter his perception of his role and his task.**

3. Professional growth should relate to life in the classroom. **The continuing education of the teacher should bear directly upon the problems he encounters in his work.**

robert n. bush

CHAPTER THREE

CURRICULUM-PROOF TEACHERS:
Who does what to whom

For the reform of teacher in-service education, which is the subject of this book, my prescription is simple: treat the teacher as a professionally competent person. To do so would right much that is wrong with education today. This is my thesis.

In the fall of 1963, I had just returned from a nine months' sabbatical leave, which I had spent studying the education of teachers in selected countries in Latin America, Africa, and the Middle East, behind the iron curtain in the Soviet Union and Yugoslavia, and in Eastern Europe. Everywhere I went I had found education in ferment; educational reform was the dominant motif. Somewhat to my puzzlement I found many of my own colleagues, particularly those on the National Commission for Teacher Education and Professional Standards, preoccupied with in-service education. A series of regional conferences had been planned for that year to analyze the status of in-service education, and I was asked to speak on the topic at one of the conferences. At that time I saw many promising things in in-service education, but I did not see nearly as much that was good as I would have liked to see and I noticed some things that, had I been inclined to be sensational, I would have labelled as shocking. Dr. Don Davies, who was active in the arrangement of those conferences, was undoubtedly influenced by what he learned from them to observe, as he recently testified before a Congressional subcommittee, "In-service teacher training is the slum of American education—disadvantaged, poverty-stricken, neglected, psychologically isolated, whittled with exploitation, and broken promises, and conflict."[1]

Whether or not such an indictment is justified, it is clear enough that there have been changes in the years following the conference. The accent in the new era that opens before us will be more upon teachers who can make even a poor curriculum come to life and who will not be locked into an impersonal mediocrity by a "teacher-proof" curriculum. Educational reform after World War II, which emphasized the building of new curricula, in its early stages seemed to take as its goal the development of a system so complete, so foolproof, that it could be operated without teachers, or at least with teachers of only limited competence. The inadequacy of this approach has now become apparent. An interesting analysis appeared in the *Saturday Review* about Educational Services, Incorporated, which has recently become a new regional laboratory. Professor Zacharias, founder of the first of the new curricula, had indicated in that report that he was joining in establishing one of the new regional laboratories because he believed that the schools and the teachers must be reckoned with if effective change is to take place. He and his colleagues now seem to agree with many others that the best-made curricula come to naught in the hands of incompetent, unwilling, or shackled teachers.

Much of the current paraphernalia and practice in in-service education has grown up haphazardly and without a coherent

---

[1] Don Davies, "Notes and Working Papers Prepared for the Senate Sub-Committee on Education," April 1967.

rationale over a half century or more. It grew in response to a situation in which teachers were, to a large degree, not well prepared. They required supervision and every possible exhortation to bring themselves up to a minimum level of competence. This condition has changed drastically over the past fifty years. In-service education has not. It now needs to be brought into harmony with the current competence of teachers. I cite a striking example.

The 1963 New York City teachers' strike, which was roundly condemned from all sides, was symptomatic of the time because it clearly reflected an urgent need in the teaching profession for a greater degree of self-determination and self-regulation. It was a sad commentary that teaching circumstances at the time should have so deteriorated as to force desperate action. The sobering question that was posed by the strikes was whether there could be found a workable alternative; and whether the profession could respond with resolution, courageously, and immediately. Now, five years later, the New York teachers make the strike of 1963 seem puny by comparison, and the phenomenon of striking teachers appears more commonly across the land. This time, however, the attitude of the teachers and the public is quite different. In their annual fall roundup of educational events, two of our most distinguished newspapers, the *New York Times* and the *Christian Science Monitor*, headlined these strikes as signaling that a professional teacher is emerging: better trained, surer of his own professional competence, and unwilling to have it hemmed in by unreasonable restraints and conditions that prohibit him from using his full competence to educate children. It remains unfortunate that strikes are necessary, but they now appear as a symptomatic clue that something constructive may be happening . . . that we may be on the verge of a new level of professionalism in teaching.

Another vastly altered condition that requires a reform in in-service teacher education is that we have not only more competent teachers, but also new and better curricula and materials for teaching and improved training programs, which are now available and which are constantly expanding.

This then is the basis for reform in teacher in-service education: a corps of more highly competent teachers than ever before, and a richer storehouse from which to draw in the development of an in-service education program—not to mention the insatiable demand for higher and higher levels of education for our whole population.

SOME PRELIMINARY ASSUMPTIONS

If one is to comment meaningfully about the reform needed in in-service education, then certain assumptions about society and education should be made clear as a framework for the discussion.

Assumption one: Education and schooling will become more, rather than less, important. I assume also that teachers will be even more crucial in the future than they have been in the past. I doubt that most or much of the learning of our growing youngsters will be transferred to the learning laboratory station installed in the home or in other places, or in completely new institutions created for the purpose. The schools, I assume, will alter their operations so as to become more intimately related to many other aspects of life. But they will grow in importance, and enroll more persons for longer periods than ever before. As the new technology develops, I predict alteration of the teacher's role, but not a diminution of the strategic importance of the teacher. Teachers with much higher training will be required if the new technology is to be developed and used wisely. It will become increasingly true that the best laid plans of the programmers and their machines can quickly and easily be wrecked by incompetent and poorly trained teachers.

Assumption two: Technology will so alter our way of life that fewer and fewer people will carry on what we formerly considered the productive work of the world, and more and more people will turn to service occupations and will have greater leisure to cultivate their own interests.

A third assumption: There will be a continued trend toward urbanization. I shall not dwell on the problems of the cities, but what I have to say will, I think, apply to the education of teachers in the cities.

Assumption four: The computer will become a *major* factor in education. The computer will care for the tremendous amount of routine record keeping and other clerical work which is necessary in the operation of an effective school. It will make flexible schedules. In computer-assisted instruction, pupils will sit at individual stations for substantial amounts of time, especially on the cognitive and skilled side of education. This will not be tomorrow, but it will be day after tomorrow. It will inevitably come.

A fifth assumption: The schools will become unlocked, and teachers will have substantially more time to work with individual pupils and with pupils in small groups. These pupils will have substantially more time to learn individually and with small groups of their peers in meaningful situations. This means that the administrative structure of the school will be greatly altered. In the past, the school has had to serve largely as a custodial institution designed to keep youngsters off the labor market, off the street, and quietly out of sight. This will change.

Assumption six: As Allen and Meade point out in their respective discussions in this book, we will use teaching talent in a way that differs greatly from present usage. There will be a differentiated staff with fewer highly qualified persons at the top of the educational pyramid, and a large team of persons with lesser training working under the direction of a fully qualified professional person. This means, also, a greatly altered use of that part of our population which is now tragically underemployed or malemployed—namely, women. Their talents will be widely used on a part-time, more flexible basis with different levels of pay and different levels of training than is now the case.

These examples, brief though they be, should suffice to indicate the kinds of assumptions on which I base my thesis about the needed reform of the in-service education of teachers.

With regard to the subtitle, may I be permitted an aside on the topic of *who does what to whom.*

In our new burst of energy concerning teacher education, we must tackle the education of teachers at *all* levels, not just in the elementary and secondary schools as in the past. The whole spectrum from preschool through the university needs scrutiny.

"Teacher education" must no longer involve only elementary and secondary school teachers. This and the next decade will be marked, I predict, for their significant advances in the field of educating college and university teachers. If for no other reason, the students, with properly increasing power in university governance, will force it. Whether it will be necessary to shame them, to bully them, to bribe them—and we will probably have to use all three—the university faculty will come to accept teacher training for themselves. Beginnings are already evident.

The problems and issues confronting teacher education at each of the different levels are somewhat different. But they do need to be seen as a totality, for what happens at one level is not unrelated to what happens at the other level. The manner in which a teacher has been taught during the course of his entire schooling, especially in the universities, is one of the most influential ingredients in how he subsequently teaches. As professional training becomes more powerful, I think this condition may become less important, but it is still going to remain a powerful determinant. Morton Deutsch warned as early as 1962 that although the explosion in knowledge that is reshaping our intellectual, political, cultural, and military environment has been stimulated by research initiated in the universities, "paradoxically, the colleges and universities have been relative laggards in applying scientific methods to the understanding and evaluation of their own functioning."[2] Nevitt Sanford of my own institution wrote in 1968 that, "graduate schools from which our teachers come, pay almost no attention to teaching. It is surprising to find that in spite of deteriorating situations, members of college faculties seldom talk about teaching, and what it is like to be in a classroom, what one is there to do, or how one is to deal with this or that situation."[3]

Most of the discussion that follows relates to the needs of teacher in-service education at the elementary and secondary

[2] Quoted in Nevitt Sanford (ed.), *The American College* (New York: John Wiley and Sons, 1962), p. 5.
[3] Nevitt Sanford, *Where Colleges Fail* (San Francisco: Jossey-Bass, Inc., 1968), p. 170.

school level. But I am impelled at this juncture to underline the need for assigning a high priority to the formation of university teachers.

PROBLEMS OF IN-SERVICE TRAINING FOR TEACHERS

Relating in-service to pre-service training

One of the most significant problems in a consideration of in-service training is the relationship between in-service and pre-service training of teachers. It is a problem on which we now seem to be constructively at work, perhaps on the brink of some significant breakthroughs as the new Education Professions Development Act provides substantial sums of money to tackle it. In 1965 at the Nineteenth National Teacher Education and Professional Standards (TEPS) Conference in New York City, under the general theme of *The Real World of the Beginning Teacher,* I set forth a concept entitled "The Formative Years." I outlined a new overall design for teacher education that tied together a six-year period in which in-service and pre-service were merged. During this six-year period the college faculty and the teaching, supervisory, and administrative personnel in the schools would collaborate closely in the training of the beginning practitioner as he moved toward the status of full licensure.

As matters now stand, a large portion of in-service education is expended on the new teachers in the form of supervisory and other inductive services and on determining whether or not these beginners should be granted tenure. I recommended then that the more experienced teachers be used extensively in this process. In working with the college specialists, who are often on the frontiers of new curricular developments, there will be mutual benefit. The most debilitating factor in teacher education, namely, the hiatus between the aims and objectives of college trainers and those of the experienced teachers, will be overcome. If the experienced teachers in the schools work together with the college and university scholars and educationists as they are fashioning new curricula and new procedures, they will develop and present a common point of view to the new practitioner as he begins to learn his role. If the new practitioner in this sensitive period is confronted with a more consistent view both from his training institution and from the field, he will more easily and readily undergo the processes of constructive socialization in the profession.

A closely related problem is that of the relationship between teacher preparation programs and actual practice. Whereas teacher preparation now follows practice, exactly the reverse should be true, or, perhaps more precisely, the two should be more closely related. The reason for this unfortunate condition is that the in-service and pre-service education programs have worked separately rather than together. It now seems true that the period of preparation required before an individual is qualified to enter teaching needs to be longer and more effective. This period would logically be labelled "pre-service." I think, however, that both those in the field and those in the colleges and universities need to engage in this pre-service program. It is also perfectly acceptable to label as in-service training all that which occurs after this point of full initiation into professional practice. If we assume a high enough level of training prior to the entrance into full practice, then the conditions that surround in-service education will be greatly altered. Under these desirable circumstances there will be a much higher degree of motivation, a much higher capacity for understanding and independence, and a much more vigorous demand on the part of those concerned to have effective training to meet their needs. Under these conditions, it is the individual practitioner who will set the standards and determine the needs rather than persons who are external to his situation.

The role of the teacher: definitions and expectations

A major issue for discussion involves the relationship of the teacher to his role. That is, we must first decide in what manner we expect the teacher to function, and we must then determine how best to train him. We must consider whether a teacher should be required to use prescribed teaching procedures with predetermined content that has been carefully tested, or whether he must be a teacher-scholar able to use considerable autonomy in making a variety of judgments about the conduct of instruction. We must also consider whether training programs should attempt to develop competence in each of the main components in teaching and to let the individual teacher put them together somehow, or whether the training program should connect them in an integrated system. There is some doubt that it is enough to develop the discrete skills of teaching without providing assistance in bringing them together.

Teaching is an extremely complex matter. In the beginning it may be helpful to break it down into specific, more simplified components. As the beginner learns to perform many of the basic skills that underlie good teaching, he should also then begin to have practice in putting these skills together, in applying them in increasingly complex teaching situations in which he is called upon to make professional decisions concerning their application. The ability to select and integrate techniques is as important as the acquisition of specific skills. During this process of professional decision making in complex situations, the teacher begins to develop his own unique style for putting these various skills together. It is probably in the in-service training program, which comes later in the professional development of the teacher, that the means of putting together the various components is best handled. However, no pre-service training program will be sufficiently long to enable the individual to develop all the specific skills he needs, and as new skills are discovered and required, it will be necessary for him to continue both in the specific skill component part of his development as well as in the more comprehensive professional decision-making arena.

In any in-service training program, we must consider the needs of each teacher, taking into account his unique qualities. We must consider the differences in teaching ability, noting that some teachers perform better in certain areas than in others, and that certain approaches may be more appropriate for certain outcomes than for others. The problem is not finding *the* best method to be used by all teachers on all pupils, but taking these variations into account and obtaining the proper matching of method with teacher with pupil with regard to the particular purposes we wish to accomplish.

In this context we must also consider the problem of the uniqueness of each situation and the question of a comprehensive in-service education program. Certainly, each teacher, each school, each community is unique. But it is equally true that certain pervasive factors make schools in one American community more like schools in another American community than they are like any selected school in France or in Russia. Role definition and role expectation vary as different persons perceive them. But there is a remarkable continuity and similarity as we move from school to school in this country.

In the training of a professional teacher, the aim must be to equip him with enough understanding from the behavioral sciences that he can understand the important factors of operating in any school situation. He must also be able to adapt his behavior according to the unique needs of any situation in which he finds himself. This is the difference between professional training and craftsmanlike skill training. The professional proceeds according to certain principles and makes adjustments according to the different situations he confronts, whereas the craftsman refines a particular way of doing something but does not provide for alterations in the design of the product produced.

With regard to the specific questions of where in-service training should be carried on, who should do it, who should determine the objectives and the methods, and when it should take place, I suggest that in-service education properly conceived is not a monolithic entity carried on in one place, designed by one individual or group following a common pattern. It needs to be a much more varied, carefully thought through, and realistic program than it now is. A substantial amount of in-service education will be carried on daily, weekly, and monthly in the context of the school situation where the experienced teacher is working. There will be short conferences, workshops in various parts of the country that individuals may wish to attend. Short and longer training periods in colleges and universities and in some of the new regional laboratories will undoubtedly be the site for some in-service education. The important point is not so much where it will take place as whether or not it is effectively designed and executed. There is probably no one best time or place. In-service training must permeate the whole educational experience and take place for shorter and longer periods of time according to the nature of the needs. Finally, for each program, the vital need is for continued specific diagnosis of teaching and learning problems in the school district, continual feedback from this diagnosis, and continued development of the materials, training sessions, and other features necessary to overcome the educational problems discovered in this way.

One of the difficulties in devising a relevant program for in-service training has always been that different people inside of and outside of the school have perceived the teacher's function somewhat differently. One of the findings of sociological research on roles is that persons in one role tend to project that role onto the role performed by others in the situation. But again we come back to the importance of casting the in-service training program not so much in terms of the respective role definitions, but in terms of resolving the educational problem with which we are confronted, always focusing on the educational needs of pupils in the particular school and the particular setting in which the teacher finds himself. If this remains the focus of the program, then the irrelevant and differing perceptions can always be corrected and brought back to the true line of their measure.

How to retrain teachers into a new form

After two and one-half years of study at our Research and Development Center at Stanford, which is dedicated to the study of the problems of teaching, we have concluded that preparing a new type of teacher is the major problem. Given the conditions we now face—a new technology, many new curricula that result from this technology, new knowledge in the behavioral sciences, and a greatly increased demand upon the schools for a more diversified education—there clearly is needed a redefinition of the role of the teacher. The teacher may at long last be able to devote more time to the more important aspects, with the burdens of routine lifted from his back. Furthermore, it would appear that in these times a fundamental reorientation to teaching is taking place, in which we move from the traditional, long-established world-wide teaching mode, which is that of teacher as teller, to a new mode, for which we have not even fashioned an appropriate descriptive term. Our best first attempts are to call it *heuristic* teaching, and the major program of our Center has as its goal the attempt to understand, describe, and develop training programs in this new mode. In our Second Annual Report, we discuss this new mode of teaching as follows:[4]

Although the idea that men must adapt to social and physical change is widely accepted, some of its consequences have not been recognized or fully accepted. If the ability to adapt to complex life situations is as critical as it appears to be, it is important that a substantial portion of educational effort should be devoted to developing individuals who are adaptive, flexible, and inventive. That our educational energies are not so devoted is abundantly clear. Although society is changing rapidly in many ways, the schools are changing very slowly.

THE INADEQUACY OF DIDACTIC TEACHING

Teaching style is probably the most static aspect of schooling. Teachers teach today in much the same way as they have for generations. The basic style is didactic, with the teacher dispensing information to passive pupils. At regular intervals, the teacher examines the children upon how much of this information they have absorbed and retained. It is the teacher who asks questions, rarely the pupil. The structure of the answers is predetermined by the context in which the questions are formulated; only infrequently does a child's schooling permit him to discover problems. The answers are known; if they are not known by the teacher, then certainly they can be found in a book. Occasionally these stretches of information-dispensing and receiving are broken by moments of creative activity. But, more frequently, the didactic method continues uninterrupted, accepted on the assumption that knowing "these things" is important.

[4] From the Second Annual Report of the Stanford Center for Research and Development in Teaching.

It is not necessary to prolong this jeremiad on the current state of teaching. Over the years, great teachers have deplored the paucity of imagination and the sterility of the methods used in most teaching, but even the fervor of the progressive education movement in the United States accomplished little.

The computer and audiovisual revolutions

What reasons are there to believe that a change can now be wrought? The answer is that a new element has been added to the social forces impinging on the schools, namely, the computer and audiovisual revolutions. Teachers' didacticism has persisted because there was no substitute for it. Children needed to learn information; the teacher was the guide to and the dispenser of that information. Not even the widespread availability of books changed this system.

The computer and various audiovisual media make possible a better information-dispensing system. In two decades or less, computers will be integral components of an electronically based educational system. These components and audiovisual systems will be used extensively as unit costs go down and comparative effectiveness is demonstrated; their educational validity is already well enough known to warrant our predictions.

Even if one were not sanguine about the development of media and computer-assisted instruction, he must recognize that the world has changed substantially because of the widespread availability of information. He has only to turn on a TV set or pick up a magazine or newspaper to have available more information than his grandfather may have had in a year. He has a sense of immediacy, of closeness to events as they are transpiring. He need not imagine what people look like; he sees them on television and in pictures in magazines. Pictorial journalism, whatever the media used, has opened up to him a world of symbols, images, and colors.

In such a world, how does one know what is worth knowing? The richness available forces a choice of what to read, watch, and remember. Such choices require principles by which one can make the decisions that lead to selection.

The didactic teaching style helps very little in enabling one to develop such principles. The didactic method is but another aspect of the information flow. The very technology that facilitates communication tends to enhance and stimulate the didactic processing in schooling. A teacher can now turn on TV in the classroom, bringing into it a better dispenser of information than he is. The day is not distant when children will go to computer terminals for access to vast libraries.

The computer and electronic revolutions have had another consequence, probably more serious. They are the symbols of depersonalization. Only a relatively few sophisticated members of our society are aware of the extent to which the machines are controlled by men. The vast majority see the computer as an impersonal force capable of making decisions for and about them, and one over which they have relatively little control. Similarly, despite all the claims about the potential educational value of television, disparaging references to its programs and processes are frequent. In our society, the machine is often seen as a threat to one's sense of identity.

It would be simple-minded to claim that the didactic teaching style has rendered human beings helpless in the face of profound technological change. It would be equally wrong not to recognize that that style, now the dominant approach to the inculcation of knowledge, does not engender ways of coping with profound social changes now occurring.

Alienation of youth and didactic teaching

Only the schools can provide a wide variety of approaches to learning. If the learner's reception of information is likely to be facilitated by technological developments, what are the likely consequences of this facilitation? Will we also facilitate the acquisition of passivity, indifferences, and alienation? That these are not unlikely outcomes seems apparent when we consider the mood of the present generation of high school and college students. Large numbers of them are alienated from their world. Others are in active rebellion against a social system that they think regards them as statistics in manpower counts rather than human beings. They charge that the educational system is forcing upon them a way of life whose values they cannot accept. They are demanding new forms of education which will help them develop as persons.

Although it has many causes, the alienation of large numbers of middle-class and minority-group youth attests to widespread dissatisfaction with American education. Many adults recognize the disparity between what the schools teach and the needs of youth, but it is the students who have pointed to the inadequacies of the way in which they have been taught. They attack the passivity of their role, the lack of involvement of their teachers in the teaching process, their exclusion from the decision-making processes which determine the nature of their education.

Vague as some of these problems seem, the prevailing mood is unquestionably to demand and provoke change in the nature of education. At present, the discontent is more apparent than the nature of the problem or the most effective way to solve it.

A decade ago, dissatisfaction with education took the form of criticizing what was called the "quality" of education. Quality was synonymous with traditional conceptions of academic achievement. The resolution of this dissatisfaction took the form of innovations in the curriculum, such as new mathematics and science programs, and greater emphasis on academic achievement. One consequence of these changes was an enhancement of the didactic mode of teaching. The good teacher became the teacher capable of increasing acquisition of subject content.

Disadvantaged children and didactic teaching

This emphasis on academic achievement occurred about five years before another profound change in American society—the explosion of the effort of the black and other minority groups to find an equal place in our society. Nowhere is the inadequacy of the didactic mode of teaching more apparent than in the ghetto schools. Many have noted the irrelevance of the curricula of these schools; few have observed that their teaching styles reinforce those very characteristics which help to maintain the inferior status of the minority-group member.

The didactic mode requires much passivity of the student. It encourages an authoritarianism of the book, where the printed word becomes the standard of truth. Receptivity to it requires detachment and delay of personal gratification.

Again, it would be too simple to blame the problems of minority youths in the schools on the teaching style to which they are exposed. It must none the less be recognized that this teaching style contributes to the alienation of minority youth from schooling.

HEURISTIC TEACHING: THE NECESSARY SUPPLEMENT

Heuristic teaching refers to styles of teaching which emphasize the development of self-initiated and self-directed pupil learning; which stress the pupil's discovering rather than absorbing knowledge; which place the student in the role of inquirer; which aim at heightening the relevance of school to the pupil's life; which are concerned with the emotional and social development of the pupil as well as with his cognitive growth. Teaching in the heuristic mode represents no one style of teaching behavior or activity. It may be characterized as imbued with the spirit and mood of inquiry, critical skepticism, invention, imagination, and enthusiasm for learning. It treats students as persons who can produce knowledge and understanding. It is revealed in sets of beliefs about the way in which knowledge and understanding are integral to personal development and the meaning of existence. It may be the essence of the varied styles of great teachers who inspire students to seek understanding.

We will not attempt here to describe in detail all that is meant by heuristic teaching. One of the purposes of the research described is to develop such descriptions of these teaching styles. None the less, one way to understand more clearly what is implied in this concept is to look at heuristic teaching from the perspective of the teacher and then from the perspective of the student.

From the teacher's perspective

Heuristic teaching styles will take many forms. We here decide the characteristics of heuristic teaching as we now see them. The concept will change as we study this teaching style in practice. Also, whether the teaching style actually produces the effects described is an empirical question. These statements should be regarded as hypotheses.

The teacher himself will be an active inquirer, making the learning process itself a subject of his inquiry. Teaching will be the means by which the teacher himself learns; he will be as actively engaged in learning as his students.

He will stress openness of inquiry. He will not make arbitrary distinctions between knowledge and living, between understanding and being, between social importance and personal relevance. He will help students seek knowledge and understanding; he will not think of teaching as giving knowledge and understanding.

The character of his relations with students will also be changed. He will appeal to the authority of free inquiry rather than to the authority of persons. He will not impose his greater knowledge or deeper insight on students, but will rely on their perceptions of his competence to stimulate them to seek him out as a guide.

From the student's perspective

The characteristic behaviors of students taught with heuristic teaching styles will also take many forms. The student will be an active inquirer rather than a passive recipient of knowledge. He will see the process of learning as a way of achieving his most significant personal goals. His definition of his goals, of what in life will have significance for him, will emerge out of the processes of learning. He also will not make an arbitrary distinction between being and learning, between personal relevance and education, between meaning and personal significance.

He will assume responsibility for his learning. He will not need to be goaded to learn, since the significance of learning will have become intimately personal for him. He will view education as a means of achieving his goals. He will see teachers not as threats to his personal integrity but as helpers in achieving and enhancing it.

Admittedly, these descriptions represent ideal characterizations of teachers and students. Realists, familiar with today's schools, will despair of achieving a system in which there are large numbers of such teachers and students.

The purpose of the Center's research and development in this problem area is to initiate progress toward this goal. It will not be achieved in the immediate future. But it can be attained within a reasonable span. For those who doubt that changes toward such a goal can be wrought, we point to the technological and social revolutions occurring in our society. These potent social forces can be made to help in the development of schooling that emphasizes heuristic teaching.

Heuristic teaching and the open school

The character of the American school must change in the coming decades if education is not to be overwhelmed by the new computer revolution, if education is to contribute to the development of the most significant aspects of children's lives. The experience of the past decade has made it obvious that curriculum innovations do little to produce profound changes in schooling. The most imaginative innovation in curriculum can be subverted into a pedestrian analysis of subject matter by a teacher who does not understand its purposes or possess the motivation and skill to teach toward its goals. A set of experiments designed to stimulate students to inquire becomes merely another set of exercises in the hands of the teacher insecure with inquiry. Comprehensive schemes for organizing subject matter are of little interest to the teacher with little zest for learning or skill in making learning a challenge rather than a chore.

Even if many teachers were skillful and motivated enough to use heuristic teaching styles, the present organization of the schools would interfere with their use. Teaching functions are undifferentiated in present-day schools, so that one teacher must perform many functions. Even though a teacher may be skillful enough to perform them, the most demanding—heuristic teaching—is likely to be slighted because the others consume so much of his energy. Moreover, the present organization of teaching does not permit teachers unskilled at heuristic teaching to avoid it, any more than it permits those unskilled at didactic teaching to avoid it.

Also, the prevailing emphasis on didactic teaching has created a generation of administrators and parents who equate learning with the absorption of information. Any change in teaching styles, particularly when it places greater responsibility on the student for his own learning and stresses inquiry, will require changes in the attitudes of both administrators and parents.

Two kinds of changes are required. First, heuristic styles of teaching must be introduced into the schools to supplement the didactic mode.

Second, schooling must be organized to facilitate both the consequences of the computer revolution and the introduction of heuristic teaching styles, creating what we have called the *open school*.*

RESEARCH AND DEVELOPMENT GOALS

The primary goal in this problem area is to create and promote the use of new teaching styles, called here "heuristic teaching." This process of creation and promotion will be achieved by describing the pupil behaviors to be elicited and fostered by heuristic teaching styles; describing actions which elicit the desired pupil behavior; creating strategies for educating teachers to use heuristic styles; initiating school programs where these styles are used.

* *Editor's note*: This conception of the "open school" should not be confused with several other usages of the term. In contrast to "open schools" concerned primarily with affect and emotional experience, Bush implies a school that emphasizes active rather than passive learning, a curriculum which takes advantage of technological resources, and learning processes aimed at cognitive as well as affective goals.

Another goal in this program area is to find ways to develop the innovative teacher. This goal will be achieved by identifying the systems and processes of change which are, or could be, mediated by teachers; developing systems for selecting and training teachers who will be agents of educational change; installing these teachers as leaders of teaching teams that will be the nuclei of the staff of the open school; developing training strategies to involve administrators in the creating of the open school and in the promotion of heuristic teaching styles.

Problems implicit in these goals must be attacked in a coordinated way. This program area will be oriented both to the innovation of heuristic teaching styles and to the study of the process of innovation itself. Heuristic styles will constitute a major innovation in a school because they are not merely techniques but comprehensive ways of teaching which permeate many teaching methods. They will change the teacher's relation to students in radical ways. Adopting this form of teaching requires the support of both administrators and parents. We must see how the teacher can innovate within the heuristic teaching styles while we are studying the styles themselves.

Training of paraprofessions

There is little question that we are already beginning to move toward a vertically differentiated teaching staff. Much attention is paid to diversified teaching functions in the new Education Professions Development Act. It is significant that the act was titled not the Teaching Profession Development Act, but the Education Professions Development Act.

Although it is too early to predict, I anticipate that some rather well-defined subordinate roles will be defined, and that we will develop programs for the specific recruitment and training of persons to occupy these roles. I anticipate that we will attempt a variety of patterns, training personnel specifically for particular classroom functions. We shall probably, over a decade or so, emerge from trying out these various plans with some that seem to work better than others. If I were to predict at this juncture, I would venture the opinion that a teacher would prefer to have his paraprofessionals already well trained and able to move in to help without excessive training on the job. The nature of the teaching teams that are developed in the different schools must, of necessity, be adapted to and developed according to the needs in particular schools. The nature of the teaching team required in industrial arts will differ from that required in English. The nature of teaching teams in ghetto schools may vary considerably from those in some suburban schools where the youngsters come from upper socioeconomic class levels.

Motivation of the teacher to improve

The frequently heard assertion that the typical teacher is not extremely anxious to increase his competencies in in-service training may be an accurate assessment of the situation. A possible reason for this is that the teacher is not interested primarily because of the system of rewards and punishments. But I believe that this assumption is only partly valid and it probably is not the primary factor. I would agree with a point Lippitt and Fox make in a later chapter that if teachers have a negative attitude toward the in-service training program offered, the attitude results less from the fact that no incentive is offered than from the program's being so frequently irrelevant to the improvement of teaching competence. In-service training programs that are relevant and effective tend to be oversubscribed.

Certainly some direct pay-off to the teacher is important. The most direct pay-off to the teacher of good in-service training programs is intrinsic to the training program itself; namely, it enables the teacher to cope with his professional task much more successfully. The problem of loading the training program onto an already overloaded schedule is a real one. If I were to outline the five most important conditions for an effective program for in-service training I would delineate them as (1) sufficient time to engage in the program, (2) conditions such that the program can be conducted with the necessary materials and supplies at hand, (3) a program that is relevant to the problem undertaken, (4) the necessary financial and other types of support required to carry it out, and (5) an opportunity to use the results of the training in the regular school situation. These are the conditions which we should strive to achieve. The in-service training program is not "a" thing. It is, as properly conceived, a vast network of endeavors of different sizes and shapes, created and continually evaluated to help with the many tasks facing teachers in the schools.

In the long run, an increase in capability will likely be a most powerful force to make for conditions that permit the program's use. If a teacher does not know how to do better, he will surely not be able to push for the conditions that will enable him to exercise this talent. If he is armed with a battery of better alternatives for performing his educational function, he will more likely be persuasive in bringing about these conditions. Without such talent and knowledge, he is in a weak position to demand better conditions or better pay. I would therefore strongly urge that the development of a higher degree of professional competence is the surest road toward increased professional status and reward.

Respective roles of teacher and supervisors in initiating and determining in-service training programs

Here we face a fundamental problem, and its exploration can bring us close to one of the major fault lines in current conceptions of in-service training. It has been asserted that the teacher may be the most reliable judge of his own technical weaknesses. It follows, therefore, that the teacher should have a fundamental voice in determining his in-service training program. The principal's judgment that the teacher may have a myopic view of what teaching can be contains just enough truth to make it misleading. There may be more myopia in the view of the principal than in the eye of the teacher. After a long period of attempting to provide in-service education for teachers, I am convinced that the teacher ought to be the one who takes the initiative, that the teacher ought to select the kind of help, from a wide array of interesting alternatives, which he wishes to avail himself of, and that, in most instances, he needs the help of an impartial outsider to enable him to make a diagnosis and analysis of the situation. For the time being, the program needs to be freed from the formal administrative structure. The evidence is quite conclusive that as now conceived, the administrator is in too strong an authoritative role with his responsibility for rating teachers for dismissal and tenure to also play a role as an impartial, objective expert who can help with the diagnosis of instructional problems. This is a problem most difficult for persons in the administrative staff to accept. They simply fail to believe that teachers' attitudes and perceptions are as they are. It is when teachers are assured of anonymity, when they are assured that the results of investigations of classroom work will not be made available to administrative superiors, that they accept eagerly an opportunity to study their own teaching and to improve it. They will reveal data about their teaching which are not available otherwise but which are essential for accurate diagnosis. They will undertake remedial measures that they would be unwilling to try under other, more threatening circumstances.

Forms of in-service education and which should be emphasized most

Four forms that current in-service education programs take are (1) expository exhortation, (2) demonstration teaching, (3) supervised trials, and (4) analysis of performance. The first has long characterized in-service education and is probably necessary, but (in my view) is much overdone and is the least important of the four.

After a noticeable absence of demonstration teaching, we are returning to this mode, which I think has great power. It is unlikely that we know clearly what we advocate unless we can satisfactorily model it. In our attempts to secure video tapes of specific instances of the skills we wish to train for, we find it easy to obtain models of negative instances and extremely difficult to find models of positive instances of the particular skills that we are advancing. In olden times it was necessary for the demonstration teacher to come in and take over the regular teacher's class. This was time-consuming, threatening, and often unmanageable. The opportunity to discuss what was going on in a candid atmosphere was not provided, and for a variety of good reasons, this form of teaching fell into disuse. Now, however, with modern technology, particularly the portable video tape recorders, it is possible to obtain models of teaching, either contrived and rehearsed or from normal classroom settings, and to have teachers view these in a setting where there is ample opportunity to engage in thorough analysis. It is possible to play and to replay, to dwell upon the crucial act at the crucial moment, and to obtain an indelibly clear impression of what is meant.

When this form is combined with forms three and four (supervised trials and analysis of performance), a very powerful means of in-service training emerges. The combined use of these three forms of teaching represents the most powerful treatment that we have thus far discovered. The exact combination and sequencing of them are the subjects of considerable research at our Center.

No fully definitive results have emerged. In most studies to date, the combination of the use of models, feedback, and supervisory discussion tends to be more powerful than any one of them used alone.

It is likely that for different kinds of teacher behavior one or another model and sequence may be more desirable. It is also a matter of diminishing returns as to how much training is required to root the new behavior in the teacher's repertory.

Use of one teacher to train another

As matters now stand, with the teacher in his isolated classroom, there is little opportunity for him to learn from his fellow teachers. Perhaps one of the most powerful advantages of team teaching still as yet not realized is the opportunity it gives for one person to learn from another person. Surely as the school becomes unlocked and as teachers begin to work with one another in the ongoing conduct of education, they will have the opportunity to learn from one another, and, indeed, this stimulation may prove to be one of the most powerful in-service educational arrangements. Teaching has tended to be an extremely lonely occupation. It places the teacher in continual relationship with younger, immature persons and has given him little opportunity to participate with other adults inside of his profession.

The question is often asked, Do teachers respond to peers as well as they do to trained experts? This seems a strange concept, for it assumes that a teacher is not a trained expert. This is an increasingly erroneous idea. It reflects an outmoded proposition on which much in-service education and supervisory work is based: that in-service education is something that an "expert" does to a "non-expert." This misconception must be routed from our plans for in-service education. A sounder conception is that of experts working together to advance their own expertness. Surely, some individuals may be at a higher level of expertness than others in a particular way. It may be that some individuals have a unique expertness that they are willing to share with their colleagues. The issue ought to be considered in the context of professionally competent persons attempting to widen their horizons, not in a noblesse oblige fashion of condescension, which characterizes supervision and in-service education in American schools (just as it also permeates our patronizing attitude toward helping the so-called underdeveloped nations).

Place of supervision in in-service training

There is a conflict regarding the place of supervision in current in-service training. The hint that the role of the supervisor is obsolete is probably warranted. The role of the principal as administrative line officer or as supervisor is also clearly in question. It is my view that the old concept of supervision, as implied in the line staff relationship and in the school organization of the past, is rapidly coming to a close. As teachers become better trained and more competent, their need is not for supervision but for a continued opportunity to improve their professional ability. With their colleagues, they also need to establish a continued dialogue of analysis and feedback regarding the effectiveness of their work. The crucial question then becomes whether or not there is need for some kind of monitoring to prevent malpractice and to insure that a softness does not creep in to prevent the highly competent person from performing at the highest possible levels.

In the preceding discussions, especially those concerning team teaching, a built-in mechanism is available so that peers are constantly discussing their work with one another and are in contact with one another; also, their work is under the scrutiny of others who are also competent. Under these circumstances the necessary safeguards are inherent in the situation. What amount of periodic evaluation is necessary to determine whether or not persons are living up to minimum standards is a difficult question. When sufficiently high initial levels of competence are established, the main monitoring required is to prevent malpractice. This can be adequately provided when the classroom is opened and subject to the scrutiny of one's colleagues. What should be built into the organization to prevent the senatorial courtesy of one's colleagues is a difficult problem, one which I am not fully prepared to discuss at this time.

The question of whether there should be a systematic relationship between classroom supervision and external training programs assumes that there will continue to be classroom supervision on an evaluative basis and other training programs on some other basis, presumably designed solely to help teachers increase their competence. There may need to be two independent operations, one for administrative purposes and one for instruction improvement purposes. My observation leads me to suggest that when you begin to link supervisory involvement, with its salary and tenure concerns, and in-service training, you almost completely destroy the possibility of providing maximum help to the teacher to understand and to improve his own practice. Consequently, I am inclined to the possibly unpopular view that these two matters should be rigorously separated; there should be only a limited amount of attention devoted to the official administrative functions, with most time, energy, and resource devoted to professional improvement. This becomes tenable when you reach a level of beginning service that assumes it is a competently trained professional who enters the picture.

Difference in training required for urban and suburban schools

A popular issue currently concerns the differences in training required for urban and suburban schools; the question can as well be raised for pre-service as for in-service education. It is fashionable now to help the disadvantaged, and so many of their needs are unique that large programs, at both the pre- and the in-service level, are being inaugurated to improve the urban ghetto schools. The needs of the poor in the cities are so overwhelming that the whole culture is giving attention to the question. Our own Center at Stanford plans to devote some of its energy to this special problem. Some time ago, the U.S. Office of Education made a sizeable grant to form a national task force to work on the problems of the disadvantaged. This group, after working inten-sively for two years, has come to the conclusion that a much wider spectrum of the population is "disadvantaged" than was ever imagined and that the kind of education necessary to pre-pare teachers for their professional tasks is as broad as the total population. To prepare teachers for only one segment such as the black, the Mexican-American, or the impoverished in Appalachia would be a great mistake. They are coming to the view, strangely enough, that a teacher ought to be well enough prepared to deal with any special group he finds himself teaching. This may be an unfair or oversimplified statement of their position, but as I understand this national task force report, it seems that this is essentially the position they have come to in their thinking. It is a position I held before they began their deliberations. I have no objection to preparing teachers sufficiently to be equally at home in the slum ghetto and in the urban affluent environment, and I admit that some teachers may have more or less personal prefer-ence for working in one of the two situations. Nonetheless, if they are incapable of working in both situations, I submit that they have not been sufficiently prepared as professional teachers. If a teacher who presumably has been prepared to teach is not suffi-ciently versed in the behavioral sciences to understand the social, economic, political, and psychological forces at work among those who are poverty-stricken, as well as those who are deeply prejudiced from the upper and more affluent classes, he simply has not been adequately prepared to teach.

There is compelling reason, as Fantini states in a later chapter, to train persons to be able to work in different situations; it is difficult to understand how they might be able to objectively work in one if they did not understand the other situation. If persons wish to specialize particularly to work in one or another type of situation, perhaps they should have some specialization added on to their basic training, but it ought to be something additional to the basic training rather than a substitution for something basic. In this sense, then, in-service education programs that build upon a presumed adequate professional base might concentrate on working with one or another type of population, whether it be persons who have special needs in reading, special problems in learning mathematics, or special problems growing out of their impoverished environment in the cities. It appears that the problems of the poor in our cities are sufficiently acute that some radical changes will be required in the total educational picture. Therefore, we may need teachers who have an unusually high degree of professional competence, not only as teachers generally but in terms of special problems. These people will be required, and in this situation in-service education programs that are specifically school- and population-centered would be most appropriate.

It must be understood, however, that the disadvantaged portions of our population, the poor and the oppressed minority groups living in the cities, suffer because of the prejudice that exists among the more affluent elements of the community, which dominate and control our society. If we are concerned with remedying the basic ills of those who are underprivileged, it will be necessary to devise new teaching programs that will overcome the extensive prejudice and the excessive racism that exist in our society. Therefore, an in-service education program is needed that will be directed toward those teachers from the more privileged parts of the society.

School-wide general programs versus individualized programs

In a subsequent chapter, Rubin argues that in-service training appears to be more effective when the total school staff is simultaneously engaged in a given training program. While there is some evidence to substantiate this generalization, we need to be clear about its implications. Earlier I noted that it is important for in-service training programs to be related to specific issues with specific problems and the specific needs of teachers who are engaged in the program. It is true, perhaps, that when a total school or a school system is engaged in some common endeavor, morale may be heightened, but this is only a part of the total question. Certainly it does not follow that everybody must be following a common program under a common philosophy in order to have a high degree of morale in the school. If the total staff in a given school or school district can engage in some projects they share in common, this may contribute to a sense of community and enhance the total enterprise. However, to attempt to beam the whole in-service training program to a common endeavor would be a great mistake. As a matter of fact, this has been one of the great errors in in-service education programs of the past. The attempt to provide a global training program that would meet the needs of all teachers—young, old, experienced, inexperienced—is simply not adequate for the degree of specialization and sophistication that is now current in educational circles.

Simultaneous curriculum development and teacher training

Should curriculum development and teacher training proceed simultaneously so that there will be no time lag?

The answer is probably yes. Should curriculum developers also be teacher trainers? It now appears quite clear that the best-planned curricula account for little if they are placed in the hands of incompetent teachers or teachers who do not understand how to use the new materials. There is a category used commonly in education entitled "Curriculum and Instruction," which suggests the indissoluble link between these two phases of education. It suggests the difficulty of separating what is to be taught from the method by which it is to be presented. The experience of the physical sciences study committee group, under Professor Zacharias, and Educational Services Incorporated, illustrates this point. It has become necessary for the scholars developing new curricula to join with the teachers who are to use them. A campaign must be developed that would give attention to the training and retraining of teachers at the same time new curriculum materials are to be developed, if the unfortunate time lag that has prevailed up until now is to be overcome. In the school mathematics reform represented by the new math, educators are finding that much of the effectiveness of a new curriculum resides in the competence of the teacher. It is also clear that not only should curriculum developers themselves play an active part in designing necessary teacher retraining, but they should also give attention to the teacher behavior required for putting the new curricula into operation.

Effective evaluation of in-service training: is it possible?

I honestly do not know how effectively in-service training can be evaluated. It has been suggested that the thoughtful judgment of teachers, as "random teacher opinions," may not be valuable. We should not underestimate the honest and thoughtfully given judgments of teachers. As a matter of fact, much of the dissatisfaction that is expressed and pervades current discussions stems from the expressions of teachers. If this is not a valid testimony, then perhaps we are ill advised in questioning the current in-service education programs. If teachers were expressing a rather uniform satisfaction with in-service training programs, it is doubtful that there would be such an effort to revamp them.

In his writings, Rubin also has suggested that the only true "index of the programs' quality lies in the teacher's classroom performance and ultimately in the students' learning." Surely the ultimate objective is to improve the students' learning, but there are intermediate objectives at which in-service education can be aimed. The alteration of teacher behavior can be considered as a legitimate objective in and of itself. It is essential, in the final analysis, to link teacher behavior to changes in pupil behavior, but there are intermediate stages in which it is not necessary to apply this full link. For example, there is a considerable body of evidence showing that the pupils need to be active if they are to learn effectively. There is also a considerable amount of evidence to suggest that the teachers do most of the talking and engage in most of the activity in the classrooms. Therefore, it may be assumed that it would be desirable if pupils became more active and teachers less overtly active in the general teaching-learning process. It would be desirable to develop in-service training programs that would attempt to bring about such constructive alteration of teacher behavior. Presumably we could evaluate the effectiveness of such programs while they are being developed. They would need to be paired later or in another context with investigations that relate the situation to pupil learning, but it does not follow that all evaluations of in-service training must be linked to changes in pupil behavior.

Surely, it is desirable to make as specific as possible the objectives of the in-service training program. Anything that can be done to increase the specificity of these objectives would be desirable, from the standpoint both of focusing effort in the training program and of attempting to measure the outcome. The job of isolating and defining the behavior that we seek to achieve seems to be the more difficult task. Devising the effective training program is not so difficult once the behavior has been identified. Here is an extremely important lesson for our whole effort in in-service training.

SUMMARY COMMENTS

In summarizing the needed reforms for teacher in-service education, I emphasize several points. First, as Allen and Lippitt and Fox stress in later chapters, we should liberally use older, experienced teachers to teach new teachers. They have much to offer and, in the process of planning and executing a program for the training of young teachers, they will improve their own competence. I refer to both experienced college and school teachers working together, presenting a united and coordinated front in the induction of new teachers during their most formative years. We are once again beginning to realize the power of the old idea in which older pupils, even though not necessarily the best ones, are able not only to help younger pupils with learning difficulties but also to overcome some of their own difficulties in the process.

Second, we need to be specific. Fewer global and so-called

inspirational types of meetings are needed. We should be precise in defining the teaching behavior for which in-service educational programs are designed. We ought to spend a much larger share of our total energy in helping teachers to build an extensive repertory of technical skills. In this way teachers will be free to apply different alternatives as they confront educational problems. We must give up the ephemeral search for *the* good teacher and begin to tailor in-service education programs for the precise needs of specific individuals and groups of teachers.

In addition, we need to consider what is coming as an "aptitude-treatment-interaction" model which recognizes that different pupils learn best in different ways, different teachers have strengths to be capitalized upon in their styles of teaching, and different subject matters and specific educational objectives are most effectively reached by different methods and materials. This is a refinement and extension of the second point above, concerning the need for greater specificity in in-service education programs.

In the fourth place, it is probably necessary at this juncture to move most of in-service education out of the administrative line. By this I mean that it is desirable to give teachers a greater degree of initiative and freedom of opportunity, and to respect the confidentiality of the data collected in the in-service training discussions. As things now stand, much in-service training has been conducted for administrative purposes, and the results have been used for rating teachers for promotion and tenure. This effectively destroys a substantial amount of the potential for in-service education. The possibilities for accomplishing what is needed remain limited as long as this condition continues. It may be possible later, when different administrator-teacher relationships prevail, to bring in-service education more directly back into the administrative hierarchy. For the time being, I join with Meade, Lippitt, and Fox in suggesting that an impartial third party, individual or agency, may need to be prominently involved in in-service training.

Fifth, we must put enough resources into the effort to insure that only programs of the highest quality will be offered as in-service education. This requires ample planning, desirable conditions for the conduct of the program, and adequate attention to the development of the materials necessary for the program. We are just beginning to realize that the developmental costs for good education materials and procedures are very high.

Finally, we must learn not to expect miracles from in-service education programs. One besetting sin in American education is an expectation of radical changes in teacher behavior and consequently in pupil behavior with only tiny investments of time, energy, and resources. Even if we markedly increase our financial supports, which now appears hopeful with federal funds, we need to realize that changes in professional behavior will take place slowly over a long period of time.

■ CLUES TO ACTION

Bush, like several of the other writers, is committed to the concept of a teacher who is professionally self-directive. Convinced that it is futile to make teachers no more than technicians, he conceives of school faculties as experts working together to increase their expertness. Like Tyler, he prefers to respect the teacher's professional autonomy, and to base professional growth activities on individually determined needs.

As the computer and other technology begin to play a greater part in instruction, Bush believes that the problem of teacher retraining will increase rather than decrease. Further, he contends that there will be major changes in the working relationships between teachers and supervisors. Whether the supervision is performed by a principal or a subject matter specialist, it will need to be based upon mutual respect and interaction rather than upon critical judgment imposed by a superordinate on a subordinate. Thus professional growth will become a matter of inquiry through which the teacher continually will seek to learn more about his craft. If Bush is right, we would do well to begin now to prepare for the impending changes. The idea of continual self-directed professional improvement should be popularized. And as administrators work with teachers, the ancient ritual of rating should be replaced with collaborative analysis.

A continuing emphasis upon the individualization of instruction, heuristic learning, and a division of labor within the teaching force also will increase the importance of in-service programs. Much as the preschool child and the disadvantaged learner posed special teaching problems, we will discover that other groups of children respond better to one form of teaching than to another. As a consequence it will be necessary to mount teacher education programs that familiarize teachers with a variety of specialized techniques. We will be ill prepared to mount these programs, however, if we do not forearm ourselves with a systematic rationale regarding teacher professional growth. Beyond this, unless we make a vigorous effort to greatly enlarge our "storehouse of in-service resources," we will be unable to mount programs that have sufficient potency.

With respect to the acquisition of new teaching techniques, Bush believes that a combination of demonstration teaching, supervised trials, and performance analysis represents the best strategy at our disposal. Logically, therefore, school practitioners should begin to acquire finesse in the use of these procedures.

Significantly, Bush's research leads him to believe that increased competence is in itself a valuable pay-off. The intrinsic satisfaction of performing ably, in other words, will impel teachers to enhance their capabilities. Although professional growth often is a slow and cumulative process, this desire to become a more adept practitioner will eventually result in a new level of professionalism, if we support the teacher's desire with a viable and meaningful opportunity for in-service growth. Bush believes that this new professionalism should embrace two primary aims: a teacher who is innovative, capable of continual self-renewal; and one characterized by flexibility rather than rigidity of teaching style. He suggests, again and again throughout his chapter, that teaching often is ineffectual simply because the teacher lacks a repertory of methods that would allow him to adjust to the particular situation. He is disinclined, as a result, to teach teachers any one way of classroom behavior. Rather, he distinguishes between professional training and professional craftsmanship, contending that the successful teacher will need to understand the various dimensions of his task and to adapt his actions to the subtleties and nuances of the learning situation. This conviction leads him to the argument that teachers can teach one another with considerable profit. He sees the experienced teacher as a tutor for the inexperienced, the imaginative teacher as a stimulus to the pedestrian, and the inventive one as an antidote to the teacher who is lost in routine convention. It is in this way that we can nurture "experts working together to increase their expertness."

■ OPERATIONAL IMPLICATIONS

1. As the reform of educational practices continues, heuristic learning, individualization of instruction, and teacher specialization will increase. **We must develop efficient programs that equip teachers to deal with these modifications in instruction.**

2. The ability to function effectively and to accomplish a specified objective is a strong form of motivation. **Teacher opportunities for professional growth must be based on the satisfaction that derives from true competence.**

3. Continual change will occur in the educational system during the foreseeable future. **The provisions we make for the professional enhancement of teachers must be characterized by three dominant aims: flexibility in teaching style, capacity for self-renewal, and receptivity to change.**

4. The findings of social psychology suggest that people with similar interests can, through interaction, contribute to one another's welfare. **Programs of professional growth should take advantage of teachers' potential for teaching one another.**

5. The effective teacher has a variety of methods that can be used to achieve his purpose. **Teacher in-service education should emphasize instructional alternatives rather than single methods.**

herbert a. thelen

CHAPTER FOUR

A CULTURAL APPROACH TO IN-SERVICE TEACHER TRAINING

Fourteen years ago I published a scheme for in-service teacher training that stressed an approach which I believed might well have potential for teachers and school faculties. This scheme called for teachers to experiment with their own classes, to discuss their thoughts in self-chosen groups, and to report to the entire faculty. The resultant ideas could then be assimilated with those from other groups, to enable the faculty to move forward on common school-wide purposes. I still see nothing wrong with those ideas as one way of calling attention to the features any successful plan would have to contain: individual creativity, psyche support, contribution to the larger society, and service to agreed-upon purposes, plus flexibility for all the elaborations that would occur to individuals.

I considered giving myself the task of outlining the details of this scheme. However, my own Ph.D. research had shown that laboratory work in freshman chemistry which followed cookbook procedures (or spelled-out details) was much less effective than that which resulted from teacher-pupil planning of the experiments. Therefore I could not propose any method of in-service training that would short-circuit action-research, diagnosis, and planning. Guidelines, yes; blueprints, no.

THE SELF-TRAINING SYNDROME

But if in-service training is not to be defined as a set of procedures to be followed, how can it be defined? At this point I began to recall the experiences I have had that would nowadays be called in-service training, and I soon realized that they are so extraordinarily diverse that no one set of procedures could possibly include them all. But would it be possible to find a common element or essential characteristic that does indeed capture the flavor of in-service training? Let me cite a few of the experiences and then see what can be made of them:

(a) Spending weekends devising laboratory setups that my physics class could use to demonstrate principles for themselves; leading class evaluation of the comparative effectiveness of the setups

(b) Speculating about new kinds of classroom activities with four teachers of other subjects while our families were picnicking together

(c) With two other colleagues, inventing and teaching a new experimental teacher-training course, requiring activities to be planned for a three-hour time block each day

(d) Participating in a faculty interest group to share ideas, to conduct experiments in our classrooms, and to concoct a report for the whole faculty; subject: social sensitivity

(e) Cooperating with a national project group in trying out their materials, writing out further materials in the same format, and contributing to a national pool of know-how; subject: critical thinking

(f) Being a teacher of classes observed by researchers; filling out questionnaires for them

(g) Participating, along with half the faculty, in a special study program planned and led by visiting university trainers; subject: child study

(h) Attending a teacher's institute series of lectures

One sees that *a* and *b* together would be characteristic of the autonomous professional; *c* requires a fully functioning team, with interaction at all levels from personal to philosophical; *d* and *e* call for member participation in activities structured by a committee; *f* involves getting some feedback but does not require the intention to do anything better or different; *g* and *h* accept a high degree of dependency and noninvolvement on the part of teachers.

As I sorted out the activities from *a* to *h*, I felt that the top three had been the most exciting and worthwhile and the bottom three the least so. What syndrome, then, distinguishes top from bottom? On the face of the descriptions, one finds intensity of personal involvement, immediate consequences for classroom practice, stimulation and ego support by meaningful associates in the situation, and initiation by teacher rather than by outsider. To this list one could also add further factors from other observations: availability of expertise, supportive climate maintained by the principal, the faculty's expectations of progress reports.

These qualities, which comprise what I call "professional dialogue," are the ones we should seek in in-service training activities. And the characteristics of the bottom activities—dependence, noninvolvement, superficial cooperation, and nonpurposiveness—have little value for meaningful in-service training.

CULTURAL DIFFERENCES THROUGH SPACE AND TIME

Having stated several desirable criteria, I began trying to imagine the sorts of in-service activities that one might be able to set up in the wide variety of schools that I have known over the past thirty years. I found I could name schools in which the top activities exist and also schools in which these activities would not even be imaginable. And I also had the strong feeling that generally speaking all the upper activities would have been much more possible thirty years ago than they are today. The difference is clearly cultural. The middle-class, suburban, affluent, educated community would have the schools whose in-service training activities are at the top. Only they would not think of it as in-service training; *it would be taken for granted as part of the way of life of the teacher*. Schools in the inner city slum neighborhoods would be much less likely to have the top kinds of activities; and in many such schools, in-service training is confined to the last-listed activity set up on a city-wide basis. In such schools a researcher can get wonderful cooperation with those teachers with whom he becomes friends; it is a personal, not a professional, matter.

What it boils down to is that the qualities of effective in-service training (professional dialogue) are already built into the way of life of some schools, and their faculties would not be easily persuaded that they need additional special activities; in other schools, however, professional dialogue is so utterly foreign to the way of life that the most an in-service program can accomplish is to be a mild diversion of no real consequence.

I further note that there is lessened expectation, even in the "better" schools, of professional dialogue now as compared with my salad days. It is as if teaching has shifted from an almost-profession to an out-and-out occupation—a conclusion that should amaze nobody. To support these assertions, I cite the following symptoms, which seem to be very much on the increase: (a) There seems to be less introspective articulation by teachers of what actually goes on in their classrooms. Talk is confined to the personalities, families, and misbehaviors of certain vivid students; classroom interactive processes (management and knowledge-discipline) are not captured in words or shared with others. They are simply taken for granted. (b) It is as if teachers do not know that alternative teaching behaviors exist or could be created. Teaching is not a process of making decisions among alternatives: it is the process of enacting the role of "teacher"; and everyone knows what that is. (c) A newly suggested procedure must be either right or wrong; there is ultimately one right way to teach and it is known to all good teachers. Throughout teacher training, the teachers have assiduously sought to learn this right way. (d) In the classroom, when one of these right procedures (that everyone knows are part of teaching) does not "work" (for example, some classroom management technique), it is not the procedure that is at fault but rather the children. The teacher would not think of overhauling his techniques; what he wants is some magic gimmick that will bring the deviate children into line and restore success to his teaching. (e) The traditional school procedures are sacred. The nation goes to fantastic lengths to keep the schools from having to change. Thus, when a large segment of the population is found not ready for first grade, Operation Head Start is set up to get the kids ready; and the sacred first grade curriculum escapes the overhauling it richly deserves. Similarly, when the school activities are so meaningless or punishing to large numbers of students that they drop out of school, job training programs are set up (at thirty to forty times the cost per pupil) to salvage these youth. (f) Then there are the administrators who come to meetings to get the package in-service training and all the time they know full well that they are not even going to call a faculty meeting.

RELATIONSHIPS BETWEEN MICROCOSM (CLASSROOM) AND MACROCOSM (THE LARGER SOCIETY)

The following propositions are offered as a means of viewing the actual and the possible relationships between the school and the larger society.

Proposition 1: The classroom is a small but complete piece (microcosm) of the larger society. It is swept by the same controversies, has the same values and behavioral norms as the community. It is by no means a *de novo* group, to be developed from nothingness to maturity. The members may be unfamiliar to one another but they create an instant culture, including a reasonably

comprehensive set of expectations, by the simple device of cart-
ing it in with them. After all, the teacher and pupils live most of
the time in the larger community, and they become socialized
into it—which means that they internalize its controls and guidelines, and then, quite naturally, they employ these in the classroom.

Proposition 2: The dominant culture of the larger society,
that which people refer to as the American Way of Life, has
shifted. The very evident middle-class Protestant ethic, maintained by the professionals and the educationally elite of fifty
years ago, has given way to the procedure-oriented, change-
resistant way of life of the majority of voters and job-holders—
and the tremendously cumbersome technologies they are chained
to. It is obvious that as participation in the larger society has
broadened, which means extending itself downward, the new
participants have *kept hold of their own culture rather than
adopt a new culture.* Elementary school teaching, like nursing, has
been a major route to higher socioeconomic or class status. The
child of blue-collar parents has, through education, become a
teacher, a white-collar person. To become a teacher he went to
one of the more inexpensive colleges, where he was taught the
behaviors that constitute the role of teacher plus some supportive
rationalizations from psychology and child development (plus
the history of his state, the evils of alcoholism, etc.). He became a
teacher by *learning to act like one;* his practice teaching—by all
odds the most influential part of the program—gave him that. He
has, then, learned the *behaviors* of a middle-class occupation; but
he has by no means internalized the way of life with its inner
motives and the style out of which the teaching profession
emerged. He can act like a teacher but, to be blunt about it, he
does not think like one; nor does teaching as an occupation have
the centrality in his life that teaching as a profession had in the
life of its practitioners fifty years ago. Upward mobility has
enriched the aspirant's behavioral repertory and vulgarized the
profession.

Proposition 3: The new dominant culture of classroom microcosm and larger society is antieducative on all grounds, both

theoretical and pragmatic. Therefore the innovations that catch on (for example, programmed learning) are likely to serve non-educative ends; that is, they will be adopted for the wrong reasons.

Proposition 4: If a substantial percentage of the classroom microcosms were to change consistently and similarly, the larger society would also change—over time. Conversely and much more demonstrably, as the larger society changes, the school feels the pressure for change, even though it has tended to react defensively and nonresponsively to any newly emerging *attitudes* or *purposes*.

Proposition 5: The teacher's job is basically to shift the culture of the classroom microsociety from procedure-oriented and change-resistant to educative, and to use his subject matter and its learning activities as the major instrument of change. In other words, the teacher intervenes in such a way as to maintain an appropriate stress on the group's natural norms; he intervenes to help the children use learning as the way to cope with the stress. You might also say that the teacher's task is to bring about group growth (toward educative norms). The activities through which each child contributes to (and is part of) this growth are the ones that will be educative.

Proposition 6: As Jackson, Lippitt and Fox, and Fischler consistently stress in their respective essays, the purpose or function of in-service training is to help the teacher himself undergo similar growth on the job. Such programs should serve to help him gain the competence he needs in order to make continual progress in transforming the classroom culture.

Proposition 7: To a professional or intellectual of the old school, the force that would drive, motivate, and animate his career would be his passionate belief in an ideal and his dedication to it. Thus we like to say that teachers are driven by the desire to help children realize their potentials, or to help society become more just or more adaptive. The emptiness of this claim becomes all too evident if one asks the claimant to show *any* connection between the realization of his ideal and the behaviors of himself and his students. No, I regret to say that teaching acts are too often means to carry out clearly defined short-range activities only, and not to strike a blow for autonomy, freedom, or other civilizing value.

This then raises the real question that probably generated the whole large project under whose auspices these ideas are discussed: Granted that the traditionally assumed professional motives for in-service training are no longer available, what forces, if any, *can* motivate teaching and teacher training?

The answer is already implied logically by Proposition 5. But more convincing than logic is what I consider an increasingly important fact: that even the teacher most insulated from reality is already finding himself *personally vulnerable* through his participation, however minimal, in the larger society. As Fantini also suggests in a later chapter, many teachers already are aware of the emptiness of their lessons, the restlessness of the children spinning out idle fantasies with the teacher, the obvious inappropriateness of present teaching methods for the poor children in cities, the nonresponsiveness of the educational establishment to events both within and without. It is this emerging sensitivity which can, I think and hope, become the basis in the present generation for humanizing education. In short, I suggest that the driving force for in-service teacher training might well be found in this phenomenon: an internalized societal tension arising from the sense of discrepancy between school and nonschool experiences of the teacher.

TEACHING: CULTURAL TRANSFORMATION OF THE CLASSROOM MICROSOCIETY

It is now time to spell out the features of the larger society that are also educationally salient in the classroom. I will, in what follows, try to show just what sort of educational havoc is wrought by accepting these features as defining the social order of the classroom.

The division of society into haves and have-nots, "separate but unequal" majority and minority groups, is replicated in the schools through homogeneous ability grouping, the purpose of which is to separate and indoctrinate children into whichever subsociety is deemed appropriate for them. Division of the children by any educational criterion, such as ability, amounts *de facto* to socioeconomic discrimination.

The existence of pluralism and subcultural diversity within our society is, according to our political doctrine, a source of strength; but most groups tend to be culturally homogeneous, and diversity between groups leads more often to conflict than to constructive controversy. In exactly the same way, differences between the culture of the teacher and his students result in a truce rather than in the emergence of a more adaptive way of life. Diversity is seen not as a source of strength but as a deviancy, and is punished. In short, conflict in the classroom is suppressed as wrong rather than taken as the beginning of insight-stimulating inquiry and growth. The teacher's opinion is regarded as the judgment of Solomon and conformity is the *sine qua non* of achievement.

It is a cardinal principle that one must work to eat, and that he must work harder if he is to eat better. The individual may strive for anything, but the rule of the game is competition. He must demonstrate within the rules that he is somehow superior or more useful to society than others; if so, he is entitled to more of whatever he wants. In the classroom, children have been supposed to take for granted that high grades are the passport to desirable things, that the children are there to strive for grades.

But all this is breaking down in the larger society. For the top and bottom groups it is *not* true that you have to work in order to eat. It is true that you have to graduate from school in order to get a job, but it is not true that only the top graduates will have jobs. Moreover, the style of one's life may actually depend more on which segment, stratum, or subculture he is socialized into than on his Horatio Alger–type merit. As students are more and more taught the same things in the same ways, it increasingly matters who you know rather than only what you can do.

Students living in modern society have plenty of evidence

that competition in the old-fashioned sense of "may the best man win" is no longer the only or most common route to success. This is evident in such school practices as automatic promotion, teacher favoritism, and the conferring of senior privileges on the strength of phony or ritualistic allegations of responsibility. Nevertheless, in spite of such evidence, children continue to be pushed into increasingly empty competition for nonexistent or worthless rewards; and both they and their teachers seem aware that the system is fraudulent.

In any situation where there is not enough to go around, the strategy of distribution through competition seems reasonable. Further, competition must be regulated by rules, and the rules should be fair and just. But any rule is bound to be more fair for some persons than for others. And any effort to make the rules more fair, through selective handicapping or subsidies, simply raises further questions of fairness. Soon one is embroiled in issues of individual need versus accessibility of opportunity; of the value of self-realization versus competence; of significance versus bias in judgment. It appears that once one has settled on a policy of competitive individual striving, he must then make an astonishingly large variety of further accommodations.

In the classroom, fairness means treating everyone alike; using only objectively measurable abilities as the basis for judgment; being impersonal, and avoiding all signs of favoritism, liking, or enmity; setting tasks and discussion topics well within the capacity of everybody; providing recourse for individuals who are unable to do the homework, have no enthusiasm for the assigned studies, and so on. Many of these conditions are antithetical to those which facilitate learning. The impersonality of the teacher, the triviality of the bases for competition, the lack of challenge of the tasks, the easy out for those who ask for it: all convey a lack of interest in individuals, a lack of respect (probably justified) for the work, and the substitution of opportunism for scholarship as the way to get ahead.

There are further difficulties, too. If one gets ahead by knowing more than others, then students will not share knowledge with each other, will insist on showing off for the teacher, and will regard knowledge only as something to be accumulated rather than used. Their only genuine coping will be with the examination situation, rather than with the learning activity. Test-wiseness will be the real objective of the course, and studying the teacher will be the actual route to success. And truth will be confused inextricably with the personal opinions of whoever has power over you. Thus the schools create the organization man.

As Fantini points out, our ingrained faith in knowlege as something to be accumulated and squirreled away—"the funded capital of human experience"—accounts for the school's foolish response to the so-called explosion of knowledge and technology: since more knowledge exists, more should be taught; and since the time for teaching remains the same, we must become more efficient. To be more efficient one had better select the sort of knowledge one can be efficient with—namely, verbal, descriptive, and memorizable. It is no accident that teaching programs, touted primarily to increase the efficiency of learning, must confine themselves to "increasing the verbal repertoire." Dewey, of course, and Aristotle for that matter, would have none of it. Both would value effectiveness of learning more than mere efficiency, and both would concentrate on the internalization of powerful principles that clarify or relate a great deal of information in the form of action-oriented (functional) trends in the real world.

Considerations such as the above raise the question of how change is to be made, how an outmoded system based on scarcity and refuted by abundance can accommodate the newer realities. Clearly some method of action research, involving diagnosis, proposal, reality testing, action, feedback, rediagnosis, and so on, is required. But the most important need is for clear purposes and confidently held values through which procedures can be assessed and modified. John F. Kennedy was exactly right in seeing that society was stagnant and that it needed "to get moving again." And the underlying difficulty was the loss of national purpose and therefore of sense of direction. Several conditions were and are responsible for this loss. First, decisions of national import arise as compromises among groups that are each acting in self-interest. Second, the present Establishment (including the industrial-military combine that President Eisenhower warned us of) has been in power so long that it is encrusted with habit and can make no new responses to newly emerging conditions; and it has also become so large and complex that nobody can grasp its whole operation. Therefore, each person must content himself with maintaining his own operations without regard for their societal context. Third, with the broadening of the societal base of participatory democracy and the consequent changes in national culture, creative discussion of purposes has been more out of reach than ever. The voter-citizen 150 years ago was not unlike his representative in knowledge and wisdom. He was a competent consultant or political partner; therefore, his opinion was valuable to arrive at wisdom, not merely to tabulate support. But at present even the best-educated voter is not competent to judge many issues. Yet we persist in thinking that all issues should be directly available to voters, and consequently the content and form of national dialogue have been reduced to the level of the majority culture. Moreover, the dialogue serves no purpose of enlightenment or goal-seeking but only political maneuvering and self-serving. Fourth, since the purposes are no longer remembered or looked to as the authoritative justification for procedures, new questions or challenges are reacted to defensively or evasively.

Under these conditions in the larger society, as Fantini also concludes, it is not surprising that much classroom education and teacher training is witless, existing simply for its own sake, or that the efforts to justify its procedures and curriculum remain extraordinarily unconvincing to a serious student of human behavior. Worse, the lack of commitment to clear and significant goals means that there is no useful way to tell whether procedures are effective or worthwhile. We know, for example, that the school affects children; so also do the family, street gang, Sunday school, policeman, television, and so forth. We do not know how the influence of the school compares with that of these other agencies, nor with respect to what. The school operates with purposes so broad that no deduction can be made as to practices, which is tantamount to having no purposes at all.

The beneficiaries of all this, our students, have only the vaguest idea about future careers, while very little school experience is felt to be a worthwhile means to any personally important end. Many teachers believe that they are basically part of the Establishment, being protected by its authority; at the same time they resent their own inability to respond creatively to children.

Finally, let us consider a rather different feature of the larger society that also finds expression in the classroom. This is a positive, adaptive process: the spontaneous, voluntary formation of relationships among individuals. In times of stress, when the formal society responds inadequately to the changed facts of life that it, ironically enough, helped to create, individuals turn to each other for help in getting hold of their thoughts and feelings. They may go on to develop programs of action. At one extreme are the separationists, setting up their own tribes and becoming occupied with each other and with their own personal subjective life. At the other extreme are the casual coffee-break groups that find cathartic release from accumulated and pent-up energy and then, serenity restored, carry on. In between are limited objective groups that start in shared disgruntlement but go on to plan action and involve others in it. Such groups may emphasize (a) self-help, or cooperative bootstrap operation; (b) persuasion, voting, and pressure tactics; or (c) survey, study, and feedback to the authorities (confrontation).

As Jennings pointed out,[1] groups form voluntarily because individuals need each other. The psychegroup forms from personal preferences of the members for one another; it is not task oriented; it is permissive; it traffics in private or semiprivate thoughts and feelings; it tends to be somewhat intimate; and its members regard one another as friends. It helps each member feel more adequate.

The sociogroup, on the other hand, is composed of individuals who want to accomplish a given purpose or task but cannot do it by themselves. The persons in the group may not

---

[1] See Helen Hall Jennings, *Sociometry of Leadership*, Sociometry Monograph no. 14 (New York: Beacon House, 1947).

necessarily be interested in one another, and their interpersonal interest may be confined to the cooperation needed in order to get the job done. The sociogroup may be convened by someone in authority who then picks the others for their expertness. Most *movements* start as psychegroups that gradually take on sociogroup functions; and usually if a sociogroup is larger than three, one or more psychegroups may crystallize within it. It is these spontaneously formed groups, emerging outside of the official structure of society, to whom we must turn for the creative alternatives that we now so desperately need.

It is important to note that the sociogroup is able to operate effectively even though it may be very heterogeneous occupationally, socially, ethically, politically, and so forth. Its strength as a productive group is, in fact, due to its *diversity,* and the condition that enables it to capitalize on diversity is the existence of the common purposes to which the members are committed.

THE REQUIRED TRANSFORMATION

Teaching has been defined as the process of shifting the classroom microsociety from the instant culture generated by putting the participants in one room to an educative culture. In such an educative culture, self-realization is supported, autonomy is developed, and the classroom itself is developed as an internalized model of an enlightened or adaptive society. We have discussed selected features of the larger society and have tried to show how these same features operate in the classroom microsociety. At this point, I should like to focus on the configurational aspects of the culture, on the fact that these various provisions are not independent of one another and that there lies behind them the unifying principle of a way of life. In other words, we are dealing with a whole, self-consistent, complex cultural pattern, and we wish to shift this whole pattern and its underlying way of life; it is not enough merely to patch up two or three of its dimensions. This, incidentally, is both a blessing and a curse. It is a curse in that to change any part of the system you will have to overcome the resistance of all parts, however loose or remote their apparent connection to the target conditions. But it is a blessing in that it makes little difference where you start the change; if you keep at it, the rest of the system will all become involved sooner or later.

Diagrams 1 and 2 portray the societal patterns of the present classroom and of the microsociety we seek. To make comparison easier, I have kept to the same categories of composition, interaction, purpose, authority, method, and indoctrination; and the arrows for the most part suggest a logical sequence of development.

In present classrooms we note that it is generally assumed that children will be easier to teach if they are grouped for *similarity* of readiness, sophistication, or ability, and that, obviously, they will achieve best and most meaningfully if they are set in *competition* with one another. It is interesting that these features are probably connected. To the extent that the alikeness of the children reduces controversy, it also eliminates the dynamic through which society maintains its vitality and individuals discover their identity. Identity seeking is limited to quantitative comparisons of self with others with respect to the traits they have in common; identity seeking becomes interpersonal competition rather than self-discovery.

The competition is directed by the teacher, and to make it "fair" he must pick tasks that are equally distant or distasteful to all the children. (If he let them dictate their interests, the person whose interest won would be believed to have an unfair advantage.) Even goals that are "fair" are too easy for some, too hard for others, and just right for a small minority. Since this must always be the case in a competitive situation, there is no point in finding out whether the goals are meaningful to the students, for changing the goal does not eliminate meaninglessness; it only redistributes it.

Since the goals are not necessarily congruent with the needs of more than a few students, the rest may not be able to tell when the goals have been satisfied. But the teacher knows and will tell the student; therefore, *satisfying the goal and pleasing the teacher are identical processes.* The child can, through teacher-study,

Diagram 1: Classroom of the present

COMPOSITION

Homogeneous group (neighborhood, economic, or academic selection)

Socioeconomically segregated; unacceptable

INTERACTION

Student competition (via achievement for grades, scholarships, approval, etc.; struggle for individuality)

Anachronistic in affluent society having no scarcity of necessities; also miseducative: directed toward accumulation rather than use of knowledge

PURPOSE

Directed at *given goals* (specified by "authorities")

Arbitrary, requiring little or no reality testing against child's actual needs; therefore must be enforced externally

AUTHORITY

Assigned by teacher (and legitimized by authority of teachers' office)

Satisfaction of the goal made identical with pleasing the teacher; teacher becomes the chief continual object of study

METHOD

Procedures specified by authority (and must be followed in order to reach the goals)

Procedures themselves made the actual goals and bases for competition; classroom aim is socialization (meeting behavioral expectations), not education (developing methods for coping)

INDOCTRINATION

For such procedures to work, pupils required to be selected for whom the procedures are appropriate; pupils must be placed in homogeneous groups

Completion of factory or product image; denial of opportunities to create new procedures; separation of upper track, productive society from lower track, welfare society

86

Diagram 2: Educative classroom microsociety

COMPOSITION

Heterogeneous group (cultural pluralism, age mixture, compatibility with teacher)

Simulating the megalopolitan world in which citizens live

↓

INTERACTION

Cooperation in activities

All students assumed to "belong"; class a supportive milieu; variety of possible rewards in multidimensional activity

↓

PURPOSE

Directed at *emergent goals*

Shared commitment to emergent goals developed through formulation and reality testing; goals serve as basis for group unity, group raison d'être

↓

AUTHORITY

Emergent goals become externalized; they then *make demands* on the class

Goal criteria become the authority for selecting among alternatives for self-discipline

↓

METHOD

Demands to be met through *inquiry* which collects diverse ideas, selects or consolidates plans, acts, evaluates, redefines goals

Use made of a very wide range of skills and contributions which the group needs; basis established for self-esteem as well as for development of individual's style of coping

↓

INDOCTRINATION

Select group to have sufficient *diversity* (resources) or orientations, values, knowledge, skills, etc.

Reaffirmation of the democratic belief that diversity is the source of strength of the open and purposive society

↓

learn to please the teacher, so that the goals remain senseless and arbitrary, and the teacher himself becomes the significant target.

Since the children cannot make deductions from goals to procedures, or from ends to means, the teacher must specify the procedures. These are concrete and require activity on the part of the student. To him, carrying out the teacher-required procedures is the heart of learning and the goal of activity; and the teacher-stated goals are only rationalizations or trust-building assurances that the teacher, at least, knows what he is up to.

Whatever procedures are set up will, of course, be more reasonable for one child than another. It is therefore desirable to select children into the class on the basis of their ability to participate effectively in the predetermined procedures. And hence we are back to homogeneous grouping and to a factory in which selected raw materials are pushed through predetermined activities for the sake of making them "competent" and also, inevitably, alike.

Before leaving this classroom design, I wish to invite you to consider how accurately the above profile fits most jobs of adults, and how such experiences in the classroom must contribute to the development of the organization man as well as to the perpetuation of the cultural pattern. I should also like to refer as kind of a footnote to the research on heterogeneous versus homogeneous grouping. Quite apart from any civil rights or historic movements in the larger society, research on homogeneous grouping consistently fails to support its superiority over heterogeneous grouping. It is safe to conclude that homogeneous grouping is preferred not for reasons of achievement but for reasons of indoctrination. By segregating the students one can indoctrinate them a classful at a time: upper tracks—college bound; lower tracks—jail and welfare bound. Obviously homogeneous ability grouping must be discarded; and, since it is only a question of time, I think it would be quite becoming to educators if we took the lead and did graciously what we will otherwise have to do later at the point of a loaded tax bill.

Turning to Diagram 2, which illustrates design 2, or the

educative classroom, I am happy to say that all the evils of the larger society and of educational systems have been corrected. This, then, is an ideal model, and education is the process of reaching toward it.

It starts with a class that represents fairly the *diversity* within the school population. Whether or not steps should be taken to make it even more heterogeneous should, I think, depend on our ability to deal with individual differences. Havighurst thinks the diversity should be that of the megalopolitan world that defines the geographic life space of today's child.[2]

The diverse populations should be assigned to teachers on the basis of *compatibility* or teaching effectiveness. Research shows that such classes are just as heterogeneous as noncompatible classes with respect to all the traditional measures. (The teacher may say he teaches bright students best, for example, but when he names the actual children who "get more out of class," their IQ test scores cover the same range as those he selects as "getting least out of class.") The big plus for the compatible class is its greater solidarity and therefore a greater ability to tolerate its own heterogeneity.

It is obvious that competition in a heterogeneous class will not do; there is no contest. For each task certain students obviously have the required ability more than others; and the others are, I think, justified in refusing to compete. The alternative to competition is to regard succeeding as an open-ended process, that is, to make success depend on factors that are unknowable at the start, rather than on stable abilities.

In the heterogeneous group, then, competition between individuals is out. A much more intense dynamic arises: natural *controversy*. This is made possible by a cooperative milieu and it is resolved through *cooperative efforts* directed toward a genuine goal-to-be-striven-for. Since nobody can initially state a real goal of the group, the students and teacher will have to put their heads together, react to clear-cut confrontations, look at their reactions, and, finally, infer the goals as the "sense of the meet-

[2] Personal communication.

ing." Goals and commitments to goals are emergent. They arise when people have good will, when they are optimistic, when they see that all of them are intrigued by some aspects of shared experiences.

For a goal to give the group direction it must be such that proposed action can be publicly judged against it; in other words, it must have operational implications and it must be possible to get clear feedback on the effectiveness of the action. This sort of goal is externalized. It acts like a demand from outside the group, but is an acceptable demand because the group created it and put it there. As a genuine goal, it is also one that nobody has the present competence to meet. The group will have to produce a wide range of skills and knowledge; and they will have to develop a cooperative way of discovering and drawing on each other's resources. This in turn will solidify each person's right to belong to the group (as a first-class contributing citizen) and thus enhance his own autonomy.

The more ambitious the goal, the greater will be the range of contributions required to meet it and consequently the more heterogeneous the class must be. And here we may find realization of the democratic ideal: that the strength of a people and the adaptive survival of their country lie in the diversity of their talents, the pluralism of their cultures, the range and scope of their purposes.

Thus we have a second coherent design, and I think there is overwhelming evidence all about us that it is trying to be born. For those who feel that my first design is too harsh (as any pure model must be) I suspect that they are seeing some aspects of this second design mixed in. Actual situations are somewhere between the two.

A further comment is in order, and that is that the description of the second design is quite incomplete compared with the first. There are simply many more relevant dimensions because the students are operating much more as "whole" persons. What has been left out is the detailing of the informal structure (for example, "small voluntary groups") of the microsociety and its processes in their relationship to formal processes. Also left out are the private purposes of the individual. When the emergent group goals give the society its raison d'être and its public authority and rationale, and when the society is productive and purposive, each individual receives the stimulation and response he needs to live far more fully and richly. He is then able to pursue within the secure public boundaries his own more private interests.

In summary, comparison of Diagrams 1 and 2 generates a great many topics as possible subjects for professional dialogue.

Composition: Formulating policies and procedures for recruiting the appropriately heterogeneous student body and dividing it into instructional groups; establishing methods for working with parents and community leaders to achieve this grouping

Interaction: Reducing competition, increasing cooperation; studying ways to increase functional interdependence in projects; enabling more students to help each other (for example tutoring, cross-age groups); finding ways to organize more effective committees, small groups, and teams for different purposes

Purpose: Seeking purposes from the situation, rather than from the teacher; enabling voluntary institutions within the informal structure (friendship groups) to inform and motivate and increase gratifications in the working organization; setting up activities to help students act out or demonstrate interests and needs that can be capitalized on educationally; detailing techniques of pupil-teacher planning; developing procedures for locating "where the group is" with respect to progress toward its long- and short-range goals; developing self-assessment techniques to be used by individual students, subgroups, and class

Authority: Moving from external authority of the teacher to the authority of the child's own tested experience; changing the teacher's role from director to consultant and methodologist; deriving purposes from the inherent logic of the situation (environment plus persons) rather than only from the desires of the teacher, textbook authors, or students

Method: From following the specified procedures to choosing among alternatives and assessing consequences of choice; from rapid convergence on one course of action to deliberate, imaginative creation of many possible courses; from seeking the right way to assessing pros and cons of all ways, and creating new ways; from submission to or imitation of the teacher to self-directed coping and to a broader range of ways in which individuals can contribute to group goals; from suppressing one's doubts to expressing them as an aid to determining wisely the next steps

Indoctrination: Consciousness of self as contributor to society, and hence as part of it—a worthy person; acceptance of interdependence as a fact of life, and understanding of the conditions that set persons free instead of constraining them; association of freedom with individual full-functioning creativity, and self-captaincy; understanding of why mutuality is required to preserve freedom; position of optimistic rationality: that problems exist, can be reformulated through use of intelligence and good will

I proposed that the driving force for in-service teacher training is to be the sense of discrepancy between community and school experiences of the teacher. This force comes from the kind of vulnerability or even personal threat that I assume any aware teacher would feel when he contemplates the snug world of the classroom in comparison with the intensely problematic real world children will have to deal with. And if the teacher belongs to any political, hobby, or artistic groups in the community, he can compare how he and his friends behave there with how he and his children behave in the microsociety.

These comparisons will have heightened impact if the teacher can really believe that what happens in the classroom does have something to do with what will happen in the community. Certainly the way English or algebra is taught in most places would justify the feeling that the classroom is not of this earth. But I think we cannot afford to fool around irresponsibly; the child is indeed father to the man, and anyone having significant contact with the child is a godmother or godfather. I challenge the English or algebra teacher to dig and dig until he comes up with plausible connections between microsocieties and macrosocieties. If he still cannot, then he has been accepting money under false pretenses all these weary years. On the other hand, if he can see a relationship between what he does in the microsociety and what his children may be expected to do in the macrosociety, then he had better get busy and make some changes because his classroom expectations are not high enough.

Let us now note that, according to the arguments of this chapter, in-service training involves (a) significant experience in the larger society; (b) conscious experiencing of the classroom as a microsociety; (c) availability of faculty members to help each other assimilate *a* and *b*; and (d) formal organization of the faculty as a purposive professional group. In the remainder of this paper, I shall consider points *a*, *b*, and *d*. Point *c* could be considered separately, but would soon be seen to be mostly supportive of the other three.

BEING OF AGE IN THE LARGER SOCIETY

It might be a good idea for the teacher to find out something about the city where he lives. To this end I would advise him to read the newspaper, see the TV news at ten, take a sight-seeing tour, take a course on the city's features, go for a walk into a new neighborhood, visit two other churches, sit under a tree in the park and watch the children for two hours, fly a kite, go to the library and find out which books circulate most and least, watch a parade and the people watching the parade, go through the local ice cream plant, spend a few hours in jail, find out what there is on the road exactly two miles west of the city limits. He should try guessing people's occupations from the way they dress and their state of origin from the way they talk.

These are *observing* experiences, just to provide the vocabulary so the teacher can find out where he is by making a list of the things he likes and another of the things he dislikes in his environment.

Then there are all the *participatory* experiences. The teacher should march in a protest, go bird-watching with a pre-breakfast group, enter a six-day bicycle race, play Winners Circle, write his brother-in-law's name on a coupon and send it in, join the neighborhood block group (if there isn't one, he should organize one), take the neighbor's four-year-old for a walk, be a volunteer helper at the hospital, help a friend go house-hunting, collect papers for the local charity, distribute campaign literature and argue with a stranger.

He should find out the city's principal interests, ethnic groups, economic resources, crime rates, income, and problems; learn the name of his alderman and the location of the nearest fire station; go to school by a different route every day; try Rice Krispies instead of Special K for breakfast.

In the thirties, it was quite common to tell teachers they should know and participate in their community. That advice was sound then and mandatory now, for the old comfortable do-nothing definition of the citizen is gone. At any rate, I propose that knocking about the city, experiencing the environment, is almost certain to contribute to one or more of the following adult perceptions and traits of just about anyone:

(a) An awareness, through consciousness of one's likes and dislikes, of one's own ideal for proper living. (And: Can I achieve these values in the classroom?)

(b) A realization that there are many ways of life, and many types of persons, and that all of them have a right to be alive and to strive for life, liberty, and the pursuit of happiness. (And: Do I allow this in my classroom?)

(c) A consciousness that one is himself still able to be moved by sights, arrested by stinks, frightened by strangeness, and piqued by fragments. This is good for the self-esteem. Further, the consciousness of alternatives to everything one usually takes for granted may stimulate some worthwhile thinking. (Like: What makes me so sure it is bad for the children to have homework sometimes?) It is fun to note that as you wander about, you just naturally think about all kinds of crazy things; and that some of the crazy things you drop right away and others you mull over or tuck away for future mulling. (And: I wonder whether the kids also think without my permission, just for the heck of it; and what they think about, and whether they think about me, and whether they connect anything in class with the rest of life.)

(d) The ability to make an assessment of the town's role and resources: What are all the materials, personnel, and messages that come into town; what are the ones that go out; what is the connection between input and output; or, as far as the rest of the world is concerned, what is the function of my town? (And: What are the inputs and outputs of our school, and of my class; and what relates them?) The city, with physical layout, transportation, distinctive neighborhoods, and so on, is the prototype of a system, a *model* for relating structures, processes, and values. As you look around the community, what are its component structures? Who is central and controlling? Who doesn't fit? How susceptible is it to change? Who has a voice in changing it? What is the place of your school in the community? (Locate the neighborhoods your pupils come from; having seen these, can you now explain some of the differences among your students?)

(e) Awareness that the community is alive with many groups, each of which, like the class, is a microcosm of the larger society: You should participate in different groups for different purposes, and compare them with each other and your own class. Be absolutely shameless in stealing ideas from the Rotary or Hillel or the block group for use in your own class. Notice especially the different ways used to get people to come to order, the variety of ways to respond to suggestions, or to warm up the audience to ask questions, or to entice persons to volunteer. Talk with other members and find out twenty-three of the forty-five possible reasons why a person might voluntarily go to a meeting. (Imagine that your children didn't have to come to class if they didn't want to. What are some useful ideas from adult groups where attendance is voluntary?)

(f) Most of all, a feeling of moral sensitivity to the larger community: Here, laid out for all to see, with no explanation or apology possible, is the physical record of the collective efforts of your fellow citizens. What does it add up to: Beauty? Despoliation? Broken promises? Sharing? Selfishness? Excitement? Depression? Sadness? And how would you like to affect all this through your experiences with the children, through what you might help them become?

The community is a midway point between the nation and the classroom. It is there to be experienced directly, endlessly, freshly. No environment smaller than the community, or even the megalopolis, can provide the stage for a man's life. To understand the full human being means to understand his relationship to the environment with respect to each of the transactions that constitute life. And once the teacher begins to see life's ecology, he can then extend it to the larger society experienced symbolically and existing only in the mind. He can also begin to see what kind of meaning the classroom, as a now rather empty corner of the child's environment, may be capable of having.

At least some of the time, the teacher should take a companion with him as he knocks about the place. He should pay attention to the kinds of ways he uses the companion: the kinds of responses he seeks from him, the kinds of questions or opinions he wants to share, the types of decisions he wants to make for himself and those he wishes to defer. He should find out what he does with a friend, compare experiences with and without a companion and see how they differ, and think about times he would rather have been alone and why. (Yes, it's like that with children, too!)

THE MICROSOCIETY AS A LABORATORY

Just as the problems of management, prejudice, and boredom one has in the classroom may stimulate corresponding sensitivities to the larger community, so intriguing, dramatic, and appealing fragments of life in the community may stimulate classroom adventures.

First there is what children have shown the teacher outside the classroom. I do not see how a teacher could watch urban poor children playing together and entertaining themselves with the most pitiful resources without sensing the way they can reach out for one another. And this strength might suggest that they could help one another in the classroom. So the teacher could experiment with making his assignments to small groups rather than separately to individuals. He could also allow some children to tutor others in reading and arithmetic. And if he did, he would be amazed at the potentials. (With students helping one another, I see no reason why everybody except the physiologically handicapped couldn't learn the three R's.)

Just as he could experiment in the classroom with strengths of pupils discovered outside, so he could experiment with his own techniques on the basis of alternatives noted outside. For example, all teachers give orders. Very well, let the teacher play with giving orders as if he were a policeman, an employer, an elected chairman, and so forth. Similarly, let him experiment with ways to acknowledge work, suggestions, and mute presence. Let him play with the logistic notion that all complex operations and structures are simply different combinations of the same essential ingredients; therefore, all persons in the community who work with human beings must be dealing with some of the same elements, and they can show one another alternative ways.

The teacher, in moving toward design 2, must encourage students to give him feedback about how things are going. They also need to plan with him at least enough to help them know what to do. The teacher should, I think, experiment with encouraging class awareness that they are a working organization with structures, direction, boundaries, and moods. In social studies it is obvious that the class as a microsociety can be used to illustrate most of the properties of macrosocieties, and the students should be invited to diagnose difficulties and nonproductive periods and make suggestions about how to remedy or avoid them. They should also be invited to experiment with special roles (chairman, monitors, sergeant-at-arms, recording engineer) as often as possible so that they can see that cooperation is necessitated by role specialization, not merely by the teacher's personal whim.

The problem of the discipline of knowledge, or the structure of the subject matter domain, is a very large one and a very sore point with anybody who thinks learning should be an experience of inquiry. To most teachers, subject matter knowledge is there in the book and never mind where it came from or what you can do with it; just "learn" it. This is maintaining design 1 with a vengeance! Our design 2 sees information as a means to accomplishing some purpose. If you cannot think up some purpose that would be served by the information, then you are in no position to teach it. This is but another way of saying that the operational level is as important as the conceptual. The discovery of "curiosity for curiosity's sake" in the case of Harlow's knothole-peering monkeys has been used to console many educational nonfunctionalists, but the monkeys actually were scanning for something to be intrigued by, and they were conducting their own investigation in their own way. My point, of course, is that they were meeting a real need they had, which is a bit different from the teacher's gratuitous empty barrage of words.

The question of what the subject matter and methods of inquiry and application can contribute to the child's experience needs to be raised over and over. Most domains of knowledge provide guidelines for meeting certain situations, solving certain problems, or accomplishing something. This is the bread and butter or consumer part. Then there are the dramatic adventures of inquiry in which the child functions as a junior historian, chemist, or mathematician to unravel some puzzle or uncover some missing (to him) fact in the field. The exciting aspect of the knowledge accumulated by man is not all those fine propositions and organized paragraphs; they are only by-products of the fantastic dialogue man carries on with nature. But the reason for having students engage in inquiry is obviously not the off-chance they will discover something not yet reported in the literature; it is so that they can learn to interact sympathetically and understandingly with the physical, biological, social, humane world. Through this prototypical inquiry experience their lives may gain built-in or internalized guidelines.

With some subjects, such as foreign language, in which

reasoning doesn't help much, the knowledge discipline can only contribute certain skills and specific information. But with other fields, the disciplines help one meet their particular, everlastingly replicated and recurring situations with efficiency, elegance, and satisfaction. Most teachers have a good deal to learn about the way real *understanding* of their subject could enrich the class efforts to become a humane microsociety.

Having seen a variety of organizations—PTA, unions, clubs, teams, offices, adult classes, church groups—the teacher may consider whether any of these could be models for the organization and operation of the class. Are there times when the class should be run like an army, a garden club, a TV panel show, an experience-swapping bull session? I would argue that for every clear objective, some special organization would be most facilitative, that such organizations do exist in the larger so .iety, and the teacher might, at the appropriate times, simulate such models.

Another major contribution of the community is in the sensitization to such qualities as justice, rights, fairness, distribution, and expectation—qualities that are usually suppressed in traditional teaching (design 1) but are vital in the larger society and *should be* also in the microsociety. The teacher may not be able to take effective action in the community; but enlightened action in the classroom is every bit as important.

THE OPERATION OF THE FACULTY

When administrators ask about in-service training, they usually want to know what to do to the faculty; and certainly faculty organization and action have their place. But I have gone to some length in the preceding two sections to insist that the crucial effort is that of the individual teacher who has a problem in reconciling his societal and classroom participation and is trying to do something about it in the classroom. I believe that any school in which in-service training procedures have a chance to succeed will indeed have such individual explorations going on.

The principal will be unable to prevent it; he will be the sort of fellow to whom teachers enjoy telling their great ideas; and he will not be able to listen to them without egging them on. In other words, the starting point or the prior condition is a decent climate and a concerned faculty, and both are set by the head man.

I do know that in-service action can be started cold in the faculty without having established an appropriate climate; but the last such instance I studied involved eighty-five teachers, of whom twenty got "involved" and three actually accomplished something. The other sixty-five pretended to be interested until the principal (predictably) lost interest himself, and then they all relaxed and forgot about it.

In-service action in the faculty begins with selective rein-forcement and encouragement of individuals by the principal. In such a climate the initiators find it easy to involve other teachers. These other teachers may just be audience, or they may have special roles, whether they know it or not. Some of the special roles one often sees are (1) a friend to talk with about one's qualms, anxieties, or big fantasies (a lounge and coffee pot help); (2) some liberal who knows about the larger society and has precise inside information about the community; (3) an experi-enced teacher in the school who knows all the children and their families; (4) someone who loves to invent new classroom activ-ities and can never teach the same lesson over; (5) the faculty as a group, meeting to hear about activities or innovations in one's classroom; and (6) a principal who not only allows himself to be involved but also sees that it is in the school's interest for each teacher to find the right sort of help from others—thus greatly extending the value of the teacher's initiation.

POSSIBLE STEPS TOWARD ACTIVATING A TRAINING PROGRAM

After the ferment is started, and perhaps a dozen teachers have been involved in informal experimentation, then one can imagine a series of steps that might follow. The reader should regard these seemingly prescriptive procedures as communication clues, which can be easily subjected to many interpretations and varied applications.

1. The teachers report, preferably with the help of slides, on their experiments. In front of the faculty, the principal may contribute a few questions that call attention to things about which he wants to express enthusiasm. Others ask questions.

2. The faculty is asked to help the researchers by suggesting next steps they might take, or questions that should really be answered before going much further. These are written on the board.

3. A panel (warned in advance) undertakes to speculate on these questions in front of the faculty; what they are looking for is evidence of underlying concerns (for example, orderliness, too much homework, delinquents, teacher overload) that may have been projected into the comments occasioned by the reports.

4. Hopefully they uncover a number of questions that interest a number of people, and these people are asked to "tell about it." If the questions are real questions, there will be disagreement expressed, and after that has gone on for a bit, it can be suggested that it would be interesting to hear from everybody and could a small steering committee be formed to develop a questionnaire and circulate it next week? A procedure is suggested (ask the panel to do it but add anyone else who was clearly highly involved and possibly strongly biased) and the committee is ratified.

5. The committee comes up with a questionnaire, which is circulated to the faculty and returned to them. The questions are relevant to the concerns identified in steps 3 and 4. The returns are tabulated and graphed and, if possible, dramatized in a skit.

6. The faculty is confronted with the tables, graphs, or skit. They go into small groups to swap views and to formulate reactions. Thus rehearsed and encouraged, the teachers may now make the same points in subsequent discussions involving the whole

faculty. The question is raised as to what major problem would be most exciting for the faculty to address itself to. Suggestions are invited and written down.

7. The steering committee reworks the list, duplicates it, and sends it out.

8. Grade groups, departments, or other divisions discuss the proposed topics, trying to think what would be involved in the pursuit of each topic. They then select the topic with highest pay-off for them and write down how they would explore it if it were chosen.

9. At the next faculty meeting, each subdivision reports its assessment of the topics. The minimum number of topics that will include all members of the faculty is selected and declared official. Tentative interest groups, several if necessary, are formed around each topic and meet long enough to set their own time and place.

10. The interest groups make no effort to plan and carry out a single experiment. Instead, they discuss all the different things people might do to throw light on the topic (for example, conditions under which assigned independent study is successful), and then encourage each teacher to commit himself to try some one method in his own class before the next meeting.

11. Concurrent with this classroom experimentation, of individuals or pairs, some investigation is conducted in the community. In the case of independent study, some teachers could investigate this concept in offices, research laboratories, detective bureaus, libraries, art studios, and elsewhere. All the investigations could be pooled in an effort to name this phenomenon or occurrence in nonschool, societal language, that is, to seek to define the more universal process of which the school's independent study is an instance. (It is only when teachers see such connections that they can help the student's school experience increase his adequacy in similar situations outside.)

12. Progress reports from the various committees are made to the faculty when appropriate, and individuals are encouraged to shift around from one committee to another. There may even be a committee for those who don't work in committees; this

would be to legitimize their individual work or nowork as the case may be.

13. It is difficult to say which of many possibilities will make sense next, and when. Next steps will become evident as their need begins to be felt.

One major sign of success is that the teachers play much more responsible and influential roles in the community, and especially that they help out with Head Start and with projects designed for the welfare of children.

Another major sign of success is that the *school* activates and works with the other youth-serving agencies in a coordinated effort for each agency to contribute what it can to the education and welfare of the children.

And, finally, the community will perhaps create learning centers that will foster self-realization for child and teacher in an environment that is cooperative, encouraging, inquiry oriented, and focused upon emergent goals.

■ CLUES TO ACTION

Thelen does not counter the recommendation of the previous writers regarding teacher-determined growth programs; he, too, believes that teachers are the best judges of what should go on in programs of continuing education. Beyond this, however, he emphasizes that meaningful conversation with one's peers is a rich source of stimulation and ego support. For Thelen, intense personal involvement is an essential ingredient in any in-service education activity that is to have significance. Not only do such group encounters provoke mutual support, but, of even greater moment, they also counteract the sense of detachment that is becoming increasingly characteristic of professional life.

The teacher, he asserts, no longer is driven by the missionary zeal that once was a hallmark of the helping profession. And it is this estrangement from the inner motives of teaching which Thelen believes should be a dominant target of continuing education activities. Along with Jackson and Bush, he urges that we rekindle the teacher's awareness of alternatives, his interest in the introspective examination of his actions, and his desire for self-initiated change. In this way we may be able to interrupt the cultural forces that are making teaching more of an "out-and-out occupation" and less of an "almost-profession."

Thelen is deeply concerned about the growing impersonality of teaching and teachers. Convinced that the classroom should mirror the larger society, he suggests that a large measure of professional growth activity be directed toward enlarging the teacher's awareness of the world around him. This, in turn, will enable the teacher to enhance the social awareness of the children he teaches. What Thelen is after, in short, is a teacher who can go beyond the constraints of the subject matter to its connections with the real world. Thus he shares Jackson's conviction that an emphasis upon teaching technique alone is grossly insufficient.

Man cannot live alone, Thelen reminds us, and it is his group life that satisfies his need for cooperative behavior. It is groups of teachers —made cohesive by the common interests of the members, and made viable by the collaborative dialogues which ensue—that can serve as an effective vehicle for professional growth. "It is these spontaneously formed groups," he argues, "emerging outside of the official structure of society, to whom we must turn for the creative alternatives that we now so desperately need." For Thelen, then, the sociogroup is more than a collection of people with a mutual purpose; it is, rather, a source of professional rejuvenation.

Midway in his chapter, Thelen sets forth the four points on which his rationale for continuing education rests: (1) opportunity to increase worldly knowledge, (2) opportunity to acquire skills for transferring this knowledge to the classroom, (3) opportunity to refine both the knowledge and the procedures for its classroom application through group interaction, and (4) opportunity to revitalize professionalism within the faculty.

■ OPERATIONAL IMPLICATIONS

1. Classrooms frequently lack relevance to life itself. **Acquiring teaching methods that result in a stronger connection between the subject matter of the classroom and life outside should be a major goal of professional growth programs.**

2. The continuing education of teachers should provide opportunities for increasing understanding of the changing society. **The training program should promote activities that give the teacher greater contact with his social environment.**

3. Some of the knowledge teachers require is most easily obtained by interacting with others in a group situation. **Groups of teachers, engaged in a mutual and open analysis of their functions, represent an effective instrument of professional growth.**

part II

THE PROOF OF THE PUDDING

Education has long been victimized by a pervasive myth which holds that it is impossible to distinguish a good teacher from a bad one. There are many different objectives in teaching, so the myth goes, and thus it is impossible to either standardize performance or hold a teacher accountable for the results obtained. In the chapters of the second section, Allen, Lippitt and Fox, Fischler, and Fantini—each in his own way—seek to demolish the myth. The essence of their argument is that the quality of teaching performance *can* be assessed, whatever the objective. We now command procedures with which to provide teachers accurate data on the fruits of their labor. The chapters suggest that, when all is said and done, it is the teacher who bears the greatest responsibility for a lesson that is either a success or a failure. The proof of the instructional pudding, so to speak, is in the learning.

We must, say Allen and Fischler, specify what it is that we wish to accomplish in the classroom. These specifications will enable us eventually to compare intent with outcome. The disparity between desire and yield serves both as a point of departure and as a road map to the goals of professional improvement. Put another way, it is the

107

discrepancy between what the teacher sets out to accomplish and what actually is accomplished that offers the best clues to the nature of the in-service education activities that are most needed. In instances, the corrective will be a matter of assisting teachers to revise their instructional techniques. In other instances, the corrective may consist of providing teachers with more information about their subject or their students. But in some cases, the writers contend, a more powerful solution may be required. Teachers use different techniques, prefer one teaching style to another, and regard some tasks with fondness and some with distaste; there are a number of arguments, resultingly, for increased teacher specialization. If, in short, we can make it possible for teachers to work at the things at which they are most adept, we will gain a substantial advantage.

Through such specialization perhaps we can aid and abet the reforms that so desperately are needed. Greater specialization, and the precision that follows from it, will allow us to design instruction from a different vantage point, to develop a curriculum that has more social muscle, and to use teaching energy with greater forcefulness. Of even larger importance, through specialization we can nurture a self-evolving teacher with much more efficiency. By restricting the scope of the teacher's activities, self-evidently, the components of professional development also are reduced. It therefore becomes easier to enrich knowledge of subject, to improve interaction between teacher and child, and, in general, to use each teacher's potential to better advantage.

Two other ideas are a recurring theme in the section. One has to do with the affective aspects of teaching, and the other with resources for promoting teacher improvement.

Good teaching performance has emotional as well as intellectual overtones. Consequently, professional growth must encompass attitudes and values as well as technical skills. In other words, what the teacher takes as his goal is fully as important as the procedures he uses to attain his goal. Talent deployed in the achievement of improper ends is, for all practical purposes, talent wasted. So, as the society shifts, and as the social changes are reflected in new educational priorities, in-service education must make it possible for teachers to keep pace.

Finally, the authors, notably Allen, Lippitt, and Fox, espouse a strong conviction that teachers can make a substantial contribution to the betterment of one another's work. The range of ability among teachers is very great. If we can somehow devise a method through which the behavior of gifted teachers is emulated more widely, perhaps we can reduce the enormous difference between the best and the worst teaching that goes on in a school.

dwight w. allen

CHAPTER FIVE

IN-SERVICE TEACHER TRAINING:
A modest proposal

Of all the tradition-bound practices in American education, the current state of in-service teacher training is probably the most indefensible. Such training as there is seems to be guided by two mutually incompatible perspectives: (1) in-service training as relevant to the upgrading of teachers' professionalism and class-room performance; (2) in-service training as a convenient way to pile up units, which will move a teacher horizontally across the pay schedule. All too often, of course, the second perspective dominates to the exclusion of everything else, and thus it is difficult to find anyone in the profession, from teacher to administrator to school of education faculty member, who has a good word to say about in-service courses. But perhaps even more ironically, the ultimate goal of current in-service training, bound as it is to the accumulation of pay-raising units, seems to be to move teachers out of the classroom, rather than to improve their effectiveness within it; the more units and/or degrees an elementary or secondary teacher accumulates, the more likely is he to promote himself out of the classroom and into a guidance position or an administrative role or, perhaps, into higher education.

Given the current structure of education in general and teacher credentialing in particular, it is not surprising that in-service training is so rooted in the conception of units taken, time spent at the university, and steps up the pay scale. Our entire educational framework is based on such time criteria, and within such a system, it is perhaps only consistent to view a two-unit course as in-service training without any reference to the course's effect on the teacher's professionalism. Indeed, it seems that we, as a profession, have committed ourselves to a pair of nonsensical beliefs that leave no room for in-service training as anything but a handle up the pay scale. We seem to believe that (1) the bestowal of a teaching credential creates lifetime professional competence; (2) inadequacies in pre-service training leave a life of irremediable professional handicaps. With this view of the relationship between pre-service and in-service training, and with a century-old belief in time as the criterion of educational success, it is understandable, though indefensible, that in-service training has become the disgrace that it is.

THE DIFFERENTIATED STAFF: A SOLUTION?

What, then, is needed to make in-service training a viable concern—to make it relevant to the professional growth of teachers and thus to the improvement of educational opportunities for students? First, I think we must admit, however embarrassing it may be, that the current structure of our educational system does not leave room for the kind of rationality we would like to see in teacher training. We have not, as a profession, gone beyond the development of vague criteria of good and bad in evaluating teacher performance. We simply have not devoted sufficient thought and imagination to the delineation of teacher tasks to know what kinds of skills and competencies are required in the various roles that teachers assume. What skills should a teacher of eighth grade United States history have that differ from those required for teaching eleventh grade United States history? More importantly, what competencies need to be developed in a teacher to help him become a stimulating lecturer that might not be necessary were he to lead small group seminars?

The tragedy of our current system is not so much that it has not answered such difficult questions, but that it provides no means whereby they can be answered and, what is worse, that it does not allow for the asking of them. Under the current system, we treat all teachers as perfectly interchangeable parts—as though there were some mystical power in the designation *teacher* that wipes out all individual differences and makes every person so labelled equally adept at teaching all varieties of students. Consider the high school teacher who has outstanding skills as a lecturer—we give him 150 students in five blocks of thirty students. Now consider the teacher who cannot lecture, but is uncannily adept at leading small group seminars—we give him 150 students in five blocks of thirty. Given the present system, how could we even begin to differentiate the various educational roles that teachers can play, and allow them to be applied to the education of students with maximum efficiency? As the system now stands, we allow the teacher to face his five yearly lots of thirty once he has a credential. He then faces the same organizational pattern for the rest of his life, receiving extra pay if he can survive long enough and pile up enough units at the university. How do we ever find out what *special* educational talents he has? How do we ever find out what skills he should have, but does not? How do we ever decide on a rational in-service training procedure that will help him to develop his own uniquely beneficial competencies? Clearly, we never get around to such crucial matters, for the system never allows us to focus on them.

What is required, then, before sensible in-service training can be developed, is a careful differentiation and task analysis of the various aspects of the teacher's role. But the current structure of education makes such analysis impossible because its monolithic nature tends to wash out and camouflage all the useful distinctions among teachers. If we are ever to pump some sense into teacher education, at both the pre-service and the in-service levels, we must find the boldness to institute an educational structure that fosters and capitalizes upon the multiplicity of educational tasks that teachers *can* perform in our schools. We need to recognize in a viable institutional form the kinds of distinctions among teachers' roles that make good educational sense: large group lecturer versus individual tutorial worker versus curriculum development specialist.

The crucial point here is not that any such distinctions we might dream up now must be instituted. It is rather that we require an educational framework which by its very nature fosters the recognition of distinctions when they arise. Operating within the perspective of such a differentiated teaching staff structure, we might begin to *develop the performance-based task delineations* that provide the key to a sane in-service program. As soon as *differentiated staff* becomes a possibility, carefully thought-out performance criteria for teachers become a necessity. A school that allowed for the possible diversity of teachers' roles would be uniquely motivated and able to analyze and reformulate the criteria by which it would judge competence in any given teaching task. Without such criteria, teacher training at any level is ineffectual, but with them it can become closely integrated to the main concern of all educators—the educational development of students.

How might a viable in-service training program operate within the context of a differentiated teaching staff? Clearly, it would overcome many of the major impediments facing current approaches. In-service training could then devote itself to its most reasonable task: the improvement of professional competence. Teachers would no longer be bound to the accumulation of units to gain better pay or to move them out of the classroom. Rather, they would be enabled to help specify the criteria by which their performance was judged. At the same time they would participate in meaningful training experiences that would help them meet those criteria, thereby earning greater rewards through their greater competence.

We have already begun to make some of the required distinctions between professional and nonprofessional educational tasks. It is important, however, that we recognize the need for extending such distinctions. We will not be in a position to select, train, and utilize teaching talent until we develop within-profession distinctions. Freeing teachers from clerical tasks is an important first step, but we must realize that it constitutes no more than a beginning. Freedom *from* nonprofessional tasks will not become educationally meaningful until we develop the differentiated criteria that provide freedom *for* creative professional growth.

THE SELF-MODIFYING EDUCATIONAL SYSTEM

Important as they are, differentiated performance criteria are by no means a sufficient solution to the problem of in-service training. A persistent source of difficulties in much in-service work has been the extent to which the training is removed, both physically and intellectually, from the classroom environment. Further, the source and setting of in-service education evoke significant aversion in most teachers. As Meade, Lippitt, and Fox also note, it is difficult to conceive of a system more likely to have minimal effects on teachers' classroom behavior than the current one, wherein teachers must go back to a university climate, readopt the roles of students, and struggle through the process of taking examinations, writing papers, and quibbling over grades. If in-service training is to have any direct effect upon the education of students, then it must become much more closely tied to particular schools, and much less reliant upon nearby schools of education and their lecture halls. A meaningful in-service program is one in which training is directed toward teacher performance goals, of immediate relevance to teachers' everyday professional experience, and I seriously doubt that anyone in the profession could honestly claim that current school of education courses meet this requirement.

The existence of a differentiated teaching staff can be of much help on this point. A school that regularly employed a few super teachers who were exceptionally proficient in the various aspects of the teaching profession would be in an excellent position to initiate and sustain in-service programs of its own. With the help of relevant university personnel, the super teachers could set up a system that assessed teachers' strengths and weaknesses in terms of their ability to meet the developinσ set of performance criteria relevant to their tasks. The university and the teachers could then offer several alternative means (ranging, let us say, from micro-teaching situations to regular lecture courses) that might help a given teacher to overcome his weaknesses or enhance his strengths. Furthermore, the existence of continually self-modifying task descriptions for the various teaching roles within the school would enable ambitious teachers at the lower levels of the wage-responsibility-prestige scale to select from a set of training experiences which would help them develop the skills and competencies necessary to move them up the ladder. It should be noted, however, that distinctions can and should be made at the same level as well as among levels. In such a way, the mysticism currently tied to promotions via time spent and units taken would be eliminated. Whenever a given position was available or soon-to-be-available in the school, it could be sought by any teacher who might demonstrate that he could meet the performance criteria set out for that particular teaching role.

It should, at this point, be fairly obvious that an in-service program based on differentiated performance criteria lends itself admirably to a kind of research that will incorporate feedback into the program and hence make it self-adjusting to a large extent. As new roles are discovered for teachers and as old ones are discarded, the various sets of performance criteria will undergo change. And, more importantly, as individual teachers undergo alternative means of training toward different criteria, a substantial and useful set of data can be gathered to answer such questions as the following: Which training procedures are most efficient in helping teachers to meet which criteria? For teachers with different initial competencies, might it be that different training experiences are optimal in helping them meet the same criteria? For a given teacher with a particular set of skills, what *sequence* of training procedures is most appropriate if he is to meet a given set of criteria? It is my hope that such meaningful research will become an integral part of in-service training programs, for then we can begin to make intelligent decisions regarding the training procedures that should be added, dropped, and modified to make them more effective for teachers of varying individual talents. We speak much, but do little, about individualizing instruction, and I can think of no more sensible place to begin a serious concern with the issue than in-service teacher training.

Clearly, an in-service program that incorporated and fed on research in the manner described above would not be likely to hit upon the final solution to the problem of in-service training. Rather, the system would constantly be modifying itself both on the basis of newly discovered criteria and on the evidence of research findings which changed its training procedures. Equally clearly, there would be extensive differences in both the criteria and the training procedures employed, dependent upon the school's environment. The criteria and training procedures relevant to a college-preparatory high school would not, at least in all particulars, be the same as those appropriate to a secondary school serving a culturally disadvantaged area. The fact that the above system differs from current practice, however, should be a source of satisfaction rather than dismay; much as we might like to believe that there is *the answer* to our in-service problems, which will apply to all times and all places, our tendency to so believe can be harmful. Just as we are beginning to go beyond the naïveté of believing in *one method* of teaching reading to all children for all times, so must we go beyond the belief that a static, monolithic system for training teachers will ever supply *the answer*. The needs and values of our society and its individuals are changing rapidly, and our knowledge of the learning process is likewise undergoing much modification. What we require in the midst of such flux are the boldness and imagination to keep up with changes and, indeed, to anticipate them. We require the flexibility and serendipity that a continually researched and self-modifying educational system and teacher training policy can provide.

Remaining at the level of generalities for the moment, I must point out one more gross incongruity that our in-service programs must learn to resolve. In the current world of teacher training there is a disturbing discontinuity between pre-service and in-service approaches. The pre-service trainee spends either a short time in intensive course work and supervised teaching or a longer time in less intensive course work and supervised teaching. He then becomes a real certified teacher, and both the course work and the supervision end for all purposes except tenure and promotion. The assumption that a teacher who receives a credential at twenty-two years of age will not change professionally in his next forty-three years of service may be descriptively accurate in the current system. And if it is, it constitutes the greatest conceivable indictment of us as a profession. If it really is possible to learn all there is to know about teaching in a one-year (or six-month) pre-service program, then it is more than questionable whether we constitute anything that resembles a profession. But if it is not posssible, as it clearly is not, then we must specify the manner in which pre-service training will partially fulfill our professional aims. We can then set forth an in-service program that helps teachers to attain their professionalism in a way that is continuous with pre-service training. It simply will not do any longer to separate pre-service from in-service experiences. We must, in the process of specifying teaching performance criteria, set out our priorities in such a way that the credentialing procedure becomes a formality, and professional growth becomes the criterion of all training experiences.

The point here is *not* that pre-service and in-service training are, or should be, identical. Rather, it is that the procedures and goals of each must become specific and defensible in a way that they currently are not. We must make some tentative decisions regarding what criteria a teacher should meet *before* receiving a credential and what criteria should be met later as part of his in-service professional growth. With such modifiable decisions at hand, we can begin to design in-service programs that have the continuity and rationality so clearly lacking now.

The difficulties inherent in the current discontinuity between pre- and in-service training are perhaps most vividly apparent in supervision practices. Certainly there are wide variations in the quality and quantity of supervision at the pre-service level, but rarely does it approach the low quality of in-service teacher supervision. The fairly common in-service schedule of two visits per year to the classroom, separated by four or five months, makes very little sense in the light of any theory of learning. If supervision is intended to be an integral part of in-service training, at *least* as a diagnostic device, then it would make much more sense for a supervisory session to be followed by specific in-service training experiences designed to overcome the teacher's observed needs. Another supervisory session should then follow immediately to determine whether or not the training has had any effect on the teacher's classroom performance.

Some such observe-train-observe schedule of supervision could be of great value for both pre- and in-service training, especially if each cycle were focused on a single performance-defined teaching skill. The implementation of such a supervisory model would, in itself, go a long way toward providing some of the needed continuity between pre- and in-service training. Furthermore, the existence of a differentiated staff and flexible school structure would provide the opportunity for schools and universities to cooperate in the processes of supervision and training at the in-service level. If the professional growth of teachers is to become the continual process it deserves to be, we must assure that supervision and training, at both pre- and in-service levels, are the conjoint responsibility of local schools and schools of education.

DEVELOPMENT OF PERFORMANCE CRITERIA FOR TEACHERS

The remainder of this paper is an attempt to set forth, in a somewhat more specific manner, some of the priorities that must be faced in any proposal to reorganize teacher training in general and in-service training in particular. What follows will be quite clearly guided by the more general principles discussed above, but at the same time it will hopefully be specific and comprehensive enough to serve as a stimulus for development in what seem to me to be the most fruitful areas of in-service training.

Our first task, obviously, is the development of carefully conceived and relevant performance criteria for teachers. *Insofar as we can deem that the reaching of some criteria is a prerequisite for credentialing,* we will be able to make a *functional* distinction between pre- and in-service training. But if we find such priority setting as difficult as I suspect we will, then we will also serve our professional interests by emphasizing the continuity of a teacher's professional growth. There are, as I see it, three general areas wherein we need to develop performance criteria that have relevance to teachers in all subjects, at all levels, and in all situations—from the traditional classroom to the multiple-role differentiated staff. There will, of course, be differences in the criteria depending upon the subject, level of students, role of teacher, and other situational variables, but the three general areas seem to me to cover all relevant teacher characteristics.

The first general area might be labelled "content knowledge." In whatever situation a teacher is operating, he is communicating *through* some content area. One of the most difficult tasks facing teacher training at any level is the specification of *performance* criteria in subject areas. We need to develop a hierarchy of criteria that will serve to distinguish the subject matter competence required of teachers in different roles. What general knowledge should all teachers in a given area demonstrate? What specialization and in-depth knowledge should a teacher in a *particular* role demonstrate? What should a teacher in a particular professional role be able to *do,* conceptually, with his knowledge of a content area? What differences in performance related to content areas are required for teachers in different situations (for example, primary versus secondary schools, college-preparatory versus culturally disadvantaged schools) and different professional roles (for example, master teacher versus staff teacher, large group lecturer versus seminar leader)? Once again, such questions need to be answered in *performance* terms that can be evaluated before sense can be derived from the pre-service–in-service teacher education scene.

A second general area that requires specification of performance criteria might be labelled "behavioral skills." To some extent, at least, the complex act of teaching can be broken down into simpler sets of trainable skills and techniques. Such skills as reinforcing student participation, higher order questioning, varying the stimulus situation, and set induction would be a few likely candidates. These skills should be analyzed in such a manner that good agreement can be obtained regarding a given teacher's success at meeting criteria of performance for such skills. Any training program that effectively places such skills within the teacher's behavior repertory is going a long way toward providing the conditions under which the teacher may be a professional decision maker. Once again, however, we need to do more than to merely bring all teachers to the same level of competence in performing behavioral teaching skills. What different behavioral skills are more relevant to some teaching roles than others? Does a lecturer need the same level of competence in reinforcing student participation as a leader of discussion seminars? Can we develop performance criteria that lead to the optimal use of such teaching skills, or should we merely assume that the skills are part of the teacher's repertory and leave the process of professional judgment as a separate area of training? Which skills are of highest priority as prerequisites for entry into the profession, and which skills are more appropriately deemed part of a within-profession hierarchy of skills to be used as partial criteria for promotion and changes in staff role? The issue here is not our competence to answer such questions immediately, but rather our willingness to institutionalize teacher training in such a manner that the right questions are asked, answered tentatively, researched, and reformulated.

The final area in which performance criteria are required is undoubtedly the most demanding and quite possibly the most important. We all recognize that effective teaching is more than subject matter plus an active repertory of behavioral presentation skills. The "something more" might best be designated as personological skills, although the label "skills" may be misleading. Such amorphous traits as respect for students, spontaneity, empathetic understanding, realness, and acceptance are intended to be included under this heading. So, too, are the vague and unspecified goals of many currently used training procedures such as sensitivity groups, role-playing, and interaction analysis. The great difficulty here is that, as professional educators, we have strong intuitions that such traits are in no small way crucial to successful teaching. Yet, unfortunately, we have never taken the time to specify what we mean carefully enough to formulate measurable criteria by which their presence or absence may be determined. Although the terms are notable by their ambiguity, it is clearly crucial that we begin to specify their meanings more precisely, for if we fail to do so, the probability is high that we will continue to leave the development of such highly relevant personological traits to pure chance. It seems to me a difficult but far from impossible task to make the characteristics of, say, a Rogerian facilitating teacher sufficiently operational to be of use in the development of performance criteria for the teacher's role. Once again, of course, we cannot be satisfied, even in the personological realm, with specifying one set of all-or-none criteria for use with all teachers in all situations. We are obligated to determine which *operationally defined* personological traits are most appropriate for which instructional situations. In this area perhaps more than the others we are faced with difficult problems in terms of priorities, sequencing the attainment of objectives, and stages of professional growth at which attainment of these goals seems most appropriate. The criteria, however, need to be developed if we wish to demonstrate that teacher training at pre- and in-service levels can have a real and powerful effect on improving and maintaining the professional competency of teachers.

Once the process of delineating such performance criteria as those outlined above has begun, we will be able to select from the various training techniques those which seem most appropriate to the teacher's professional interests. Given the great diversity of teacher characteristics which will always exist, and given the soon-to-be realized diversity of teacher roles and tasks, it is imperative that we find and invent alternative means whereby in-service programs can help teachers attain any given criterion. In the process of meeting content area performance criteria, for example, there are innumerable possibilities beyond the standard lecture course. Programmed instruction, computer-assisted instruction, directed reading arrangements, seminars, video tapes, and film presentations all represent possible means by which any particular content aim might be achieved by a teacher with his own unique background. Given a sufficient amount of research on the success of teachers with varying abilities in meeting content criteria through alternative routes, we might eventually develop the competence as a profession to predict the optimal training sequence for any given teacher in attaining any given criterion. But until such research has been done, and in order to foster it, we have the responsibility to specify the criteria, provide alternative routes, and carefully analyze the success of different techniques in bringing individual teachers up to criterion performance. Limited only by our own imaginations, we ought to be able to assure that *any* teacher, no matter what his particular weaknesses are, will be able to meet *any* criterion through *some* in-service training procedure.

In the area of behavioral skills, the hope is once again that we can devise numerous alternative means for the attainment of each specified performance criterion. In-class observation, supervised micro-teaching sessions, simulated teaching situations, seminars, lectures, programmed instruction, and even computer-assisted instruction loom as currently existing possibilities. Again, our goal should not be the development of one super method which will be applied to all teachers, but rather a wide variety of approaches that can be researched within the in-service program so as to design optimal training for individual teachers. The proper sequencing of training experiences for different teachers in the acquisition of different skills will be an interesting research problem here, as will the development of priorities for deciding when a particular skill is most relevant to a given teacher's professional growth. Most challenging in terms of inventing training techniques, however, is the problem of optimizing a teacher's *use* of behavioral skills once they are part of his portfolio. Can we devise experiences for teachers that will help them to develop the decision-making capabilities necessary for effective use of their bag of behavioral tricks? Should those experiences be the same or different for teachers entering different educational situations? Do we have the imagination to create *different* training situations that will help different teachers to attain the same level of competence in such decision making?

In the personological area, interestingly enough, we already have a fairly extensive set of training experiences, but we have very little evidence as to what the results of the training are. When we have begun to specify desired personological skills more precisely, we can employ and evaluate the effectiveness of such techniques as modeling procedures sensitivity training, role-playing situations, simulated teaching experiences, and interaction analysis. Many of these techniques have been used in teacher training programs, but their relationship to teachers' classroom performance remains rather vague in the absence of well-specified personological criteria. With such criteria in the making, we can start asking, and perhaps answering, some important questions concerning the relationships among specific personological skills, teacher aptitudes, situational variables, and student performance.

DIAGNOSTIC AND EVALUATIVE PROCEDURES

The final, and as yet unmentioned, key to a successful teacher training program, pre-service and in-service, is a systematic and relevant set of evaluation procedures. In the past, evaluation has all too frequently been considered a mere formality, necessary for the appeasement of those who grant project funds. But in any teacher training program that takes change and self-improvement seriously, evaluation is the pivotal point. For a teacher training program designed according to the broad principles set forth in this paper, evaluation must play at least four key roles.

First, diagnostic procedures are continually necessary to assess the extent to which teachers in the field have met the various criteria appropriate to their roles, and to new roles they might wish to assume. The teacher requires the assistance of supervisors, evaluators, and perhaps some video tape self-viewing in order for him to determine how well he meets the criteria of performance set out for his role. By knowing the criteria and his relationship to them, the teacher can decide on the necessity, or lack of it, for his participation in various procedures as a means to increasing his professional competence. The teacher must have access to self-evaluative procedures to help him in making professional decisions regarding his own skills and possibilities of improving upon his talents through alternative training experiences.

Second, evaluative procedures are necessary to help administrators determine which teachers have met which performance criteria, so that they can be placed in the appropriate educational role with the appropriate rewards for their professional talents. It is absolutely crucial, in terms of both developing sound in-service training and keeping valuable talent in the teaching profession, that we begin to employ evaluation and promotion procedures based on performance rather than time criteria. In order for us to make sure that good use is made of existing talent and that better talent is drawn into the field, we must see to it that teachers know the criteria by which their professionalism is evaluated, and that the criteria used are directly relevant to their teaching experiences and talent. Until such sensible procedures are implemented, we will continue to hire, promote, and train in our current haphazard fashion.

Third, we need a systematic means of evaluating and researching the appropriateness of the teacher performance criteria we employ. It is a necessary, but not sufficient, condition of successful in-service training that precise criteria exist, but it requires a careful investigation of the relation between teacher performance criteria and student learning to create a truly functional teacher training program. It is simply not enough to rely on intuition as a guide for specifying the criteria to be used in evaluating teachers' performance. We must develop research models that will supply us with the necessary information regarding which performance-defined skills have which effects on which students. It is not an easy research task to attack such complex situations, but an in-service program that viewed the development of professional skills as a lifetime process, not a one-shot deal, would be the ideal setting for investigating the effects of trainable teacher characteristics on student learning.

Fourth, and most important if in-service training is to have the flexibility it requires, we must develop self-regulating research models to help us make decisions about the effectiveness of our training methods in reaching the goals we have set for teachers. Such research models must provide feedback to the system of alternative training procedures as a way of adding, dropping, and modifying those procedures. The models must be such that additions to evaluative procedures and performance criteria can be made on the basis of information arising out of training modifications. And, even more centrally, the models must provide initiative for the investigation of aptitude-treatment interactions. We need to gather systematic data on the teachers going through an in-service program so that we can obtain the kind of research that will tie particular sets of individual variables to optimal sequences of training experiences as means to particular goals. In brief, we need to know what kinds of teachers require what kinds of experiences in what order and at what times to help them meet given performance criteria. In this area, as in other research efforts tied to a viable in-service program, it is imperative that feedback operate in both directions. That is, the findings of research must direct changes in in-service training on a general and individual scale, but at the same time, changing developments in the training and its priorities must direct shifts in the focus of research.

THE DIFFERENTIATED STAFF: ADDITIONAL POSSIBILITIES

The general structure of an in-service program based on differentiated staff and self-regulating research provides a host of other alternatives for more effective use and development of teacher talent. Consider, for example, the current structure of teacher supervision. During pre-service training, teachers are more or less supervised by university personnel and, perhaps, a senior teacher. Credential in hand, however, the teacher is observed twice a year by an administrator to determine competency for tenure, and thus all processes remotely resembling adequate supervision come to a halt. Teachers rarely, if ever, observe each other in the classroom, and any attempts to do so are frequently viewed as threatening. In point of fact, of course, much could be gained by both sides from a process of supervision which involved teachers helping their colleagues. If school schedules became more flexible and staff use more functional, teachers would have blocks of time free at various points during the day, week, or month that could profitably be used to observe and supervise their colleagues at work. The supervised teacher would gain much from the introduction of several new perspectives on his teaching competencies. The supervisors would gain at least as much, not only in increasing their powers of effective observation, but also in being exposed to new alternatives in modes of instruction and teaching skills. As an addition to an effective in-service program, the establishment of supervision and observation opportunities among teachers holds great promise. The process of having teachers supervise fellow teachers could go a long way toward developing and spreading new teaching techniques and at the same time could promote the development of relevant performance criteria by sensitizing teachers to the problems of evaluating their own teaching performance.

The processes of supervision in general, and colleague supervision in particular, become more valuable the more precise we are in defining criteria for teacher performance. Insofar as our criteria are vague, supervision is not likely to have an appreciable effect on teachers' classroom behavior, no matter who does the supervising. But with sufficiently specific criteria on hand, educators can implement completely new models of the supervisory process that make small demands on teacher time but yield much by way of diagnosis and remediation. Given tightly specified criteria, one teacher can be quite efficient at diagnosing and helping to remedy his colleagues' teaching difficulties even in a five-minute period of observation. In fact, with usable criteria available, it probably is much more useful, for both supervisor and supervised, to engage in eight five-minute observations, each centered on a specific skill, than one global forty-minute encounter.

Another fruitful possibility that could be opened up by introducing flexibility and differentiation into the school structure is the more efficient sequencing of in-service experiences. As schools begin to offer independent study programs, flexible scheduling, and other organizational innovations, they free various blocks of teacher time that could well be used for in-service training. The hope here is that such scheduling innovations will free teachers from their current nine-month, nine-to-five syndrome. Under current practices, any in-service training that is to occur must fall neatly into evening classes, vacation seminars, or summer courses. With a more flexible system of scheduling in the schools, however, such need not be the case. With more flexibility possible, in-service experiences of whatever length could occur at the times in a teacher's career when they seemed most helpful and relevant. With sufficient flexibility, teachers could greatly widen the scope of their professional activities to include attending research conventions, consulting with school systems, working on curriculum projects, supervising other teachers, and any number of other things that might contribute directly or indirectly to their classroom performance. With a modest amount of ingenuity we can begin to break the nine-to-five rut and open up possibilities to assure that the in-service experiences of teachers are of the greatest possible variety and of the highest degree of relevance in terms of their sequence in any given teacher's career.

Flexibility and differentiation would again be of great value in shedding new light on some of the uninspected assumptions of in-service training as it currently functions. For example, we tend to operate on the premise that the purpose of in-service education is to adapt teachers to existing, or soon-to-exist, slots in the school framework. Thus, even when we have developed performance criteria, we are all too likely to assume that it is the teacher who must be somehow changed so as to fit the system, rather than allowing for the possibility of adapting the school structure and even its objectives to the particularly outstanding features of a given teacher. If, for example, a school happened upon a teacher of unusually high competence in lecturing to large groups, it might well be worth the school's educational while to hire him and so adapt its organizational structure as to provide him with large groups to lecture to. Or consider a teacher who is eminently qualified to teach a subject matter that is not part of the school's "standard" curriculum. Might it not be a valuable idea to adjust the school to his talents as a means of expanding the exposure of students to varied materials and developing new areas for curriculum research? In the past the dictum has simply been that the teacher must adapt to the educational system and its fixed slots. But there is clearly room for bringing in people with outstanding and relevant talents, and adjusting the slots to fit them. We might learn a great deal about the limitations and the possibilities of in-service education by drawing on currently existing talents, while trying to develop those talents which we have found necessary to classroom success in various situations. There is much that we can gain in terms of delineating new criteria of teacher performance and new modes of training by remaining open to the use of talents that do not fit our preconceived educational ideas.

We have, as a profession, missed a considerable number of possibilities by failing to capitalize on the useful combinations that might be developed between in-service training and curriculum development. The scheduling flexibility referred to above could again be of much help to free teacher time so that such combinations might function. If, for example, teachers in a particular curriculum at a given school could meet regularly during the day, possibly with the assistance of appropriate university staff, they could become jointly involved in a local or national curriculum development endeavor. Such active involvement in curriculum matters would be beneficial in at least two ways: First, it would constitute a valuable in-service training experience; that is, it would force teachers' attention to the difficult but crucial problems of specifying curricular outcomes for their students, as well as efficient means of reaching them. Second, such work would expose them to the kinds of problems (particularly those related to specifying desired educational outcomes in performance terms) and the kinds of university personnel that could form the core of an in-service program. At the national level, the teachers would be more likely to become familiar with new curriculum materials and to learn to use them effectively in their own particular situations. Such efforts could become a crucial aspect of in-service training, especially when new teacher competencies are required for new curricula to be used efficiently.

We need, in short, to be much more imaginative in our consideration of the relations among curriculum development, school structure, and in-service training. An in-service program that is appropriate to one structure and one curriculum might be totally misguided for a different school structure or a different curriculum. If in-service experiences were closely tied to changes in both curriculum and structure, changes in any one of the three areas would free the other two *and might reduce* some of the current delays in implementing useful innovations. It might, for example, be worthwhile to initiate curricula in a full-fledged but trial-stage manner so as to investigate what new approaches to teacher training and school organization would be necessary to make the curriculum work efficiently. Or, if a particular school placed great priority on the development of a new curriculum, it might make good sense to deliberately *increase* class size (or toy with the institutional structure in some other way) so as to free the teacher time required for such investigation. Or, if a school wished to institute a new curriculum, it might create free teacher time for in-service procedures so that teachers might be helped to make the best use of the new materials. The point is that enough flexibility in structure allows for much imagination in combining a school's efforts at improving curriculum and in-service training. There is no necessary conflict between these areas, and a successful in-service program in fact depends upon its ability to both react to and initiate changes in the curriculum. And, once again, a cycle of research is required to net the greatest gain from the entire process. The school that is not prepared to research the effects of its deliberate increase in class size (even though the increase was incidental to a curriculum project) is letting extremely valuable information go down the drain.

To summarize, one might say that nowhere in the educational enterprise is there a greater need for innovation than in the provisions for teacher in-service education.

■ CLUES TO ACTION

In contrast to the previous writers, Allen's position is a good deal more prescriptive. Not only does he believe that it would be desirable to differentiate among teaching roles, allowing teachers to perform the services for which they are best suited, but he also suggests that we can and should delineate the various tasks that comprise instruction. Only in this way, Allen argues, can we achieve the position essential to effective schooling.

Once teaching tasks have been accurately defined, and teachers are working in the area of their special endowment and competency, it will be possible to diagnose a teacher's professional needs with greater exactness. And of even greater significance, it will be possible to design efficient training sequences through which the individual's needs can be accommodated. Mindful of stylistic differences, he cautions us against a system of in-service education that is predicated on any single method. Clearly, however, Allen does not believe that we will ever reach the point where all teachers are absolutely equal in ability. Rather, he conceives of a system in which there are a few "super teachers" attached to each school faculty. As a teacher gradually increases his ability to perform the most difficult of the teaching tasks, he draws closer to the ranks of super teacher. Acknowledging that professional growth is highly idiosyncratic, Allen there concurs with several of the preceding writers in recommending that programs of professional growth allow for self-adjusting mechanisms so that a teacher is able to increase his proficiency through whatever procedures are most efficacious.

Although he concedes that there are alternate routes to professional development, Allen is adamant about the importance of performance assessment. He believes, in short, that a teacher who lacks a knowledge of his subject matter, or who has not mastered either the required pedagogical skills or the art of interacting with his students, can be helped by careful retraining intervention. In order to make such interventions, however, it is necessary to know the precise nature of an individual's weakness. Consequently, a teacher's performance must be measured against a yardstick of relatively precise criteria.

Quite often one finds an imperfect fit between a teacher's unique talents and the needs of the organization. Allen maintains that if we are to overcome this incongruity, we must endeavor to modify the organization as well as the individual. Put another way, if we persist in seeking to shape teachers to the organization, we shall dissipate a large amount of the human resources available to us. Organizations and systems are not ordained in heaven, and there is no reason why they cannot be altered in order to capitalize upon the special skills of a given individual.

We must, Allen counsels, distinguish between the mastery of the knowledge and skills that are the prerequisites of fine teaching and the ability to make appropriate decisions regarding the use of content and skills. Superior teaching, in other words, is a matter not only of capability but also of knowing when to do what. Accordingly, in our efforts to enhance the continuing education of teachers we must go beyond knowledge and skill to the more difficult elements of judgment. It is in the sharpening of this sense of judgment that teachers can be particularly helpful to one another. Allen endorses, in this regard, the recommendations of the several previous writers: the collaborative sharing of teaching ideas represents one of our most promising avenues of continuing teacher education. In fact, Allen believes in such collaboration so strongly that his arguments constitute, implicitly, an entirely new approach to the supervision of teaching.

It is obvious that at this point we do not know enough to implement the kind of professional growth programs advocated by Allen. A considerable amount of careful research stands between our present situation and the one he envisions. It is likely that such research will materialize in the period ahead, however, and his recommendations therefore are less utopian than they might appear.

■ OPERATIONAL IMPLICATIONS

1. Professional growth must be attacked with precision. **It is essential to specify performance criteria for the various tasks teachers perform.**

2. **Individuals have unique talents. In order to capitalize upon these differences we must make use of differentiated staffing.**

3. Like all other learners, teachers respond to different kinds of training stimuli. **It is desirable to establish specific performance criteria with respect to subject matter knowledge and behavioral and per-**

sonological skills, and to develop alternative growth programs that lead to the attainment of these levels of performance.

4. Many available methods of professional growth have received scant attention. **It is essential that we greatly enlarge our range of professional growth procedures.**

5. Professional growth and systematic research on professional growth can aid each other. **It is imperative that we begin to exploit the potential available from research.**

6. Some knowledge and skill are best acquired before the teacher enters service. Some can be acquired only after the teacher is in service. **We must determine, in the development of teachers, where, when, and how particular skills and understandings are best nurtured.**

7. Curriculum development and teacher professional growth share a common ground. **Much would be gained if we took advantage of the opportunity to interrelate the two.**

8. The teacher's performance represents the only rational base for determining reward and assignment. **Promotion, tenure, and teaching specialization all stem from an appraisal of performance.**

9. Little professional growth will take place without provision of adequate time. **Teachers' work schedules must be reorganized so that there is routine opportunity for the continuance of their professional education.**

10. The teacher's talent must be used in whatever way it best serves the learning of the young. **We would be well advised to adapt schooling to exceptional teachers rather than to require them to follow predetermined patterns.**

ronald lippitt
robert fox

CHAPTER SIX

DEVELOPMENT AND MAINTENANCE
OF EFFECTIVE
CLASSROOM LEARNING

The theories presented in this volume concerning the continuing education of teachers have already resulted in many instances of practical application. In this chapter we will endeavor to present some of these specific instances of application, for they have great value both as examples and as a stimulus to action. For this reason we depart from the narrative structure used in other chapters and adopt an outline form, which will make the ideas and suggestions more readily accessible.

In this analysis we will focus on ways to help the teacher play his key role in the learning process of students. We will bear in mind the total context of the learning situation, noting the following features: the peer group strongly determines attitudes toward learning, toward the teacher, toward participation in the school program; interactions with older siblings and parents determine support or rejection of learning, both at school and at home; the administrative policies and socioemotional climate of the school building will have a strong influence on the teacher and his students; and the physical ecology, grouping practices, schedule, facilities, and available resource materials will provide the opportunity structure within which the teacher and students will be able to shape the learning experience.

Focusing on the teacher and the development of his role, we can think in terms of directly helping him to improve his performance, or we can think in terms of improving the conditions that would support good role performance.

In the analysis that follows we have selected several critical areas in which one might intervene to improve teaching practice. In each of these areas we have presented (1) assumptions about the process of improving teacher performance; (2) some implications of these assumptions, formulated as goals for teacher training; and (3) some illustrative designs and training activities relevant to the particular goals. The analysis is concluded with a summary of our teacher education model, some observations on what is required to initiate and maintain such a model, and the continuing evaluation design that is needed.

AREAS OF INQUIRY

The following areas of inquiry and practice have been selected as the framework for our analysis:

1. What strategies will lead to the initiation of a program? What approaches can be used to involve the teacher in the need to participate in a program of learning opportunities?

2. Who are the appropriate targets for in-service training activities? Who needs to be reached by a particular training program?

3. Who should be the training specialists?

4. What framework is necessary in the training activities to provide continuity between initiation of a program and subsequent support of efforts toward change? What will be the role of supervision?

5. What should be the content, methodology, and design of the learning activities?

6. What types of support materials are needed to facilitate and implement training activity?

1. **Initiation of an in-service training program for teachers**

   A. **Several assumptions**

   (1) Most teachers have experienced a wide variety of attempts to influence them to change their performance or to improve themselves.

   (2) Many of these experiences have not appeared relevant to any felt need of the teacher, and have resulted in defensive attitudes.

   (3) Most teachers have participated in some of these activities and have been disappointed by the impracticality of the help offered.

   (4) Most teachers who have attempted changes as a result of participation in in-service training activities have experienced frustration or lack of support at the moment of real risk, when the changes are first being tried out. If the effort does not result in success, they either give up or accept a change that has little significance.

   (5) Most teachers have experienced feelings of guilt after committing themselves to "try something new" if they have then not followed through.

   (6) Most teachers have a number of other important roles in professional associations, as parents, as citizens, and as private persons. These other roles compete for time and attention. ₁

   (7) Typically the stimulus to participate in in-service training is an unwelcome imposition of authority, or an inept invitation to volunteer, with no previous involvement or warm-up opportunity to explore the potentialities of the training.

(8) Education as a profession has not developed norms or procedures that support and reward participation in continuing education, as one would find in medicine, industrial engineering, or even agriculture.

B. Implications of the assumptions for approaches to teacher involvement

Several implications for successful involvement of teachers in professional growth activities seem to follow from the foregoing assumptions:

(1) Teachers need to be involved in the identification and articulation of their own training needs whenever possible. This does not mean they "know what they need" in all respects, but the process of articulation, with resource help, is a major way of securing involvement and commitment to personal growth effort.

(2) Wherever possible, teachers should have an opportunity to taste before commitment, to see or experience a sample of what the in-service learning experiences would be like before they become involved.

(3) The relevance and feasibility of a particular learning program or innovation should be communicated as often as possible through accepted peers, or "persons like me," so that the natural defenses of caution and distrust can be dealt with.

(4) It should be clearly indicated at the very beginning that there will be follow-up support available as part of the learning activity.

(5) Joint sanction and participation by key elements of the peer culture, as well as administrative leadership, should be sought.

(6) The administration should involve the teachers in establishing a mutually satisfactory time, place, and principle of funding for the professional development activities.

C. Illustrations of designs for the entry or involvement phase of in-service teaching training activities

 (1) *Diagnostic group interview inquiry*

  In one school a team of parents, teachers, and students were trained to operate in pairs to conduct group interviews (between five and seven in a group) of parents, teachers, and students. They sought responses to questions about the most-needed improvements in the classroom teaching-learning process, and most-desired improvements in the performance of teachers. These data, recorded on a prepared recording schedule by one member of the interviewing team, were analyzed by the joint action-research team, who prepared a feedback report to the teaching staff on "challenges for professional development." This provided the basis for involvement and content of the in-service training activities.

 (2) *Micro-laboratory for projecting desired goals*

  (a) To provide an opportunity for all the staff to become involved in the in-service program, a single session event was set up, as a regular faculty meeting. This meeting was designed to provide a basis from which teachers could make their own decisions about participating in the total program. To open this hour and a quarter micro-laboratory, all staff members began by engaging in a brief personal fantasy period in which they came in as strangers, in a year's time, to observe themselves on the job. They were to describe the actions and events that would most please them as evidence of outstanding professional competence.

  (b) In the next phase of the lab, trios of colleagues shared their goal fantasies, helped each other make them more concrete, and asked each other for explanations of the particular change goals.

Then each staff member did a "force-field analysis" of the factors inhibiting movement toward
his goal, and factors supporting movement. This
sharing of personal development aspirations and
problems led to clear identification of several
clusters of faculty with the same professional development interest. This was the springboard to
intense involvement in a professional development program.

(3) *Sharing of innovative teaching practices as an initial
training activity*

(a) One of the most motivating entries into professional growth effort is the opportunity to share
and to become acquainted with new teaching
practices. In School X a nominating blank was
used asking every teacher to describe any atypical
practice used by himself or a colleague to increase the motivation to learn for all or part of a
class.

(b) At least one innovative practice was elicited from
almost every staff member. These were shared in
a "sharing of teaching institute" that provided a
springboard for most teachers to become involved
in observing, learning about, and planning some
new teaching practices.

(4) *Research derivation session*

Another procedure for getting started is to present,
usually as a brief written statement, a number of research findings focused on classroom process, for example, teacher-pupil interaction and relationship of
sociometric status to achievement motivation. This
presentation is followed by intensive work on formulating implication statements, then a brainstorm of all
possible alternatives for action, followed by a process
of selecting preferred alternatives for personal action.

(5) *Nominating peers to become in-service trainers*

The staff from one group of buildings helped to select

two fellow teachers who would constitute, with the principal, a training team. This team received training in the techniques of being leaders for the in-service training activities in the building. The nominees did become teams and worked with their peers in new training activities.

(6) *Personal inquiry and consultation*

Each member of the staff received a form designed to conduct a self-inquiry into personal needs for professional development and long-range individual goals. These inquiries then became the basis of consultative sessions to plan for the needed personal development experiences and sequences.

This is a small sample of the models for initiation which serve as resources for the beginning phases of in-service education programs.

2. **Identifying appropriate targets for in-service education programs**

A. **Assumptions**

(1) Current in-service education is focused primarily on the teacher as an individual and is seen as a continuing acquisition of concepts and skills in anticipation of future use, much in the pattern of pre-service professional training. Transfer of such learning to the problems of daily classroom life and school operation is minimal.

(2) Major responsibility for in-service education has been delegated to colleges and universities. This situation, as Meade also notes, has accentuated the isolation of the teacher's professional growth activities from the realities and relationships of the school setting.

(3) The professional development problems of teachers are not solely matters of individual growth but must be seen in the context of a group process, of team relationships, of total staff development.

(a) Improvement in education demands change in behavior on the part of the teachers, rather than just the learning of something new. Such changes are most likely to come through a process of problem solving in which the teacher is centrally involved.

(b) The change potential of a teacher is determined in part by what he perceives to be the expectations of his peers.

(c) The effectiveness of change activities on the part of teachers or teacher groups is enhanced if the sanctioners (administrators, students, parents, school board members) are involved as participants.

(4) The development of an effective problem-solving team requires more than direct focus on the problem to be solved. Clarification of role relationships, the establishment of supportive group norms, the gaining of skill in performing a range of functions needed in effective group operation, the development of a climate of openness, trust, and mutual support—these are learning goals which require involvement of the total team in the in-service education program.

B. Implications of these assumptions about targets for a teacher education program

If the foregoing assumptions about the appropriate targets for in-service teacher education are accepted, a number of implications may be drawn:

(1) Most in-service education activities should be carried on within a setting in which the people who work together have an opportunity to learn together. This is likely to be in the local school building, within the school system, or in a setting where the appropriate staff members can retreat for concentrated work together. It is not likely to be on the college campus.

(2) Activities should be designed for and should include such groups as:

    (a) Teaching teams (two or more persons responsible for the conduct of learning activities for a specific group of students; included may be teachers, paraprofessionals, student teachers or interns, volunteers).

    (b) Special task force groups (teams created to work on specific problems, or individuals associated to support each other in the pursuit of common interests).

    (c) School building staffs (including building administrators, teachers, special teachers, and service personnel).

    (a) Vertical teams (selected representation from central administration, local building administration, teachers, pupils).

    (e) Cross-sectional teams (elementary teachers, secondary teachers, parents, students, administrators, supervisors).

    (f) Groups serving continuing functions within the structure (administrative councils, research and development committees, curriculum councils).

(3) Attention should also be directed toward the personal development needs of individual staff members. Appropriate opportunities should be provided for assessment and diagnosis, planning of strategies, and pursuit of in-service growth activities appropriate to the personal professional growth needs of the individual. This topic is more fully developed elsewhere by Fischler.

(4) A multiple entry strategy is indicated. The professional development program should provide simultaneous opportunities for staff members to engage independently in personal growth activities. They should, in addition, be able to join in role clarification and development activities with peers who perform similar

roles, and to join with appropriate colleagues in cross-role team development efforts.

C. **Illustrations of ways in which various target groups may be involved in in-service development activities**

Although the school system with a dynamic in-service teacher education program will be supporting a wide variety of activities simultaneously, each activity will be initiated in response to a felt need or as a result of diagnostic efforts that point toward specific training goals for the individual or group concerned. The following examples are illustrative of some of the possibilities:

(1) *Administrative council*

A superintendent and his administrative council members decided to hold a one-week preschool laboratory session for all members of the council. Factors leading to this decision were concern by principals about the extent to which they controlled the budget for their buildings, discomfort over the fact that agendas for administrative council meetings were set solely by the superintendent, and lack of clarity among central office staff about who was responsible for various preschool workshop activities. Three resource persons from a nearby university and from the National Training Laboratories were retained to assist in designing and initiating the training program. Several two-hour sessions were held in advance and a series of follow-up activities was provided during the succeeding year.

(2) *School building staff*

A new elementary school was to be opened in February. During the summer the staff for the new building was identified, and provision was made for a two-week start-up workshop prior to the opening of school. School was to be opened and carried forward during the first semester in facilities shared with a junior high school. Focus in the workshop was on establishing a staff climate, identifying and agreeing on areas for initial staff experimentation and innovation, and developing norms that supported open communication, sharing, and involvement. At one point in the workshop a group of parents and some students were invited in to serve as consultants.

(3) *Teachers with a common interest*

Teachers in several school buildings throughout the system, both elementary and secondary, volunteered to work with a university team in gathering some data about the interpersonal learning environment in their classrooms. During the summer they were assisted in analyzing these data and in developing some action alternatives for improving the situation. During the next year, as each teacher tried out his plan, he continued to meet once a month with his colleagues and the university consultants to share progress reports, analyze difficulties, and explore adaptation or revision strategies.

(4) *Total system as target*

One school system determined to study itself and improve its capacity to manage change processes effectively on a continuing basis. It started by gathering some data on the state of affairs. School board members interviewed interested groups of citizens. Administrators and teachers were asked about their perceptions of how things were going, what influence various groups or individuals in their system had upon policy and program decisions, what they believed the priority goals for the system were, and whether or not they thought students, administrators, and school board members had similar or different priorities. Student councils were encouraged and helped to gather data from various student categories about the extent of their involvement in learning activities, relevance of the school curriculum, and so forth. An analysis of these data then stimulated an extensive series of staff and student sessions in which implications were explored and action plans were developed.

(5) *Individual teachers*

As a routine part of the annual conference held between the principal and each teacher in one school system, time is spent in helping the teacher diagnose his personal professional growth needs and in developing a plan for dealing with such needs. They examine problems in gaining continuing certification, current deficiencies in skill or conceptual background, and growth needs in relation to immediate or long-term professional goals. The resulting professional development plan may include such activities as encouraging the teacher to apply additional diagnostic techniques in his own classroom (such as interaction analysis, pupil feedback devices), and participation in selected national or regional conferences.

(6) *Cross-role training groups*

Throughout the school year in the B——— school system, there are held five-day laboratory sessions of cross-role teams from various schools. Each team is composed of three parents, three students, a school office worker, and an administrator. Laboratories are designed so that six or seven such teams can attend concurrently. A team of outside resource people work with a within-school-system team in planning and carrying forward the program. Focus is on improving communication among individuals in the different roles, identifying common interests, and developing skills in cooperative problem solving.

(7) *Continuing committee*

Another school system has an "R, D, and T" (research, development, and training) committee. It is a mechanism for developing policies, identifying priorities, and providing opportunities for these functions to be performed within the system. The committee is composed of the associate superintendent for curriculum, the personnel director, the coordinator of research, an elementary principal, a secondary principal, and an elementary and secondary school teacher. This committee recognized its need to spend some time in developing its own resources and improving its working relationships. It spent an initial three-day weekend in attempting to clarify its own functions, in exploring effective ways of utilizing the various committee members, and in developing initial action plans. Periodically, now, they set aside time for working on process issues within their team, utilizing outside resource people in broadening their perspectives and in reassessing their goals and activities.

(8) *Task force*

One elementary school staff decided it wanted to improve its effectiveness in working together, utilizing the range of resources possessed by various members. They appointed a group of five of their colleagues to work for a semester in exploring the various alternatives, such as team teaching, and to develop some proposals for staff consideration. The committee affiliated itself with an "innovations workshop" being conducted by the county intermediate school district in cooperation with several universities. Use was made of various outside resource people. Members assigned themselves reading; some visited other schools. Constant attention was paid to keeping the rest of the staff informed and involved as the committee weighed alternatives and developed recommendations.

(9) *Teaching team*

A teaching team for the second grade group in S——— Elementary School is composed of a senior teacher serving as team coordinator, a second teacher, a student teacher, a paraprofessional teacher assistant, a volunteer parent, two sixth grade students, and a secretary. This team recognizes that it needs to work along two lines: one, to build its skills in working together; two, to seek ideas for organizing learning activities that utilize wisely the various resources represented in the team. The in-service development plan for this team includes the regular use of a consultant from the central office, time given for interpersonal growth of the team and for assessing progress toward team goals, and periodic development sessions where outside resources are brought in to help with particular problems or projects.

3. Who should be the in-service educators?

Just as the trend is away from relying upon campus courses and summer institutes for in-service teachers' education, so it is clear also that not all of the qualified instructors for in-service activities are at the university. What assumptions can be made about leadership and trainership resources?

A. Assumptions

(1) The leadership and technical resources for meeting the in-service professional development needs of teachers are to be found in a great variety of locations: at the institutions of higher education, in the regional educational laboratories, in state departments of education, in business and industry, in the Institute for Applied Behavioral Science (NTL), in the professional staffs of teachers' organizations, in neighboring school systems, and within the local school system.

(2) If in-service education is to be a continuing process, leadership for designing and conducting in-service education activities must be drawn from among those who understand and are a part of the local situation. On the other hand, expert leadership resources must also be vigorously sought and used from the outside scientific and educational community. So that these leadership efforts may be coordinated, an effective "inside-outside" team relationship needs to be established.

(3) If sufficient leadership for a wide variety and continuing sequence of in-service education activities is to be provided, much of it will need to come from within the local school system.

(4) Teachers, while being themselves a part of in-service education activities, may also need to become the persons responsible for conducting the in-service training of teacher aides, parents, and students.

(5) Preparing a teacher to train others requires training activities different from those which are required to train a teacher to teach.

(6) Both conceptual resources and procedure skills are required in the conduct of in-service training. If they are not found in the same persons, it may be necessary to seek a training team that includes these resources within its membership.

B. **Implications of these assumptions about personnel resources for a teacher education program**

(1) A systematic program is needed to develop personnel resources and skills from within the system for the conduct of in-service education activities.

(2) Continuing administrative coordination is needed for the considerable job of seeking out and procuring the variety of necessary professional resources from across the region and the nation.

(3) Outside consultants or trainers should seldom be used on a "one shot" basis. Advance briefing, joint development of plans, cooperative handling of training events, follow-up activities, and evaluation should be included.

(4) Teachers should be helped to become more skillful in managing some of their own in-service education—training in problem solving, in seeking and utilizing resources, in developing alternatives for action, in evaluating the results of innovative efforts. In other

words, teachers as well as students may profit from "learning to learn" activities.

C. **Illustrations of ways in which appropriate personnel resources for in-service education may be identified and utilized**

(1) *Inside-outside team*

The responsibility for in-service education cannot be wholly delegated to the university graduate schools. Neither is it sufficient for the local school district to rely only upon its own internal resources in this day of expanding specialization and knowledge explosion. The answer may be in the use of a collaborative arrangement in which two or three persons from within the system and one or two from without meet over a period of time to plan and carry out a block of in-service activities.

(2) *Special training of individuals within the system*

A pool of special skills and talents may be built up within the system. One school district, for example, sent one person each summer to the Educational Leadership Laboratory of the National Training Laboratories at Bethel, Maine, for a period of four years. These four then became consultants to others in the system in the designing and conducting of training activities. Another school system helped a group of teachers become knowledgeable about practices in other schools that were directed toward the improvement of self-concept in learners. These teachers are increasingly called upon throughout the entire system to consult with teachers who want help in improving learner self-concept.

(3) *Sharing of resources among school districts*

Special competencies and skills developed by personnel within one school district may be shared with other school districts as needed. For example, one principal has become expert in assisting staff groups to analyze their climate of staff relationships and to engage in productive exercises to increase openness of communication. This principal is released to help a principal in another school district conduct a weekend laboratory with his staff. Several school districts in eastern Michigan are establishing a consortium to facilitate this kind of exchange.

(4) *Outside consultation on a continuing basis*
Leadership from the outside can often be utilized most effectively if it is involved under a continuing consultation arrangement. The retainer fee, long-term contractual arrangement, or a joint appointment may provide the framework for such relationships.

(5) *Teacher independent study arrangements*
A major resource for teacher professional development in service is surely the teacher himself, utilizing the increasing variety of packaged materials, kits, programmed learning sequences, and laboratory units. Curriculum laboratories staffed by experts in retrieving the latest and most relevant conceptual and instructional materials can aid the teacher in such individualized study activities.

4. **Providing for a continuity of professional development activities and mechanisms in support of change efforts**

A. **Assumptions**

(1) Pre-service education is only the beginning of professional training. Professional development must continue throughout a teacher's career if he is to keep up with changing conditions and new knowledge.

(2) Responsibility for continuing professional growth has traditionally rested with the individual teacher, to be managed on his own time and at his own expense.

(3) School systems have therefore given low priority to providing funds and staff for the conduct of in-service education programs.

(4) Such professional growth activities as yearly teacher institute days, speakers for faculty meetings, and pre-school workshops have not provided for much continuity of effort.

(5) Most effective "supervision" is directed toward the support of professional growth.

(6) Many teacher efforts to utilize ideas gained from in-service education activities are abortive because of lack of support at the time of the "try efforts."

(7) Changing behavior usually requires an unfreezing process within which an individual (or group) has a chance to examine questions of relevance, value, risk, potential support, and priority, and to develop commitment to change.

(8) Rewards for engaging in professional growth activities have been modest—slight recognition by either superiors or fellow teachers, and salary increments that have come automatically with the completion of a set number of college credits.

B. Implications of these assumptions about continuity of professional development activities

(1) Teacher education is continuing education. Discontinuities must be minimized between pre-service and in-service education, and between the in-service professional growth opportunities provided by one school system as compared with another to which a particular teacher may transfer.

(2) A mechanism for the long-range planning and coordination of the professional development program of a school system is needed. The process should involve the various professional role groups that will be affected by the program.

(3) Time must be built into the schedule and work load of the staff for professional development activities. Scheduling cannot be done on an *ad hoc*, overload basis.

(4) In addition to providing for continuity of personal

professional growth, an in-service education program should give attention to the sequence of activities required in the development of a team, a school staff, or an organization. The following phases or types of activities might be included:

(a) Involvement in initial problem identification and planning of strategies (for example, involvement in the preparation of a proposal, if project funding is being sought from outside sources)

(b) Data gathering and diagnosis of specific problem areas

(c) An unfreezing or start-up activity, usually a block of time in a setting conducive to concentrated interpersonal and group activity

(d) Skill development and team building activities

(e) Retrieval and utilization of resources

(f) Explorations of alternative courses of action

(g) Documentation and evaluation

(h) Sharing with colleagues

(i) Reassessment of goal priorities and initiation of new problem-solving efforts appropriate to the goals

(5) The supervisor should be a specialist in helping teachers diagnose their professional growth needs, designing activities that can contribute to meeting such needs, and arranging for such activities to take place. Beyond this, however, the supervisor is a key person in supporting the teacher in his efforts to initiate changes as a result of his learning. He provides interested and sympathetic follow-up, additional resources, suggestions for modification or adaptation of plans that are not working, and ideas regarding next steps.

(6) Norms of the teacher peer group need to be supportive of professional growth efforts. They should encourage colleagues to experiment, to innovate, to take initiative in suggesting school improvement, and to share results with others.

C. Illustrations of ways in which continuity and support for professional development may be provided

(1) *Contract negotiation process* is used by teachers to insure that professional development activities are legitimized and financially supported, and that teachers are involved in planning for them.

(2) A *personal professional growth plan* is developed or redeveloped as a part of an annual teacher-principal evaluation conference. Decisions are made with regard to the kinds of collaborative arrangements that are needed in order to carry out the plans.

(3) *An in-service education committee* is established in the school system to assist with the identification of training needs, establishment of procedures, arranging for evaluation and feedback, and planning for the future. Such a committee should be cross-level, with representatives from teachers, principals, central office, students, and parents.

(4) *Base-line data* are routinely gathered on school system variables affecting the climate for professional growth and change. Assessment is made of such variables as the following: how individuals perceive the influences on their own decisions or decisions made by others; the extent of innovations; openness of communication; perceived support for change effort; congruence of goal priorities among various role groups within the system. These data are analyzed for evidence of progress toward professional development goals, and for setting new priorities.

(5) *Released time* for in-service education is provided in one system by sending pupils home each Wednesday at noon. In another, one grade level at a time is released for a day so those teachers may engage in workshops, visitation, or other professional activities. Sabbatical leaves at half pay are increasingly provided. Another system provides, in its negotiated contract, for

one in-service education day per month, to be used by building staffs as deemed most appropriate.

(6) One school system provides for the *joint appointment* of a college staff member to the public school staff to supervise student teaching and follow-up on first-year teachers within the system.

(7) *Helping teachers* are employed to provide special at-the-elbow support for first-year teachers.

(8) *Teaching teams* provide for gradual induction of student teachers and younger teachers into the full teaching role over a period of years.

(9) A full-time coordinator of manpower development programs gives leadership to the initiation and maintenance of in-service training activities for all levels of manpower—administrators, teachers, special personnel, teaching aides, older students doing tutorial work—and for the recruiting and training of volunteers to work in the schools.

5. Design, content, and methods of the training program

A. Assumptions

(1) In a large proportion of in-service training activities the content is preselected and preorganized by the trainer without involvement of trainees as to training needs, readiness, level of sophistication, variety of individual expectations, and so forth.

(2) A significant proportion of the trainees in most in-service programs enter the program because of extrinsic motivations (for example, credit, salary incentive, promotion ambitions), which tend to support a learning role characterized by conformity and a minimal amount of initiative.

(3) The methods of most in-service training activities emphasize cognitive learning of the preselected learning content.

(4) The design of most in-service training activities does

not emphasize the integration of concepts with role performance skills and planning for application.

(5) Very little inquiry method is used as the model of learning in in-service education.

(6) The learning of new behavior patterns is very unlikely to occur as a result of acquiring information about relevant basic principles or about the desirable behavior patterns. In this respect the acquiring of new behaviors in teaching is often different from the learning of innovations in agriculture, medicine, and industry.

(7) Most learning of new behaviors in education comes from personal adaptation of someone else's discovery rather than exact adoption of the model or idea.

(8) Most designs for in-service education have no provision for continuity of support or for evaluation of the efforts to utilize what has been learned.

B. Implications for improvement of training content and design

(1) Trainees must be involved, voluntarily, to define and clarify personal training needs. The design of the training must rest on this teacher involvement.

(2) The learning activities must link conceptual learning with action implications for the individual.

(3) The total sequence of in-service learning activities should be organized as problem-solving efforts in which the teacher-learner takes the initiative for inquiry.

(4) The in-service education design must allow for and plan for individual differences in readiness, sophistication, focal concerns, and content needs.

(5) A major concern of learning designs must be to activate and link the cognitive, affective, and action aspects of the self.

(6) Provision should be made in the design for appropriate

continuing support of efforts the trainees make to use the in-service training experiences.

C. Illustrations of in-service training designs and methods

The following sample illustrations of different types of in-service designs take into account the assumptions and implications summarized above.

(1) *Development team problem-solving design*

From the diagnostic start-up inquiry, several clusters of problems and desires for change were identified. These were reported to the staff and all staff had the option of exploring the formation of development teams with colleagues having similar interests. The trainer met with each team to help attain clarity of goals, and to clarify the needs for outside resource persons and materials. In addition to spending time on their own, the teams met together once a week to report progress, to get critical reactions to plans, and to coordinate development projects. The trainer helped the teams look at their own team process, at their skills in involving others, and the preparation for trying out their ideas.

(2) *Start-up laboratory with follow-up support sessions*

The total staff of a school building worked together for five days before the beginning of school. Each day had the following type of design:

8:30 to 10:00	Sensitivity training groups led by outside trainers with administrators as regular members. Emphasis was on study of interpersonal relations within the staff.
10:00 to 12:00	Staff planning committees working on a variety of curriculum and staff operation activities, with administrators and special personnel as consultants.

1:30 to 3:00   Skill practice activities (for example, micro-teaching experiments with children as resources, work on teacher-parent communication with parent groups).

3:00 to 4:30   Faculty meeting, led by principal, with trainer in role of observer and consultant; trainer shares observations as to productivity of decision making and other meeting activities.

4:30 to 4:45   Evaluation review of day sheet.

Before the end of this period, plans and commitments were made to a regular sequence of follow-up support activities and team assignments.

(3) *Confrontation and search laboratory*

Students, parents, several teachers, and the administrator worked before the laboratory to prepare a series of taped confrontations or critical situations which teachers cope with, either in the classroom or in other aspects of building operation. These situations were chosen from a teacher survey. During the in-service training program each teacher had an opportunity to react to each confrontation, to compare his response (which was taped) to those of colleagues, to discuss the problem situation with consultants and peers, to read selected reading material relevant to each problem, and to request a second opportunity to handle each confrontation. The trainers were impressed with the high level of motivation to use consultants and to do reading after the stimulus of the confrontation.

(4) *Program of identifying and sharing innovations*

(a) A nomination blank was prepared and distributed to all teachers of the system, giving them a chance to nominate a "teaching invention" of their own or of a colleague that they felt was making a significant contribution to the learning of pupils.

(b)   Several hundred descriptions of practice were received and screened by a committee of teachers, administrators, curriculum specialists, an educational researcher, an educational philosopher, and a behavioral scientist. They generated a series of rating scales that helped select thirty practices for the sharing program.

(c)   In sharing institutes the inventors of these practices were used as resource persons. The trainers helped them to communicate their ideas nondefensively. The trainers also helped their colleagues, in the inquiry sessions, to explore each practice in depth, to think through the relevance for adaptation, and to project the learning needed to successfully use the idea. Much cross-class and cross-building observation and consultation was stimulated by this in-service program.

(5)   *Human relations laboratory*

(a)   The faculty participated in an intensive weekend laboratory which focused on inquiry into interpersonal relations and personal and group behavior. The weekend included a series of interpersonal sensitivity training sessions; skill practice in giving and receiving help; presentation of concepts needed to understand problems of authority, conflict, inhibited communication, and self-rejection. Another important aspect was the consultation and peer discussions on applying one's learnings to the classroom situation.

(b)   An opportunity was provided for a bi-weekly, two-hour session on human relations with an "open group" situation of all staff invited to attend. Attendance was remarkably high and continued to hold up throughout the year, with the

staff deciding to have another weekend laboratory six months later.

6. Types of support materials and facilities needed for in-service training activities

A. Assumptions

(1) Audiovisual and other training materials can supplement but not substitute for interaction with a trained
trainer.

(2) Most training materials are didactic communicators of
content rather than stimuli to inquiry.

(3) Training materials can be a unique opportunity to observe or share in experiencing phenomena and models
of practice beyond the access of the group.

(4) Most physical facilities where training activities are
conducted are too inflexible and inadequate acous-
tically to permit the development of creative teaching
designs (for example, flexible furniture, space, and
acoustics for individual, small group, and large group
work; use of tape recording and video recording and
playback; walls and newsprint pads for appropriate
reporting and communication designs).

(5) Quick retrieval from libraries and other resources is
usually not available as part of training activities.

B. Implications

(1) Resources should be available for the production and
utilization of tapes, video tapes, and rapid production
of written materials.

(2) A large flexible space should be available so that those
involved can efficiently move back and forth
between total group sessions, small group work, and
individual work.

(3) Selective and rapid retrieval of documents, books,
journals, films, and tapes should be possible.

(4) Protection from interruption is necessary, but isola-

tion should not be so great that resource persons and materials cannot be secured as needed.

C. Illustrations of use of training materials and facilities

(1) *Skill practice exercises with video feedback*

In one in-service program it is regular procedure for each trainee to cope with the same confrontation (for example, difficult child behavior, reaction to principal's behavior), each one seeing his own feedback on video immediately and having an opportunity to try again after reflection and consultation. Then the total group views all the episodes, discusses differences in style and strategy, and works on preferred alternatives.

(2) *Micro-teaching with overhead projection of observations*

As the teachers take turns conducting micro-teaching episodes with pupils, the other trainees observe the teaching. They can at the same time watch on the wall as a skilled observer records on the overhead projector transparency observation blank the coding of teacher-pupil interaction. The observers are becoming trained to perceive more fully, and the data are used for a feedback discussion with the teacher immediately after the teaching session.

(3) *Producing taped confrontations*

The in-service training group is divided into quartets, with each foursome producing a taped episode to be used as a practice situation by their colleagues. It has been found that there is great training value in preparing training materials and assuming the training role with peers in the in-service program.

(4) *Tape listening*

In one in-service program there is a regular tape listening period in which the group listens to and analyzes one of their own group sessions and the role of their teacher in working with them. Alternatively they review an excerpt of teaching behavior that one of the trainees has volunteered to provide for study.

(5) The trainer brings in, for group use, one of the available training resource packages (for example, "The Vicious Circle"). The group uses these phonograph records in the session to stimulate reaction to the recorded episodes of teen-age–adult conflict. They also use the reading materials and discussion guides to work on techniques of changing the negative cycle of relationships between the generations.

(6) *Immediate production of resource materials*
In an institute on the sharing of classroom teaching practices each innovator who is being interviewed about his practice has his description of practice written directly on a duplicating master by the delegated recorder, so that within half an hour after the interviews are completed, the descriptions of all the practices can be run off and every participant in the institute can have a complete folder of the practices.

(7) *Brainstorm "art exhibit"*
The in-service training group is broken into trios to brainstorm all the ideas they can produce about individualizing instruction in the classroom. They record these on large newsprint pads and put them on the wall with masking tape so that at the coffee break they can review the products of all the groups and select ideas from all groups to use in the next phase of their problem solving.

Concluding comments

As we have reviewed the dimensions of the in-service training function in the preceding sections, we have identified a number of activities and skills that are the core of what we conceive to be the needed ingredients of in-service training. These add up to an action-research problem-solving model of in-service training that places it in the context of planned change within a structured social system. These ingredients include the following:

Identifying needs for change

Designing action-research projects

Working with outside resource people

Diagnosing the learning climate

Serving as a member of a school building or school system change-agent team

Learning about innovations developed by other teachers or by national projects

Utilizing the resources of school system personnel

Increasing interpersonal sensitivity to authority figures, peers, and students

Deriving implications for learning from research findings

Gaining support from colleagues

Sharing results with others

Contributing to the development of these skills are arrayed a wide assortment of in-service training activities, each of which may contribute in its own unique way:

1. School building faculty meetings focused on professional problems

The traditional school meeting is devoted to administrative matters. The agenda is set by the principal, and the group norm against raising any question that will prolong the meeting is invoked. There is need to explore the possibility of brief but focused in-service educational projects that might involve thirty to forty-five minutes of the meeting time. Principals may need to have available resource materials that will assist them in conducting such meetings and directing them toward a sequential learning experience for staff.

2. Principal-teacher consultation

The use of the principal by the teacher as a resource person provides a most effective opportunity for in-service education. The teacher needs to know what kinds of resources the principal might contribute and how to best work with the principal to take advantage of his resources. The principal needs to develop skill in sharing his resources effectively.

3. Teacher consultation with university-based resource persons

University resource people are notorious "in and outers." Effective utilization of the skills of the university-based scientist or educational specialist requires careful planning and a measure of skill. Orientation of the specialist to the kind of help needed, some opportunity for free exchange of ideas, extension of the relationship over a period of time so that as attempts to apply are undertaken or new obstacles encountered, there can be some checking back with the original resource— all are possible ingredients for the effective use of the consultant. Skill can be developed and the process improved if it is a subject for study in itself.

4. Building a temporary structure within the school system for support of a particular action-research project

The use of temporary structures has been described by Miles.[1] It involves organizing in order to implement a particular innovation or change project. Such systems not only contribute to the realization of the goals of the change project. They can also be utilized to further the learning of the participants.

5. Utilization of a curriculum materials center for retrieval of basic research, innovations, and tools

A most valuable in-service education activity occurs with staff involvement in the retrieval process under the leadership of a curriculum materials specialist. Teachers may help in various ways: searching for potentially useful materials; setting up schemes for classifying and arranging them so that they may be accessible when needed; developing evaluation

---

[1] Matthew B. Miles (ed.), *Innovations in Education* (New York: Bureau of Publications, Teachers College, Columbia University, 1964).

or screening procedures; perfecting ways of arranging for the most useful materials to get to the staff member most in need of them at the proper time; and setting up procedures for retrieving from colleagues materials and tools they have created or adapted and making them available to others.

6. Sessions for the sharing of practices

Opportunities to share with colleagues, through face-to-face discussion, some of the innovative practices that particular teachers have developed have proved to be stimulating and helpful. The sharing process can be perfected in a number of ways, such as defining more exactly what kinds of information are helpful for a teacher wishing to adopt the practice, presenting evidence regarding success or failure of the practice, sharing hunches about ways a practice might be further improved or adapted to other situations. Some school systems have institutionalized these sharing sessions, holding them once a month or building them into a portion of each faculty meeting.

7. Clinic sessions with teachers from other systems

Clinic sessions (periodic meetings of teachers associated with similar change projects from different school buildings or school systems) provide opportunities for support and sharing of ideas often not existent within the normal school faculty communication system. An esprit de corps may develop among persons engaged in similar projects that results in continuing interpersonal support and motivation. It appears that most teachers are freer to share the problems and obstacles they face in carrying through their change efforts and in receiving help if the persons involved are not directly connected with their day-to-day working environment.

8. Internship with other projects on a released-time basis (curriculum projects, university-based development, or research activities)

During the past year, one school system has released a high school teacher to work with the Social Science Education Consortium in Purdue, not primarily to further the teacher's graduate degree work but as an internship program planned to feed back directly to the system. The Ann Arbor school system regularly releases an outstanding elementary school teacher for a year's internship with the University of Michigan's teacher education program. The released staff member serves on the university faculty supervising student teachers, assisting with the teaching of methods courses, and becoming involved in the variety of program-planning activities connected with the undergraduate teacher training program. On completion of the year's internship, the teacher returns to the public school classroom. Other arrangements involving less of a total time commitment could also be described, including the involvement of classroom teachers in field testing of materials in collaborative work with university-based curriculum development projects.

9. Sensitivity training laboratory

Human relations sensitivity laboratories provide the participants with opportunities to learn about themselves and about the operation of groups. Use of the "T group" or training group, in which no agenda is provided and no leadership or rules for operation are imposed, provides an exciting opportunity for participants under the direction of a trainer to focus upon the processes that occur while the group is engaged in interaction. Aspects of group behavior such as the development of norms, patterns of influence, communication systems, and internal leadership can be studied through such an experience-centered learning situation.

10. College class

The more formal college class, possibly arranged through extension procedures to be taught within the school setting, offers opportunity for systematic review of theory and the development of concepts relative to particular aspects of the school program. Frequently some adaptation of the course can be made so that it speaks more directly to the particular needs of the school system involved.

11. Membership on an inside-outside team responsible for developing change strategies for the school or school system

The University of Wisconsin is experimenting with the establishment of Research and Development Centers within the school buildings as an instrument for instigating and furthering the process of change. The Cooperative Project for Educational Development working in five regional centers of the country has established the inside-outside team as a central device. Through it, the project can assist school districts in examining the mechanisms for instigating and supporting change efforts within the school system. Teacher membership on such a team constitutes a unique opportunity for in-service development.

12. Summer work sessions

A block of time for intensive work by curriculum committees or other action-research staff groups can provide opportunity for intensive work on aspects of their projects. Usually such sessions plan to involve resource people and result in products that can be shared with others.

13. Preschool workshop

Schools reserving a block of time at the beginning of the school year for staff preschool workshops are often able to launch particular change projects at this time. Total staff involvement can be sought, special resources brought to bear in identifying and clarifying the problem, and beginning steps taken to establish a plan of action.

Thus, there appears to be a wide range of types of activities that can contribute to the in-service program. The specific content of such activities may include emphasis on at least five different types of experiences.

First, resource identification and retrieval experience need to be emphasized. Effort would be made to identify sources of innovations, and sources of knowledge and expertise; to develop criteria for selection of innovations for trial, and documentation and description techniques; and to work on ways of establishing effective working relationships with scientists and other resource people. Second, there should be emphasis on *conceptualization.* Conceptual schemes, such as various models for describing the process of educational change, the circular process of interpersonal behavior, and theories of instruction and curriculum need to be studied and their application to specific problems of the classroom explored.

A third area of emphasis is *diagnosis.* The force-field analysis technique for diagnosing factors affecting change potential has proved to be a useful tool. Opportunity should be provided to become acquainted with other diagnostic tools such as post-class reaction forms, sociometric measures, and tools for measuring peer group standards. Skills of analyzing and interpreting the diagnostic information should be developed so that needs for change may be identified.

Sensitivity training constitutes another area of emphasis. The sensitivity training group could be one approach. Diagnosis and study of the communication structure of the faculty and teacher self-analysis programs would also contribute to a better understanding of self and others. Self-assessment programs are excellent examples of this type of activity.

A final category of experience that might be provided is that of skills *practice.* Each of the foregoing types of activities may give rise to the need to develop particular skills. Skills-practice exercises directed toward utilizing force-field analysis, using the outside consultant, developing change strategies, and sharing practices in a helpful way are examples of this type of emphasis.

Management of the in-service education program

Finally, it may be suggested that the development of an in-service training program focused on the continual problem-solving process of the school system be managed by an in-service education *team,* with a coordinator to facilitate its plans. The team would be charged with identifying the needs for training as they grow out of the action-research program, designing the scope and sequence of a particular year's training activities for the school system, and identifying the kinds of resources needed to staff such an in-service education program.

A team, rather than an individual, is recommended so that there may be several lines of communication between the persons or groups actually engaged in problem-solving activities and those responsible for supporting such activities with the necessary in-service education.

In conclusion, it has been the thesis of this chapter that involvement of the classroom teacher and his colleagues within the school system in a scientific problem-solving process is essential to the building of a self-renewing school system. Within such self-renewing systems the process of innovation and educational change will be enhanced. If teachers are to play their roles in such a system, they need the continuing support of an in-service education program geared to helping them obtain the concepts, the sensitivities, and the skills required.

■ CLUES TO ACTION

Lippitt and Fox remind us that the peer group has a strong influence on the individual's behavior. Just as the attitudes of the class affect the child, the attitudes of the faculty affect the teacher. It follows, therefore, that a teacher is not likely to aspire to sustained professional growth if the aspirations are not shared by his colleagues.

Like the previous writers, Lippitt and Fox emphasize the teacher's involvement in his own learning. Not only do they suggest that, whenever possible, the teacher should participate in identifying the growth experiences which will be most useful, but also they suggest that the growth activities should, at the outset, assist the teacher to develop his capacity for self-direction. And in so doing, the authors illuminate one of the significant differences between pre-service and in-service education, for only after the teacher has begun to teach can he become adept at identifying and analyzing his professional problems, evaluating potential correctives, and initiating stylistic changes in his techniques. Partly because of the importance they attach to peer influence, and partly because of their great respect for group processes, the writers strongly favor collective teacher education. "The professional development of teachers," they say, "must be seen in the context of a group process, of team relationships, and of total staff development." Although they do not rule out individualized learning, they believe, as does Bush, that much is gained when co-workers engage in collaborative programs.

In their arguments Lippitt and Fox underscore a number of weaknesses in our present approach to teacher in-service education. They believe, for example, that the design and management of an in-service education program must be done by someone who is intimately acquainted with the environment in which the teachers operate. This would imply that professional growth programs should be specifically tailored to the situation that exists in the particular school. Moreover, they see little point to growth programs that do not integrate underlying principles with performance skills. The teacher, in other words, must not only understand what to do but why to do it. And, more importantly, they recommend that professional growth activities have a cognitive, an affective, and a behavioral dimension. Thus a continuing education activity designed, for instance, to familiarize a teacher with a new instructional technique must deal not only with the technique but also with the encouragement of its use. If the average teacher does, indeed, have skills that he often lacks the motivation to use, the writers' argument has considerable significance.

Better teaching, they say, requires more than familiarizing the teacher with something new: it requires fundamental changes in the teacher's behavior. A great many teachers, nonetheless, participate in in-service activities because of one extrinsic factor or another. Lippitt and Fox contend that unless the person's motivation stems from an intrinsic desire to teach more effectively, the degree of professional growth is minimal. As a consequence, it is essential to evoke a strong desire to improve among teachers. It is perhaps for this reason that the writers insist so strongly upon the use of a trained specialist to facilitate growth. Their convictions in this regard are unmistakable: there is no substitute for interaction with a training agent.

■ *OPERATIONAL IMPLICATIONS*

1. Because many teachers have had unsatisfactory experiences with in-service activities, it is critical that teachers be involved in the identification and articulation of their own training needs. **When teachers are involved in the initiation and organization of training activities, conditions are enhanced for peer support, shared effort, and eventual utilization of new insights and skills.**

2. A problem-solving approach has the greatest potential for resulting in real learning. **Therefore, most in-service education activities should be carried on within the setting in which the learners nor-**

mally work together. **Using the inquiry method, staff members can effectively learn to identify and analyze their own problems and to participate in achieving solutions.**

3. Personnel resources for in-service training reside in a variety of locations, including people within the local system, district consultants, university consultants, and consultants available through national educational programs. **A systematic program must be developed in which "inside" and "outside" resources can collaborate to provide leadership and assistance to teachers.**

4. If efforts to change the performance of teachers are to succeed, there must be a framework to provide continuity of action and assurance of support. **Professional growth programs demand long-range planning and coordination, appropriate sequencing of activities, and evaluation and support of change efforts.**

5. Many resource materials and technological aids are now available, and many useful kinds of training facilities have been designed and developed. **Training programs should provide the teacher with the opportunity to learn to use current resource materials.**

6. Group efforts at problem solving encourage the sharing of acquired skills and of tested methods for dealing with common problems. **Thus teachers themselves can contribute to a growing body of knowledge that will be of significance to the entire profession.**

abraham s. fischler

CHAPTER SEVEN

CONFRONTATION:
Changing teacher behavior
through clinical supervision

In-service education today is still being conducted in two ways: (1) Teachers may attend extension classes taught by professors of education from universities or state colleges. These classes normally take place from 3:30 to 5:30 in the afternoon, or in the evening. Teachers come after a day's work, sit passively, and listen to the pearls of wisdom expounded by the professor. (2) Teachers may take courses at universities or state colleges, picking up units toward a salary increment.

In either case, there is no study with which I am familiar to indicate that there is a relationship between courses taken and productivity in the classroom. There is no research study to support the assumption underlying our present salary schedule— the assumption that a teacher with sixty hours beyond the bachelor's degree is having a greater effect on the learner's outcome than a teacher with thirty hours of added credit.

In education we tend to make changes without building in a research design that will enable us to determine the effect of our change. We tend to believe that if we do something, by definition it is a good thing. If we spend millions of dollars to upgrade the profession, then we should approach this process in a systematic way, gaining information and assessing and reassessing our goals. Any program aimed at changing teacher behavior, therefore, must have built into it a clearly defined method of evaluating the effect of the program.

Piaget's theory of learning and teacher change

Piaget's theory is broken down into four component parts. He states that a student must be faced with a *discrepant* event or confrontation. This is an event that does not fit the intellectual model the student possesses, which enables him to view his world in an orderly fashion. The event does not fit the prediction the student has in his mind of what should occur. Once the student has met the confrontation or observed the discrepant event, he goes through the processes of assimilation, accommodation, and equilibration. These are the processes of modifying his intellectual model to take into account the discrepancy so that once more he has reached a state of equilibrium. The state of equilibrium may be a complacent state. The task of the teacher is to know when the student has reached the state of equilibrium and then to introduce the next discrepancy, which forces the student to constantly refine and redefine his intellectual model. Now let us examine the same theory as it relates to teaching.

Until the present time we have been taught in administrative and supervisory courses that when we enter the classroom, we should "make ourselves scarce." We should not do anything to increase the anxiety of the teacher. Therefore, we usually sit in the back of the classroom and record an occasional note based on a subjective appraisal. Later we meet with the teacher to discuss our observations and criticisms. This occurs approximately three times each year with nontenure teachers and somewhat less frequently with tenure teachers. In our discussions with the teacher we tend to avoid direct confrontation. We tend to approach our dialogue in a vague manner, and we try to select one or two items to discuss in a rather supportive manner.

Since the observer does not have a record of what actually took place in the classroom, nor a time line against which to reconstruct the lesson, there is a great deal of difficulty in analyzing the lesson. The teacher's perception of the lesson and the observer's perception of the lesson are usually quite different. The principal or supervisor is in a higher position than the teacher. Therefore, the principal makes recommendations and the teacher normally nods his head and accepts them. There is little room for dialogue. Since the principal does not return the next day, the influence of this technique is nil.

With the advent of modern technology, we can begin a more effective way of supervising our teachers. If our teachers can be trained to use a half-inch television system, they can place the camera in a position within the classroom where the camera can pick up the maximum amount of information. I am suggesting that the television camera (with no operator) is probably the most objective tool we have to observe what is taking place in the classroom. If there is no operator, then there is no way to build in human bias. The camera remains fixed with a wide-angle lens, which allows for the widest amount of information to be recorded on the tape. If an operator is present with the above system, the operator begins to select what he feels is important and this immediately introduces a bias.

In a school system that has no television recording system, a teacher can put a tape recorder in his classroom and at least pick up the verbal communications. Since about ninety per cent of what occurs in the classroom is verbal, the tape recorder does enable the teacher to examine the sequence of questions, the types of verbal rewards and punishments, and the different patterns utilized to handle the verbal communications. If, in addition to the tape recorder, we can also provide an observer to pick up what the students are doing, this then provides a fairly accurate record of what took place in the classroom.

In some school systems, the supervisors and principals are

trained to be recorders. They enter the classroom and take a seat where they can see the maximum amount of interaction. The observers might utilize Flanders' Interaction Analysis or MACI's Interaction Analysis. There is now a more enlarged form of Flanders' Interaction Analysis that was developed by Amidon and Hunter.

Rather than spending time now to analyze the accompanying scale, I shall return to this later in the chapter.

CLINICAL SUPERVISION

In clinical supervision, the observer keeps a time line by recording as profusely as possible. He soon develops a shorthand that enables him to keep an accurate record of what takes place in the classroom. This is probably the least objective method and yet, short of technology, it is the only method I know whereby one can accumulate enough information to begin to analyze in relation to the behavioral objectives the teacher planned for that lesson. The observer does not write down good or bad things. In fact, what he records should be free of values. He must record as rapidly as possible the perceptions he is receiving. There will be a time when he will focus on the teacher, on what he is saying or doing. Suddenly something might catch his attention in another corner of the room. He would write what he sees or hears there. Thus, it is a record of those things which the observer focuses upon at different times during the course of the class.

Analysis of data

Whether the data is collected on a television system or tape recorder, or by an observer, order must be made out of chaos. Thus, the supervisor or principal goes into his office and looks at what he has recorded. He tries to identify recurrent patterns utilized by the teacher. At this time, he may or may not know the objectives of the lesson. It is far more important to analyze these data for recurrent patterns than it is to worry about whether the patterns inhibit or enhance the objective.

Modified Categories[1]

Teacher Talk	1. Accepts feeling
	2a. Praises
	2b. Praises using public criteria
	2c. Praises using private criteria
	3. Accepts idea through:
	a. description
	b. inference
	c. generalization
	4. Asks:
	a. cognitive memory question
	b. convergent question
	c. divergent question
	d. evaluative question
	5. Lectures
	6. Gives direction
	7a. Criticizes
	7b. Criticizes using public criteria
	7c. Criticizes using private criteria
Student Talk	8. Pupil response:
	a. description
	b. inference
	c. generalization
	9. Pupil initiation:
	a. description
	b. inference
	c. generalization
	10a. Silence
	10b. Confusion

[1] From Edmund J. Amidon and Elizabeth Hunter, "Interaction Analysis: Recent Developments," p. 389. In Edmund J. Amidon and John B. Hough (eds.), *Interaction Analysis: Theory, Research and Application,* copyright 1967 by Addison-Wesley Publishing Company, Reading, Mass. Reprinted by permission of the publisher.

There are normally an infinite number of patterns a teacher might utilize in any situation, but any given teacher uses only a finite number. Our first task is to observe each teacher and determine which recurrent pattern this particular teacher utilizes in different situations. From this we can determine the strength of any teacher. Having determined the teacher's strength, and having the behavioral goals, we can determine which patterns might be advantageous for the teacher to utilize in order to achieve a desired objective.

It is important to illustrate what the term *pattern* implies. During a class a teacher might ask a question, receive a student response, and reward the response by saying, "Good," "Bad," "That's correct," or "That's incorrect." This would be one type of teaching pattern. In another section the student might ask the teacher a question and the teacher might respond. This would be a different recurrent pattern. Every time the student asks a question, the teacher responds. A third pattern might involve the students working individually and the teacher walking around the room and examining different students' work. The teacher might stop and talk to one student, and then proceed to a second student, and to a third. In a discussion class the teacher might remain silent for a long period of time as a student-student-student-student interaction occurs. These are just a few patterns one might see emerging after observing a class for forty minutes or more.

Confrontation

In many cases it is advisable for the supervisor or principal to duplicate the raw data collected in the classroom. Thus, when the teacher enters for the purpose of the analysis session, the principal hands the teacher the sheet. As a cup of coffee is being brought in, the teacher has an opportunity to see what the principal has recorded. There is no secret in this system. All information collected is shared with the teacher.

Under the old system when the principal would say to the teacher that such and such occurred, the teacher might be totally unaware of that particular incident in the class. The teacher's perception when he stands in front of the room or works with children is entirely different from an observer's perception of the same lesson. The teacher cannot process all the cues simultaneously. He might be focusing on the verbal communication taking place between a student and himself, while the observer might be focusing on what three or four other students are doing. If no record is kept of the lesson, and if no sequence is kept of the questions that were asked or the activities that took place along a time dimension, then it is almost impossible for the teacher to reconstruct the lesson in any accurate manner. But, if the teacher is given a set of notes taken by the observer while the observer was in the classroom, the teacher can more easily reconstruct the lesson. Naturally, if there was a video tape recording system in the room, both the teacher and the principal could sit and observe the lesson together without any comments. This helps the teacher relax and, at the same time, enables the sequence to be established. If a tape recorder is used in conjunction with an observer, the observer might ask the teacher to listen to the tape recorder, and relax. However, if neither of these devices is utilized, the principal has to give the teacher the opportunity to look at the notes and reconstruct the lesson in his own mind.

If the rules are established before this kind of analysis takes place, teachers usually do not become anxious about the fact that the observer is writing constantly. If the teacher knows that whatever is being recorded will be given to him later, his anxiety is usually eased.

The teacher now has in hand a written record of what took place in his classroom, events that were recorded to the best ability of the observer. The teacher's lesson plan represents that which the teacher hoped to see occurring in the classroom. Thus, the record becomes a *confrontation* between the lesson plan and the observed behaviors. The teacher's lesson plan should have been developed in a manner that indicated the kinds of behaviors and outcomes he was seeking on the part of his students; and the observer's records should reflect the kinds of behaviors that occurred in the classroom. The discrepancy or the compatibility of lesson plan to the observer's record is the point on which the dialogue focuses.

This procedure follows closely Piaget's theory of the "discrepant event." The teacher, after looking at the record, analyzing what took place, searching for his patterns, categorizing his patterns as they relate to inhibiting or enhancing the objectives, and searching for alternate strategies that could be used to achieve the objective, is going through the processes of assimilation, accommodation, and equilibration.

At times, teachers tend to blame students rather than themselves. If the teacher says that this student never performs in any other way, the principal can focus his attention on alternate strategies of correcting this student's behavior. The principal should accept the discrepancy that the teacher observes and wishes to speak about, and not oppose this discrepancy too quickly. It is important that the principal not let the teacher psychologize; instead, he should encourage the teacher to speak from the observation record. There is a tendency for the teacher to talk about extraneous matters rather than to focus on the data, the analysis of these data, and the inferences one might draw from them.

The dialogue between the principal and the teacher could start and end in many different ways. For example, if the principal recorded and analyzed the first six or seven questions asked by students and found that they were for the purpose of clarifying what the students should do—the assignment—then the principal might ask the teacher to attempt to reconstruct the total lesson. The teacher, having the notes, could start by saying, "Well, I started by giving some directions." "Can you read the directions?" the principal might ask. The teacher, with the aid of the notes, might be able to recall the directions given.

They might then discuss the next series of questions, and it might become clear to the teacher that the next series of questions were asked by the students because of the incompleteness of the assignment. If it becomes obvious that the teacher sees this problem, the principal might ask, "How could you have reworded or used a different strategy in order to accomplish the same goal—that of giving students the directions before today's lesson?" The teacher's job is to try to search for alternate methods of accomplishing the same goal. The principal, on the other hand, must listen to the teacher attentively and perhaps offer some strategy that had not been considered. The principal should never put himself in a position of insisting that his particular strategy is better than the teacher's strategies. Rather, the purpose of this dialogue is to increase the possible alternatives a teacher has at his disposal, before he constructs the next lesson.

A teaching pattern of itself possesses no value. Let us go back to one of the illustrations previously used: teacher question–student response–teacher reward. If a teacher said that he wanted to review factual information for the first five minutes of a class in order to be sure that the students had a common base for analysis or synthesis, one could argue that this pattern would enhance the achievement of his overall objectives. In fact, it is nothing more than a linear program, being presented orally instead of being written down. However, if the teacher suggested that he wanted a discussion (by discussion we mean maximum student participation, minimum teacher interference), we could assume that this pattern inhibits the achievement of the stated objective. This pattern forces the teacher to make the next input, each time he rewards the student with the remark, "That's good." If the teacher is responding after every student's comment, that is, talking approximately seventy-five to eighty per cent of the time, the students are talking only twenty-five per cent of the time. If we want to reverse this process, we must help the teacher develop other strategies to accomplish his goal.

Let us use a second illustration: teacher question–student response–student response–student response–teacher summary. If the objective of the lesson is to have the students verbalize the relationship between two or three ideas, this type of pattern prevents the teacher from getting the feedback he needs in order to determine whether the students are capable of performing the task. In most cases the students begin to realize that they do not have to listen to one another. They soon find out that the only important thing is what the teacher says at the very end. Thus, they tune in only when the teacher speaks and fail to listen to what their classmates are saying.

Another common type of teaching pattern is the following:

A student misbehaves in the back of the room for one reason or another (he might be talking to a colleague or looking out the window). The teacher calls the student to attention. However, the teacher doesn't drop back and help the child to make the transition from the point at which he tuned out to the current state of affairs. Thus, the child tries to pick up the thread, but if he has not been paying attention for some time, it becomes almost impossible for him to leap into the activity and become an active learner. Therefore, it is very likely that the student will misbehave a second time. Alternatively, when the teacher calls the student to attention, he could ask him a question to which the student might not be able to reply. The teacher could then reword the question to determine where the student was prior to his loss of attention, and then work with the child to the point where he is ready to participate as an active learner in the sequence.

Peer interaction

Until now, I have been using the word "principal" or "supervisor." However, if we move into team teaching with two or more professionals responsible for the same group of students and for the achievement of the same objectives, willing to have their professional behavior analyzed by their peers, we can train teachers to become objective recorders, and the dialogue could take place between two or more teachers. We have evidence from studies done in Carmel, California, that this kind of professional dialogue produces teachers who are capable of viewing alternate strategies before selecting the strategies they think most appropriate for the achievement of a specified objective.

Micro-teaching, a relatively new training device, is a useful tool in clinical supervision. It provides an opportunity for a teacher to take a small group of students and develop certain techniques for handling different learning situations. The observer or television system becomes a record that is reviewed by the teacher, either with another teacher or with the principal or supervisor. Once a teacher identifies the type of skills needed to perform in different situations, this particular technique is utilized as a strategy for aiding the teacher to develop the necessary competencies. Thus, shorter portions of a particular class can be recorded and analyzed in order to aid the teacher in developing certain skills. This experience is within the dimension of training, not that of education. It is a method of training the teacher to develop the ability to use silence, nonverbal cuing, or probing questions, or to set the stage for discussions. Each of these could be viewed as a small micro-teaching technique, and teachers can train themselves to become effective with the technique. However, mastery of the technique does not mean that the teacher knows when to use it. The situation is analogous to one described to me by a scientist, who observed: "It is one thing to know about the germ theory of disease and it is another thing to wash your hands before you eat." Knowing about the germ theory doesn't insure that a teacher will know when to utilize it to achieve a stated behavior goal.

Systematic analysis

The concept of clinical supervision developed from a basic important assumption—that every teacher has certain strengths and that the supervisor's task is to provide as many alternate strategies as possible, so that the teacher can eventually capitalize on these strengths. It does not entail a preconceived notion of what the teacher ought to be doing on any one day. It is concerned not with what the teacher is doing, but with the *quality* of what the teacher is doing. In the interaction analysis matrices, what the supervisor observes is the frequency with which the teacher does certain kinds of things. However, it is very difficult to get a quality picture of what the teacher is doing. The observer records that the teacher is asking a question, or giving directions, but he does not record the question or the kind of directions. The recorded observation then becomes a gross picture of what is happening in the classroom; however, when the observer tries to develop a finer analytical tool, he has to move toward the analysis of the interaction evidence itself. In the interaction analysis it is very difficult to distinguish between Level 1 and Level 5 questions (utilizing Bloom's Taxonomy). However, it is important for the teachers to become aware that there are different levels of response elicited by asking different types of questions. If a teacher is fully aware that the question he is asking can be answered only by the student who is capable of operating at a high level, then when he receives a response from one student, he drops back to help the others reach this capability. If, however, the teacher just continues on and accepts the response of one student, thinking that all students are capable of performing at this level, we have the problem of students drifting farther and farther behind, with the few bright students getting all the rewards.

Clinical supervision enables supervisors to analyze both the verbal interaction occurring in the classroom and the nonverbal interaction. Nonverbal cuing is a very effective tool for (a) maintaining control and (b) continuing a discourse among students. A teacher can maintain control by looking toward a student, by nodding his head, by raising an eyebrow, and by using many other types of nonverbal communication. It is my hunch that when nonverbal communication fails, the teacher resorts to the verbal. Thus, it is important to see what type of nonverbal behavior the teacher is utilizing in order to maintain control in the classroom. For instance, I consider myself a pacer. I never could teach comfortably behind a desk and therefore constantly walked back and forth and between the rows of students. This type of behavior allowed the students to focus on me continually and thus prevented them from tuning out during the lesson.

Another advantage of clinical supervision is that it enables the teacher to keep a permanent record of as many classroom visitations as the observer makes. Thus, even if peers or paraprofessionals are recording, the teacher has a series of lessons. By having five or six of these to examine, the teacher can analyze even further the quality and frequency of the interaction. It also enables the supervisor or principal to see whether the teacher is trying new strategies during the course of the year. Since it is relatively free of value judgments, the record could be shared by a number of teachers. A dialogue can be built around a particular lesson for which we can reproduce the recorded observations and ask for other ways of accomplishing specific objectives.

A third advantage of clinical supervision is that it provides no bag of tricks for a teacher or principal to utilize. By this I mean that there is no panacea to the educative process. Each teacher must work on developing his own strength. Each one must try to determine what patterns will be effective with a particular group or student in order to achieve a particular objective. It forces the teacher to analyze the interaction between the student and himself rather than merely to select something because he feels it will work.

It also removes from the principal the necessity of forcing the teacher to make a particular selection. It enables the teacher to remain in full control of his classroom and the kinds of decisions he makes in relation to the teaching and learning process. However, it does not prevent the teacher from trying new strategies that were mentioned as alternatives to the accomplishment of certain goals.

Also, the principal avoids being cornered in the kind of position in which a teacher could say, "You told me to do this; therefore, I did it." The principal merely makes suggestions of alternate methods, but never insists. If the principal wants a teacher to try a particular method, the dialogue might go something like this: "Tomorrow, I would like you to try a particular technique because I would like to observe the changes in the students' behavior. I know you normally would not teach this way, but I am interested in the students' responses to a particular strategy. So, why don't you try it, and I will return tomorrow and observe the lesson."

Notice that the principal is taking full responsibility for the consequences of tomorrow's lesson. If it fails, the principal says, "It is my fault." If it is successful, the principal does not have to say anything, but hopefully the dialogue that follows will enable the teacher to understand that this was a positive strategy in terms of the achievement of a specific objective with a certain group of students.

If we listen to what the "militant teacher" is telling us, we learn that up to now the administrators have been hiding behind public relations and avoiding their professional responsibilities.

They are saying that very rarely does a principal even know what is taking place in the classroom. "His salary schedule is tied to our salary schedule, so that when we get a raise, he automatically gets his raise." They contend that the principals have not been forceful enough in taking leadership for quality education. That is, the teachers have had to become militant and go out on strike in order to raise more money for education. In fact, they say that the principal has abdicated most of his responsibility for the improvement of instruction.

SUMMARY

Clinical supervision provides a vehicle for the principal to re-enter into a dialogue with his teachers in relation to the instructional program. It provides the opportunity for the principal to collect data, to observe the interaction, and to offer suggestions as possible alternatives. Since the principal shares his writings with the teacher, everything is honest. There is a built-in integrity to this system. If any alternate strategies are agreed upon, the principal and teacher record them. This process leads to a genuine intellectual relationship regarding the achievement of professional goals. Thus, through this method, principals can once again assume a respectable position in the educative activities of the school. It puts them on firmer ground to make the kinds of decisions the superintendent expects of them: decisions about whether or not this is the kind of teacher who should be given tenure. If the superintendent were concerned with instruction, this record—the raw data and identification patterns—could be sent to the superintendent in order for him to see what is actually going on in the classrooms of his school system. Naturally, this is applicable only if the system is small. In a larger system, the assistant superintendent in charge of certain areas could also know what is taking place in the classrooms.

In summary, then, a teacher's behavior will not change if he is complacent. The observational record that is made by the utilization of technology or by an observer writing in the back of a classroom becomes a confrontation for the teacher. The dialogue that takes place focuses on the differences and similarities between the lessons planned and those which took place in the classroom. This dialogue, based on an analysis of alternate strategies that one might utilize in order to achieve stated goals, helps increase the repertory each teacher might consider during the planning of his lesson. The whole purpose of in-service education is to increase the effectiveness of the teacher in the classroom. The greater the teacher's repertory, and the more he knows about the effect of each teaching strategy on the expected performances of young people, the more apt he is to select that strategy which is most effective for a particular group or individual.

■ CLUES TO ACTION

Fischler, in a definitive departure from the previous chapters, provides us with an opportunity to consider the teacher education requirements posed by a specific teaching strategy. He describes the confrontation model, in which the child learns by confronting a discrepant event and then working through the assimilation, accommodation, and eventual internalizing of the material. Using this model, Fischler describes the factors involved in helping the teacher to guide the student through the successive stages. Heavily committed to the potential of technological apparatus, Fischler is convinced that one of our greatest failures is the refusal to engage in direct confrontation with the teacher. The teacher himself, in other words, must be aided to understand the direct consequences of his instructional action, through the process of confrontation.

Fischler believes that the camera provides us with the optimum tool for developing the teacher's insight. He believes also that since most classroom transactions are verbal, the audio tape recorder can be utilized. The ideal situation, however, is one in which the video camera is combined with a trained observer who records the responses learners make to the instruction. In this way the relationship between the teaching goal, method, and effect can be judged accurately.

As the training agent seeks to assist the teacher to function more effectively, Fischler emphasizes that it is essential to concentrate not on the particular goal or objective but on the recurrent patterns that manifest themselves in the teacher's instructional style. It is these patterns, the nexus, so to speak, of the teacher's teaching, that should establish the point of departure in organizing an individualized program of professional growth. The growth itself—for Fischler—is a matter of helping the teacher to accomplish his self-determined task more efficiently. Since an individual cannot hope to take account of all the evidence stemming from an analysis of what goes on in a learning episode, the role of the observer is to assist the teacher to clarify misperceptions in his interpretation. The confrontation is achieved by forcing the teacher to recognize the disparity between his aims and his results.

Like several of the previous writers, Fischler wants the teacher to learn in much the same manner as the child learns. He conceives of professional improvement as a systematic analysis of cause and effect. It is the teacher's behavioral pattern, in short, that represents the connecting link between aims and outcomes. Where the outcomes do not correspond satisfactorily with the aims, the patterns must be altered. Thus real growth does not, for Fischler, stem from unstructured tinkering, but rather it is a consequence of the deliberate effort to analyze and modify behavior. Arguing that a teaching pattern per se has little operational value, Fischler does not want a particular teaching strategy imposed upon a teacher. Rather, through dialogue, he hopes the teacher will open himself to better alternatives.

Fischler is convinced that teachers, working in two-member teams, can improve their performance by mutual criticism. He believes that not only can teachers learn to become objective recorders, but also (in keeping with an argument of Meade's) they can develop a receptivity to the objective analysis of their work.

He takes pains to point out that the kind of clinical supervision he envisions is more training than education. It will influence not what the teacher does but how well he does it. He implies, therefore, that other professional growth activities will be necessary to increase the shrewdness and significance of the teacher's instructional aims. In sum, Fischler lends his support to the conviction espoused by Allen, Meade, Lippitt, Fox, and Jackson: namely, the teacher must have a better understanding of the results of his labor.

■ OPERATIONAL IMPLICATIONS

1. The modification of behavior is facilitated by a direct confrontation with the outcomes of the behavior. **Teachers must have an opportunity to analyze and evaluate their results.**

2. In order to analyze the consequences of teaching behavior, teachers must have recourse to some objective record. **There is great advantage when teachers can analyze their behavior through (a) sys-**

tematically recorded observations, (b) audio tape recordings, and (c) video tape recordings—or through any combination of these.

3. In general, teaching consists of patterns of actions rather than of isolated tactics. **Clinical observations, with their accompanying permanent objective records, provide the teacher with an opportunity to analyze the quality and frequency of his interaction patterns. Written or taped observations give him access to both the verbal and the nonverbal aspects of his teaching patterns.**

4. The discrepancy between teacher perception of a lesson and the observer's record of it is a useful basis for identifying teaching strengths and weaknesses. **Whenever possible, teachers should be asked to compare their goals with their actual results.**

5. Clinical supervision provides a vehicle through which principals and teachers, or teams of teachers, can enter into a dialogue based upon open and honest consideration of alternative strategies for reaching teaching goals. **Teacher teams should be encouraged to engage in cooperative analysis and evaluation of teaching performance. Principals and teachers should work together to be jointly responsible for the improvement of instruction.**

mario fantini

CHAPTER EIGHT

TEACHER TRAINING
AND EDUCATIONAL REFORM

A major movement to improve public education has been under way for almost two decades. Sufficient money has now been spent to permit us to conclude that money alone is not the answer. Although funds obviously are a necessary ingredient in the formula, our experience suggests that we tend to use money to do more of what has always been done. In the main, additional dollars are used to amplify and replicate past errors. Our inability to achieve dramatic improvements in schooling leaves us with two options: we can continue our present course in the hope that more money, energy, and time will eventually produce more effective schools; or we can seek more rapid and efficient solutions, which, necessarily, will also be more revolutionary. The arguments set forth here, in essence, represent a proposal for revolution. The proposal is born out of a conviction that we presently are consuming money and energy in defense of a system

189

that is obsolete and that cannot be substantially improved without fundamental reform.

It should be clear that authentic reform involves something more than nondescript tinkering. Whereas segments of the reform can be attacked separately, the full-blown reform of an institution does not occur until these isolated efforts are joined in an integrated movement. The reform needed must be of two sorts. First, there must be a fundamental realignment of the partners in the educational enterprise; students, teachers, administrators, and the public itself must pool their collective efforts in the improvement of the schools. It goes without saying that such collective endeavor cannot happen until the partners communicate to the point where they understand one another's conviction. Second, there must be a major alteration in the substance and process of education. That is, the things which are taught and the way in which they are taught must be made more relevant to the realistic concerns and interests of the students. In short, a fundamental criterion of curriculum significance must be that of meaningfulness to the learner. It is obvious that educators cannot achieve a reform of this dimension alone. In all probability, the teacher training institutions will need to play the dominant role in efforts to promote the interaction of the different partners. Moreover, these institutions will need to look beyond the schools to the community itself, since public education is only a part of the overall social system that must readjust to changing societal conditions. Until the reform is achieved, we will continue to suffer from outdated behaviors dictated by an outdated system.

The case of so-called disadvantaged children serves as a ready example. The results of our attempts at compensatory education, a program launched by the Ford Foundation some years ago, are not encouraging. The schools have not, in retrospect, received a fair return on their labor or money. The failures stem not from insufficient funds, too little effort, or a lack of incentive; they stem from a shoddy methodology and an impotent system. Those of us who have worked in compensatory education and who have been witness to the agonizing constraints of our tired educational machine have, from time to time, become depressed and even bitter. Convention, tradition, and bureaucratic rigidity are strong enemies. Moreover, compensatory education is a small sample of the dilemma that faces the establishment as a whole. And it is particularly illustrative of the problem of teacher retraining.

A legitimate attempt to innovate and improve cannot, *a priori*, ignore any solution that departs from custom and honored mystiques. If we persist in searching for correctives that the present system can comfortably accommodate, it is obvious that the range of alternatives will be greatly reduced. In brief, we cannot enable teachers to extend their competence to any significant degree if we limit ourselves to that which is convenient and customary, and it is foolish to equip teachers to work with a system that is inherently self-defeating.

We are in a period of rapid societal change. The changes are manifested in the conflicting ideologies of the young and the old; in the growing belief among many that education perpetuates social inequality; in racial revolt, in the rising expectations of the disadvantaged; and in the harsh facts of poverty, both black and white. It may be that we are giving ourselves to a hopeless attempt to make an old educational system fit a new social structure. Humans are reluctant to yield old patterns for new ones. Change requires both an excursion into the unknown and a corresponding loss of security. The evidence nevertheless is incontrovertible, and as our changing social system continues to evolve, public education will need to be reformed. In lieu of what is likely to be a futile attempt to repair one breakdown after another, and in lieu of approaching teacher training through a rationale which has already demonstrated its inadequacy, we might more profitably determine the kind of education we need and reform schooling and teacher training accordingly. In this spirit, what follows is a consideration of some of the more pressing elements of needed reform.

After a half-century of teacher training it has become profoundly clear that teachers learn to teach not in the training institution but in the schools where they serve. What goes on in the training institution may provide a preface to the real world of the classroom, but it does not produce an able practitioner. Away from a learning child, teachers cannot learn to teach any more than lawyers can master trial law outside the courtroom. Beyond this, all schools are not the same and every teacher must adapt to the situation in which he finds himself. If the school is the real laboratory of the teacher, it follows that we must revise the relationship between pre-service and in-service training. The imbalance between theory and technique needs to be corrected so that theory acquires meaning through pragmatic use. The teacher in training must spend more time with children and less time with the abstractions of the lecture hall. A larger percentage of the training must be given by master teachers, rich in successful practice. The training methods must reflect, to a far greater extent, what we know about the way humans acquire attitudes and skills instead of reflecting a kind of blind faith in the written and spoken word. And of greatest moment, teachers must have a rigorous orientation to the social environment in which they will function. In some classrooms, for example, a tolerance for student hostility is crucial; in others it is equally important to understand the compelling incentive of college entrance examinations.

Thus, to infuse teacher training with vitality and potency we must direct our attention to those forces which really shape teacher behavior: to the organization of the school, the exigencies of the curriculum, and the political forces within the profession. Unless we can understand these forces and take advantage of them, we are likely to make slow progress in the development of teachers and, concomitantly, in the improvement of instruction.

If the training institutions do not strive toward these goals, they may not survive. There are two reasons for this: first, their clients are already demonstrating signs of rebellion, and, second, their obsolete objectives contradict the requisites of a changing world. The training institutions, in sum, must reform in their own self-interest.

The school's traditional academic objectives have considerable bearing upon its inability to keep pace with societal shifts. Since the inception of public education in America, what little change has occurred has largely been a matter of method rather than goal. The worship of academic scholarship and factual knowledge has led us to a gross exaggeration of the importance of subject matter. A command of information is no guarantee of happiness, and success in life is not a corollary of a college degree. In part, our unwillingness to heed the demands of those who are dissatisfied with the schools has been testimony to our great dependence upon a curriculum of academic fact. When one analyzes the present social conflicts confronting the society, it is evident that the realization of full human potential, the elimination of prejudice and racism, and the enhancement of fruitful human relationships cannot be achieved through instruction that limits itself to one historical period or another, a knowledge of phonics, or the ability to diagram sentences. Because of our ancient conceptions of the purpose of schooling and our traditional beliefs about appropriate subject matter, we are forced to bend improvement programs in whatever ways are necessary to accommodate conventional expectations. Resultingly, it has become more and more difficult to make the public school curriculum relevant to the social scene and, concomitantly, increasingly difficult to initiate necessary improvements.

Throughout the nation's schools we can find an almost unlimited number of instances where traditional teaching procedures yield unsatisfactory results, largely because they have little congruence with the learning styles of children. A given child, for example, learns best in a situation that is concrete, inductive, and more kinetic than verbal. However, since such teaching is contrary to tradition and a departure from the prevailing system, it rarely takes place. Furthermore, since teachers are trained in traditional approaches and equipped to fit the typical system, they are unfamiliar with the necessary pedagogical techniques. Time and again the child is hurt by his inability to match the teacher's style. Similarly, with almost incredible tenacity, we persist in teaching the ghetto child about irrelevance. If we wish him to learn some simple arithmetical computations, we are likely to present him with a problem concerning the number of gallons of milk a farmer must obtain in order to acquire so much butterfat. In short, the traditions of schooling have become so sacred as to require that we ignore the learner's experience and his frame of reference. We do not teach about bus transfers, court bail, and unemployment simply because we have never done so. Most importantly, however, our preoccupation with content and skills has caused us to ignore values and emotions. Success as a person depends less upon what one knows or can do, or even upon the amount of money one earns, than upon his feelings about himself and life. These, nevertheless, usually are outside the pale of the accepted curriculum. Feelings, attitudes, values, and concerns, in short, are not allowed to intrude upon the memorizing of the world's rivers or the poetry of Kipling.

The overemphasis of cognitive learning and the corresponding disregard of the affective (feeling) aspects of education have also resulted in a lost sense of identity among students. It is not so much that the schools have sought to dissipate the black child's feeling of blackness or the Mexican child's pride in his cultural heritage; rather, it is that the schools have not utilized ethnic identity as a springboard to social involvement and have neglected the ethnic factors that underlie the individual's self-concept. Apart from sins of historical omission, distortion, and the perpetuation of tribal myths, the typical curriculum is based upon white, middle-class beliefs. It sets forth specious notions about life in America that the Puerto Rican child, the black child, and the Mexican-American child know to be nonsense. Within their blackness, Negro children span the same range of human individuality as do white children. Aside from reconciling himself to the fact that he is a black in a white society, the black youngster must still resolve such questions as: who am I? what am I? and, what do I do with my life? The minority child is thus shortchanged on two counts: his heritage and uniqueness are ignored in the school despite the fact that they are major considerations in the real world; and his personal sense of identity is overlooked in the press for academic learning. Perhaps it is worth noting that identity loss is a problem for all students, not just for those of minority stock.

It is not surprising, therefore, that in the cities something of a small war between the parents of minority youth and the schools has developed. A decade or so ago these parents were philosophical about their children's school failures. Told by the educator that their children were four years behind accepted levels because of "cultural deprivation," the parents accepted, as a quirk of fate, that their children were predestined for academic failure. Today, however, the revolt of the clients has changed this. Spurred by the black power movement, the more general quest for civil rights, parents of Mexican, black, and Puerto Rican children are demanding that the schools meet their legitimate responsibilities. The parents' attitude is simply that the schools exist to serve youth, whatever the nature of their educational needs, and that they must be made to face their problems instead of avoiding them. As a consequence, the moment of *accountability* is drawing close.

Despite the educator's professional training, his knowledge and expertise, and despite the layman's lack of sophistication regarding teaching and learning, parents in ghetto communities are issuing ultimatums. They have recognized, with penetrating clarity, that education, perhaps more than any other social institution, perpetuates white supremacy. The parents' position, reduced to its simplest dimension, is that the schools are cheating their children. Schools are supported by public dollars to serve the public good. The schoolman is trained, hired, and paid to educate the young, and he must be accountable for his performance. Our theory, research, and esoteric experience notwithstanding, a growing body of parents have decided that it is the public's province to decide what kinds of schools it wants and what kinds of standards ought to prevail. Although these parents are willing to leave implementation and method to the professionals, they are a good deal more dictatorial about the results they seek. If Johnny cannot read, as is often the case in the cities, it is not Johnny but the school who is at fault. With a problem of this degree of complexity, confrontation is inevitable. Unhappily, our usual practice is to respond to confrontation with defensive maneuvers.

The Ford Foundation has played a substantial role in the effort to improve the education of the inner-city child. My experi-

ences in New York, Boston, Philadelphia, and Washington have
led me to believe that there is a predictable cycle to the rebellion
of ghetto parents. The ghetto community comes to a realization
that its schools are inadequate. This awakening is followed by
somewhat primitive and inept efforts to alter affairs in the
schools. In defense, school administrators overwhelm the parents
with rhetoric, logic, and research findings. Unable to comprehend
or debate the profession's arguments, but unshaken in their expectations, the parents seek the assistance of politicians. In due
course, a small group of militant and highly vocal parents emerge
as the leadership force and commence to speak for the community. Whether or not they actually represent the ghetto community at large is a moot point. Sociologically speaking, there are
probably many educational communities rather than one. In
addition, politicians are swayed by activists rather than pacifists;
therefore, those who speak are likely to receive attention whether
or not they are representative. Ultimately, political force is ex-
erted and the schools begin to express concern about political
meddling and external interference.

The voice of the ghetto may well be a sign of things to come.
Although parental attacks on education are somewhat more
prevalent in the cities than in the suburbs, attitudes of the public
are taking on a new importance everywhere. In the future,
parents may be less willing to defer to the professional expertise
of schoolmen and more determined to control the policies of the
school themselves. Suburban communities would do well to begin
to assess the sentiments of their public and to make sensible use
of the available lead time. It may well be that a calculated effort
to judge public concerns now and to bring the schools closer in
line with community expectations is the best hope of forestalling
the hostility and rebellion that could easily characterize the
future. In the minority communities, per se, it seems to me that
there is no alternative but to accept the parents' demands for
legitimate involvement in the control of their schools, and to use
communication and collaboration to improve matters. Even so,
there is a possibility that in the beginning stages many parental
groups will take the position that teachers and principals are
hired hands, paid to accomplish ends set by the parents.

The evidence in the Koerner Report and in a number of similar studies is incontrovertible. There are close connections between education, civil rights, and class mobility. From the point of view of the minority community, the schools are part and parcel of a white society—a racist society—and lack of good education is a major obstacle to a better life. For the parents of the disadvantaged it makes little difference whether the professional educator is a racist, whether he is the willing pawn of a racist society, or whether his intents are honorable but incapable of overcoming the system; in any instance, the school's perpetuation of discrimination and inequality is the same. The important question, of course, is whether the society and its schools have the courage and the strength to do what must be done. The difficulties, admittedly, are awesome. To compound matters, the more militant parents may appear to hinder rather than help the cause. Nevertheless, the task is a matter of both morality and survival. We must begin to put the urban schoolhouse in order. We must find ways to improve the professional development programs for teachers who work with minority youth. While many teachers and principals have contributed magnificently, there are also those (their master's degrees notwithstanding) who look upon the black child as inferior and incapable of learning, and thus set in motion the classical self-fulfilling prophecy.

Minority youth itself has also manifested indications of an emerging hostility. The black adolescent, for example, feels that his school serves as an instrument of assimilation. Because of a desire to assert his own identity, he may regard assimilation as undesirable. If one is Puerto Rican, an accent may be unavoidable. In the spirit of the melting pot dream, moreover, it may not be something to be ashamed of. Black and brown students alike are beginning to understand that the good life ought not to depend upon a denial of what they are. Their arithmetic achievement scores notwithstanding, blacks and Puerto Ricans can count. Sixty per cent of the school population in New York City is either Puerto Rican or black. Their teachers, however, are predominantly white. Not only is "whitey" in control, but nonwhites are rewarded in proportion to the extent to which they emulate white values and customs. Pride, a search for self-identity, and the realities of social life thus breed hostility in minority youth. When 4,000 Philadelphia high school students march through the streets with a list of demands, their actions may be regarded as hostile, senseless, anarchic, or impudent; they must nevertheless be reckoned with. In view of a mounting minority antagonism to white teachers, the problems of teacher training are obvious. We are called upon to prepare teachers to enter classrooms where the students are antisocial, antiestablishment, and antiwhite.

These brief references to the conditions that exist in school and community set the stage for an analysis of the changes which seem in order and some speculation regarding the implications for teacher training. We can infer from the protests of minority youth and from dropouts in general that schooling must be more than the acquisition of substantive knowledge and academic skills. This inference is reinforced by the concerns that have been expressed by business and industry. The growing interest in T-group training, basic encounter groups, sensitivity training, and similar activities designed to make the individual more fully functioning suggests that we have underemphasized the affective aspects of education. With an intelligent realignment of our methods of teaching and our choice of subject matter, it is conceivable that the schools might spare business and industry the need to develop the psychological health of their workers, and might also reduce the dissatisfactions of youth who feel that their schools have failed them. Most children learn, early in their school experience, that it is unwise to exhibit real feelings in school. They learn that the school and the society alike have preconceived notions about proper attitudes, feelings, beliefs, and behavior. We commonly graduate from the high school a young man or woman who is prepared to enter a choice college, who has a B average or better, who has "made it" in the eyes of the school—and who is a desperately unhappy human.

However, we cannot deal with such things as identity, self-confidence, and emotional stability unless we are willing to reformulate our objectives in schooling. Do not mistake me here. I do not suggest that we eliminate geography, history, or the study of the Byzantine Empire from the curriculum. Rather, I mean to imply that a more rational set of objectives, coupled with a more sensitive approach to teaching, can produce substantial improvement in both cognitive and affective learning. Clearly, if we do not teach the black youth the Constitution of his country, we fail him as surely as we do when we teach him to hate his blackness. The compelling need for reform, to repeat an earlier point, stems from both the shortcomings of the present system and the changing social order, which has made many of our ancient practices obsolete.

The demands of the black community for an educational program that deals directly with the black child's sense of identity, and that serves to familiarize him with his own unique cultural heritage, have given rise to a legitimate new set of humanistic objectives. As educators, we have always been committed to the needs of the individual child. But we have barely been able to translate these needs into operational programs, largely because the public majority considered the programs to be frills. The demands of the black communities are helpful to the educator's cause as a legitimizing force; they reaffirm the public's right to help determine the educational policies of the schools. At present, the black community has made it clear that the traditional curriculum has little relevance to the life concerns of their children. Their demands, resultingly, have become a legitimizing force for curricula reform. This, let it be said, is as it should be. The American educational system is predicated upon the assumption that it is the public itself which should determine the educational objectives.

To initiate new objectives it will be necessary to establish a different yardstick on which to measure teacher performance and the accomplishments of the school. The teacher who is interested in enlarging the human potential of his children, or in overcoming a student's tendency toward prejudice, or even in improving the quality of the human relationship within the classroom, must now run a sizeable professional risk in order to pursue his interests. Although our courses of study make frequent reference to the humanizing aspects of education, and although school spokesmen habitually speak of its importance, the fact of the matter is that teachers and schools are judged predominantly by the academic achievement of the student. The school that is successful in holding a disenchanted adolescent, for example, is likely to receive little credit; if the student is below par on a standardized test, his presence damages the school's reputation. It is not the profession but the parents who are responsible for this situation. Usually, the parent, dissatisfied with his child's school, is concerned primarily with the youngster's inability to perform at grade level. In the more privileged suburbs, parents are equally dissatisfied when their offspring do not perform two or three years above grade level.

The corrective strategy is sequential: we must expand the humanistic aspects of education and corresponding new behavioral objectives must be established; to do this, it will be necessary to alter the public's attitude as to the purpose of schooling; and, to modify public opinion, the schools must communicate in greater depth, increase community involvement, and develop a clearer sense of mission. In time, the school must accept a greater responsibility for the welfare of each child entrusted to its care, and it must solicit the various kinds of support necessary to discharge this responsibility. Above all, we must forego our temptation to tinker with a system that is already tinged with social obsolescence, and must instead substitute bold new approaches to the educative process, approaches characterized by new targets, new concepts of achievement, and new standards for judging success. And only after such a transformation has taken some shape can we hope to train the teachers we need. We cannot provide for the authentic professional growth of the teacher until we devise a school system that fits the sociology of our time.

We cannot avoid the need to change, if only because the society cannot sustain present circumstances for very long. If we are able to overcome our disabilities, and there appears to be no good reason why we cannot, our profession will be much the better for the effort. The improvements in the inner city, for example, will also have considerable merit elsewhere. Apart from deleterious aspects, the race crisis may be a useful stimulus to interrupt the status quo and alter the system. Monolithic bureaucracies are not easily changed, and it usually takes a sequence of intolerable events to prompt major innovations. The alienation between teachers and parents that has become so manifest in ghetto communities probably exists on a much wider scale. Not only is there an absence of and a disregard for educational opportunities and cooperative collaboration in community life, but parents seem increasingly to distrust the school's motives and procedures. The teacher and parent are natural allies. They are the determining force in shaping the child and the primary agents through whom intellectual and emotional development are managed. As a first step, therefore, we must seek to improve parent-teacher understanding and cooperation. Parents are the first teachers, and appropriate home activities in the preschool years can aid and abet what is to come later in the school. Similarly, when parents and teachers both understand and respect their mutual objectives, they can complement each other's efforts throughout the child's formative period. Collaboration of this sort obviously depends upon effective and continual communication.

When the demands of parents in ghetto communities are analyzed, it is apparent that, in the main, their expectations do not differ very much from the general aspirations of all parents. They want their children to learn, to prepare for a satisfying adulthood, and to acquire a sense of adequacy and competence. What *is* different in the ghetto, however, is that parents are demanding greater authority in the control of the school. It is not only that they are opposed to what is now going on; they also are not certain that the white establishment can be trusted to look after the welfare of their children, and they resent their position as helpless victims of school discrimination. Given a better understanding of the purpose of schooling and a greater voice in determining policy, it is unlikely that they would argue for much that is contrary to the *stated* intent of the schools.

The antagonisms of the hostile minority youth are further testimony to our communication failures and to our cavalier attitude toward the educational consumer. Admittedly, some of their demands are irrational. Although the insistence on a black principal, for example, is understandable, the request that collard greens and grits be served in the school cafeteria is obviously silly. But it behooves us to consider the underlying basis of the demands rather than their specific nature. Here again we must face the criticism squarely, respecting it where it is valid and clarifying its misconceptions through better contact with the public—with community leaders, parents, and students themselves. Since the growing political power of minority groups and their increasing ambitions for social action cannot be checked, it would be foolish to ignore their hostilities and to fail to take advantage of their constructive energies. The ghetto school could become a battlefield of social protest, black parents pitting their mechanisms of obstruction against the defensive tactics of white school administrators, reducing education to a meaningless war symbol. Moreover, the oppressed learn from one another, and it is probable that all disadvantaged classes will eventually have their day in court.

In a sense, then, the challenge to educational leadership will test not only its ability to reform an outdated system but its ability to fabricate a strategy of reform that can forestall the negative actions of the dissatisfied public. The reform should not be regarded as a meaningless sop to minority communities. Instead, the teacher training institutions must collaborate with other partners and deploy their own energy in the coordination of the other available energies. In brief, the teacher training institutions are in the best position to orchestrate a collaborative and forceful program of correction. Therefore, it is imperative that the teacher training institutions themselves understand the pressing need for a new system. Beyond this, they must give prudent thought to their own role in the reform, and to the mechanisms through which they can invoke necessary collaboration. If a concerted attack of this kind is not launched, we shall fail despite our best efforts because we will devote ourselves to the improvement of a system that is already obsolete. If the necessary alterations are approached with intelligence and an honest spirit of intent, it will benefit education generally. The structure of the system must be overhauled—not its decor. Those who over the years have worked to make the educational process better and to improve the learning environment of disadvantaged youngsters may feel embittered and maligned by the turn of events. There may be resentment over the artificial aspects of the crisis and its more irrational characteristics. Social change invariably poses hardships that violate reasonableness. It is imperative that we rise above our defensiveness and our damaged feelings in order to bring the full measure of the profession's competence to bear upon the problem.

The basic elements of the needed reform are unmistakable. Because much of the school population suffers from emotional disabilities and psychological unrest, the base of our instructional program must be extended to include to a far greater extent experiences that make for a more stable personality. Since racial discrimination, poverty, unemployment, and a general social malaise are the crucial societal dilemmas of our time, they must be dealt with forthrightly in the school. It is imperative that the curriculum be made more realistic and more relevant to the fundamental concerns of youth. We must devise instructive procedures through which to deal with the problems of alienation, identity confusion, disconnection, and the pervasive belief that the good life is possible only for white, middle-class society. Put another way, the schools must become more congruent with the life of their clients and must overthrow convention and conformity in order to revitalize the school by making more imaginative use of learning opportunities in the community. While we should not negate traditional content and the obligation to familiarize the learner with man's accumulated wisdom, we must seek to link substantive knowledge with the practical concerns of life. In the cases of the black, the brown, the white southern migrant, and other disadvantaged groups we must avoid a tendency to inadvertently eradicate their cultural past. The diversity that characterizes our nation is a precious commodity. Out of their heritage and history, the black and the Mexican—like the Pole, Frenchman, and Italian—have contributed substantially to our national strength. Minority children must learn to take justifiable pride in their ancestry and their heritage.

Reform movements are difficult. They are not easily initiated, they are hard to sustain, and the more ponderous the bureaucracy, the greater the amount of effort required to diffuse their momentum. It is not surprising, therefore, that we have for a long time sought to avoid reform by a variety of stopgap measures. Aside from sporadic gains, these have been spectacularly unsuccessful. The reform is overdue, and it is now time to get at the hard core problems.

The crucial problem is how to achieve the reform within the provisions of the democratic system. In view of the plurality of people's educational objectives, there cannot be any wall-to-wall solutions. Nor can we arbitrarily scrap the present system in favor of any particular change.

Instead, we must seek a variety of options so that there is room for a choice among alternatives. If some prefer to stay with the status quo, their preference must be respected. And if others want something else, they, too, should have their wishes honored. What we need, in essence, is a system of choice. Only in this way can we reform rationally.

Some of the options will succeed and some will fail. Those which succeed, however, will add impetus to the reform and to a continuing search for better schools. Thus, programs of teacher professional growth should stimulate options and depress mandates throughout the mainstream of the educational process, for it is in the diversity of man that our strength lies.

■ CLUES TO ACTION

The reader may sense a certain repetitiveness as different writers refer to the same point. Although these repetitions could, of course, have been omitted, they have been retained largely because the repetition serves to lend weight to their importance. Fantini, for example, adds additional weight to a number of earlier implications: school is the real laboratory for professional growth, and we therefore need to work for a closer bond between pre-service and in-service learning; and the initiation of the necessary change must stem from the deliberate intervention of administrators.

More importantly, however, Fantini extends the consideration of teacher education to the larger community and to the social forces at work. Convinced that the schools need a revolution, he suggests that it would be foolish to mount programs of professional growth that equip a teacher to deal with an already obsolete educational program. Put simply, he believes that the school is becoming a decadent institution and he not only wants the continuing education of teachers to anticipate the future, but he believes that teachers should acquire skills and attitudes that enable them to perpetuate a new kind of educational system. Not only does he advocate a broader base of educational decision making, but he feels that the profession and the public can together work toward the improvement of the schools. Such collaboration, he argues, will lead to education that better serves the public good.

Like Thelen, Fantini is worried about teachers' lack of sophistication regarding their social environment. "Teachers," he says, "must have a rigorous orientation to the social environment in which they will function." He believes, furthermore, that the teacher's behavior is heavily influenced not only by his training but by the curriculum, the school organization, and the political pressures within the bureaucracy. Both implicitly and explicitly, he suggests that the curriculum has failed to take note of the child's frame of reference, and teacher education has failed to respect the teacher's frame of reference. These failures result from a lack of sensitivity on the part of the institutions and the people who train teachers.

Warning that hostility and rebellion could easily permeate the future of public education, Fantini would like to see far greater emphasis upon the emotions, both the student's and the teacher's. We cannot hope to help children develop a sense of identity, self-confidence, and a more stable personality if we do not rethink our educational objectives and revise the substance of our teacher education activities. In addition to a curriculum that more closely parallels community expectations, he asks for new pedagogical techniques—techniques that enlarge the student's potential for humaneness—and for new criteria with which to judge teacher and school effectiveness. None of these, however, is possible unless we are willing to function more imaginatively and to take greater professional risks.

Essentially, Fantini calls upon educational leadership to devise a strategy of educational reform with which to overthrow an outdated system. Like many of the other writers, he wants a complex rather than a simplistic system. With better parent-teacher cooperation as a point of departure, the public's conception of schooling must be altered, a widespread interest in the humanistic elements of education must be championed, and new behavioral objectives, reflecting a more dynamic and relevant educational program, must be instituted. And, crucially, the teacher training institutions must not only understand these reforms, but they must endeavor to produce teachers who can put them into effect.

■ OPERATIONAL IMPLICATIONS

1. The schools belong not to the profession but to the people. **Students, parents, teachers, and administrators must collaborate more closely in the setting of educational policy.**

2. The existing school system is obsolete. **The educational profession must undertake to initiate a series of major school reforms.**

3. It would be shortsighted to base the continuing education of teachers on an outdated school. **Professional growth activities should anticipate the reforms that are needed.**

4. Teacher retraining must become more pragmatic and more vital. **Truly superior teachers must be involved to a greater extent in the growth activities of their colleagues.**

5. The behavior of the teacher in the classroom is affected by a multiplicity of forces. **In addition to more rigorous programs of teacher professional growth, educational leadership must work for a curriculum, a school organization, and an ideology that do not counteract the objectives of teacher continuing education.**

6. The humanistic aspects of education will be increasingly important in the future. **The in-service education of teachers should anticipate this fact and should give increasing attention to the emotional development of teachers.**

part III

TIME AND DESIRE

As the preceding two sections have demonstrated, professional growth is a complex phenomenon. Teaching competence requires not only a knowledge of subject and child, a command of technique, and an appropriate sense of purpose, but also an endless desire to become more adept. This desire is the touchstone of the self-evolving teacher.

To evolve and mature, however, one must have at least minimal conveniences. One must, for example, have some means of gaining insight into his strengths and weaknesses. It is also necessary to have whatever apparatus is necessary for shoring up deficiencies. And, crucially, one must have time in which to grow. This last requirement is most likely to be treated cavalierly. As enrollments increase, costs escalate, and dollars become scant, we may, in false economy, under-estimate the importance of in-service development. In so doing, we will continue—if not extend—our tolerance of flawed performances in the classroom.

In the final section of the volume, Meade, Fischer, and I place many of the arguments set forth earlier in context. These final chapters prescribe what must be done: first, we must set standards of quality teaching; second, we must routinely determine whether or not these standards are being achieved; third, we must make it possible for the teacher to recognize whatever is delinquent in his teaching performance; and, fourth, we must provide the time and other resources that permit the teacher—in an orderly process of self-evolving professionalism—to improve.

All of this, admittedly, is easier said than done. Nevertheless, despite the obstacles, it *can* be done. If forced to choose between a strong teacher and a weak textbook, most school administrators would unhesitatingly choose the competent teacher. Teaching competency affords protection against poor instructional material, but no learning program will hold up against the abuses perpetrated by shoddy teaching.

The willingness to provide time and other resources, consequently, is in effect a test of the importance we attach to quality teaching. It is a measure of whether we will see fit to heed Meade's admonition that "we acknowledge the great importance of teacher in-service education and assign it high priority." In the long run, money and energy devoted to the support of a self-evolving teacher may prove to be the most sensible expenditure we can make. One needs only to recall his own captive years in classrooms to realize that some teachers make a difference in our lives and others do not. From this point of view, the importance of teacher professional growth seems unquestionable. The merit of devoting time to the cause seems equally unquestionable. What matters, of course, is that the time be used wisely.

edward j. meade, jr.

CHAPTER NINE

NO HEALTH IN US

There is perhaps no better summary of the state of in-service education today than the words of Thomas Cranmer: "We have left undone those things which we should have done; And we have done those things which we should have left undone; And there is no health in us."

In-service education—the continual updating of the practitioner in the classroom—is clearly suffering as much from the sins of omission as from those of commission. The list of what has been left undone is long and varied, and in the vacuum created by these failures, often trivial and inconsequential substitutes have flourished. What should be a vital component of teacher preparation has been allowed to remain piecemeal and haphazard. What should inspire teachers to maximize their potential is too often regarded by education management as either an onerous burden or an incidental ritual.

211

OUR SINS OF OMISSION

Our first and perhaps our greatest omission is one that affects the entire enterprise. We have failed to probe in depth the interplay between teaching and learning, to examine all the divine ways in which learning occurs. Jackson and others remind us elsewhere in the volume that we must begin to look at the classroom transactions with new eyes. For the most part we still are content to see teacher training as a matter of equipping the teacher to tell children about one kind of knowledge or another. But the body of knowledge is unstable. It changes and grows. Yesterday's fact is replaced by today's inquiry. And often fact A and fact B are not nearly so important as the relationship between them and the relevance they have to the lives of the children we teach.

The social curriculum, all those experiences of the school and classroom that are basic to the development of competence in the art of living, has escaped our attention almost completely. Social scientists who have studied the changes our society is undergoing have much to tell us about the institution which is the schools. If we ignore their findings, we will operate from a partial, and often misleading, understanding of the drama that daily is staged in our schools.

One aspect of that drama, something we call "learning," has been the subject of much study, albeit more intensively with rats and pigeons than with children. And, curiously, more of the study has been concerned with individual learning, despite the fact that almost everywhere children in school are still taught in groups. Even in the laboratory, the research has dealt more with individual rats and individual pigeons than with groups. It would seem, therefore, that the child, no less than the rat or pigeon, learns as an individual, even if in some—or many—instances he does so in group situations. Perhaps it is time to acknowledge this fact of life and to make the necessary readjustments in our approach to schooling. As a consequence of all this research, moreover, learning theories are not in short supply, although they may sometimes conflict. Viable theories of teaching, based on helping people learn, on the other hand, are scarce; some would say nonexistent. In their place are random observations, some of which undoubtedly are more accurate than others. The trouble is that we do not really know which are accurate and which are not. But we tend to act upon most of these observations as if they were a kind of gospel. Thus we are imprisoned within our own shortsightedness. Worse, we are led into an acceptance of the view that "teaching" is "what teachers do." Our faith in the notion that "teaching is what teachers do" would not be so damaging if we carefully examined what teachers are expected to do. Unhappily, this is too rarely done. Evaluation of good and bad teaching in the absence of some performance criteria becomes a capricious exercise in authority. In turn, planning in-service education without performance criteria becomes an exercise in futility. And developing those criteria without a sense of purpose and commitment is perhaps the highest folly.

We have had little success in defining "good teaching" in terms that would allow for evaluation of performance. The problem here may be not so much the paucity of answers to the question, What is good teaching? as the question itself. When a question seems insoluble despite continuing efforts to deal with it, one does well to re-examine the question to see if it can be put in some way that does lend itself to an answer. If we continue searching for that elusive good teaching, we may be committing ourselves to a dilemma from which there is no escape. As with love, teaching is a many-splendored thing, and its richness and power derive from stylistic differences, from a repertory of skills, and from a sensitivity that allows the teacher to do what is right for the student. Perhaps our question regarding good teaching should be thought of pluralistically.

No program of in-service education will be efficacious unless it is based upon a realistic understanding of the many elements of the teaching act as it affects learning. The monolithic structure of education makes such differentiation difficult, but is nevertheless essential for two reasons. First, although much that we do in the preparation of our teachers assumes a homogeneity of type and ability, teachers are individuals. They vary in the same manner and degree as other mortals. In a profession that prides itself on its concern with the individuality of the clients it serves, educators seem curiously myopic about individual differences in their own ranks. It remains true, nonetheless, that both teachers in training and teachers in service have different strengths and weaknesses. Training programs that respect this fact promise to be more productive than those which assume a basic sameness among people who teach the young. If individualized instruction is to be anything more than a pleasant slogan, it must begin in our teacher education programs both because it is desperately needed there and because only in this way can it serve as a model for the teacher-to-be. Second, the trend toward teacher specialization is inevitable for several reasons. Specialization will come as a result of the great complexity of the educational system; it will come because teachers themselves, in their growing professionalism and autonomy, are beginning to perceive the benefits of a division of labor; and specialization will be necessary if we are to begin to distinguish among what is best done by learners individually, by learners with technology, and by learners working with other humans. Moreover, humans are of different orders of talent and training. The school lends itself to a logical division of labor, a division that we still do not make with any real precision.

Assuming that a finer analysis of the teaching act can be achieved, we must still deal with those deficiencies in our in-service programs that stem from "what has been left undone." Disunities bear much responsibility for the unhealthy state of our teacher in-service education efforts. The basic disunion is that between pre-service and in-service programs. Beyond this, many secondary ruptures occur within the framework of the in-service system itself.

From the standpoint of licensing, the distinction between pre-service and in-service is clear. People prepare themselves to be teachers. At some stage in their academic careers, they are certified by state and/or local district and are allowed to begin their practice. The basis for such certification varies from place to place, and emergency procedures often permit some or all of the credential requirements to be waived or postponed. Once an individual is permitted to teach, the pre-service stage is complete and the in-service stage is begun. This arrangement obviously does not guarantee greater competency from one stage to the other, nor does it indicate that people in the pre-service stage require markedly different experiences from those in the in-service stage. This being the case, what, for example, is the logic in limiting the activities of the college training supervisor to pre-service candidates?

The college supervisor, or the college consultant, as he might more properly be called, many of whom are scholars from academic disciplines, should act as a content resource for teachers. Generally he is concerned primarily with the teacher's treatment of his subject. He does not view himself as central to the direct supervision of the techniques of teaching. Furthermore, this role is better left to the schools, specifically to the teacher supervisors or teacher trainers. The college consultant should be available, when needed, to help the teacher understand the nature and perspective of contemporary knowledge and instructional techniques in the intellectual discipline in question. In addition, the college consultant ought to work closely with the in-school teacher trainers, assisting them to help teachers achieve a better blend of content and method. For only in this way can his contribution reach the mainstream of schooling.

THE ABUSE OF TRAINING

In the way of our world, most in-service activities appear to serve three functions. First of all, they provide a method for arbitrating advancement on the salary schedule. In the absence of other criteria, academic units are often the only basis for rewarding teachers. Second (and paradoxically), they are a route out of the classroom, often promoting to some other capacity the very teachers they are purporting to help become more effective. Third, they are temporary rescue missions, instigated to help teachers overcome a pressing crisis, perhaps the introduction of a new and different set of textbooks.

Each of these functions is subject to criticism. Massive evidence exists to explode the myth that there is a positive correlation between amount of traditional training and quality of performance in the classroom. Aside from the fact that this evidence constitutes an indictment of current training procedures, it is also clear, or should be, that tying salary to accumulated units works to the disadvantage of both the in-service program and the educational system as a whole. It offers an incentive that debilitates the educational value of professional growth, and it fails to provide any tangible reward for better teaching performance—which is, perhaps, the proper realm of salary considerations.

If the situation were reversed and teachers were rewarded in terms of their achievement, in-service training might become in fact what we claim it to be in principle: a program through which understandings are deepened and skills are sharpened. The classroom would be the real test of the in-service program's value. In such a system it is likely that teachers would demand effective in-service assistance.

The present state of affairs suggests that we have as yet been unable to resolve a crucial issue: should the teacher assume responsibility for his own professional growth or should the system? Although it would be easy to make a case for shared responsibility, the fact remains that if we wish to guarantee quality teaching, the guarantee must be made good by one party or the other. Ultimately, in other words, either the individual must decide for himself whether he has adequate competence and then do what is required to bring himself up to par, or the organization—the school—must judge his competence and provide the necessary corrective measures. My own inclination is to place the charge on the system. I do not mean by this that the teacher is to be reduced to a puppet, for puppets will never provide us with the kind of classrooms we need. As in all learning, the teacher must play a significant part in his own growth. I mean, rather, that it is the system, as represented by pupils, parents, the public, teachers, and school leaders, which must set standards of performance as well as provide the incentive and opportunity for their realization.

Like most other workers, teachers must look to their organization for an indication of what is expected. Moreover, it is the organization's leadership who must be accountable for its good and bad points. It therefore seems reasonable to assume that we can avoid an unnecessary impasse by expecting school systems to determine the kinds of competencies they wish their teachers to have, and to permit the teachers to acquire these competencies in whatever ways the teachers think best. Such an arrangement obviously would require that school systems afford teachers an adequate opportunity for professional development and that teachers respect the necessary limitations on the provisions which can be made.

Another consequence of this kind of reorientation would be that teachers would undoubtedly take more initiative in acquiring the competencies for which they feel the greatest need. One of the shortcomings of present practice is the failure to capitalize on one of the best sources of information regarding teacher needs: the teacher himself. If more relevance is required in in-service activities—and there seems to be widespread agreement that this is the case—it would appear sensible to involve teachers in the planning and execution of their own improvement programs.

CREDENTIALS AND COMPETENCIES

One of our most serious problems is the lack, almost a complete lack, of teacher criticism of their own performances and those of their colleagues. It is considered almost unethical for teachers to seek fault in their teaching, let alone in that of others. Why does self-evaluation, and the spirit behind it, virtually cease when a person becomes a teacher? Visit any faculty meeting and listen to the conversations. Rarely, if ever, are there critical analyses directed toward an examination of what teachers do in relation to helping pupils learn. Once bestowed, the teaching credential is taken as an eternal guarantee of adequacy.

It seems certain that if the expectation of continual evaluation of teaching—together with clear criteria for judgment—were firmly rooted in our professional ethos, classrooms would profit. Clearly, education would be improved if teachers were to criticize their performances objectively and face their strengths and weaknesses squarely as many other professionals do. I have always been impressed, for example, by defense and prosecution attorneys who separately and jointly review their respective work in a particular case and assess each other's labor—both good and bad. Why can't teachers do the same? A hallmark of the true professional is his ability to exercise critical judgment of his own performance. This searching for weakness is partly a matter of competitiveness, partly a quest for perfection, and partly a human desire to be a winner rather than a loser. These desires are in a sense typical of all of us. That they are infrequently manifest among teachers is less a failure of people than one of organization. It is the working climate in which the teachers function, in other words, that largely is responsible for promoting an endemic resistance to self-criticism. The end result of this circumstance is that mediocrity is allowed to flourish. The routine assessment of performance depends essentially on attitude, on a desire to know, and on the ability to judge accurately. Given a working environment in which self-criticism is not only permitted but encouraged, and one in which the acknowledgment of error does not produce punishing censures, it would be relatively easy to develop the necessary attitude and judgmental skill. It seems to me that little professional growth can occur until the teacher becomes aware of his weak points; therefore, it would seem imperative that we make it safe for teachers to judge themselves accurately. The freedom to fail occasionally, after all, is a small price to pay for improvement.

This active involvement of teachers would go a long way toward reassuring them that they can function as professionals, capable of participating in the control of their own growth. The illness metaphor I have used to describe the state of in-service education itself does not fit the teachers in the field. To view teachers in terms of a pathological model would be to assume deficiency and illness that can only be remedied by the prescriptions of an outside expert. This line of thinking will not do. First of all, the negative expectancy is bound to exert a damaging influence. The self-fulfilling prophecy must surely operate on teachers as well as on students. While it may not always be true that teachers perform according to what is expected of them, the reverse is almost never true. Most often teachers perform according to the frequently shallow expectancies they sense in those who administer and supervise schooling. Also, if diagnosis and remediation are placed solely in the hands of outside "experts," the teacher is deprived of the privilege of participating in his own development. The lessons of the social sciences are instructive here: humans prefer to be captains of their own souls and they respond to what they perceive to be worthwhile in life. And, last, the illness model leads to sporadic attacks on in-service problems, that is, to symptomatic therapy rather than to needed reform.

Just as it is counterproductive to view teachers as objects to be manipulated, so it is futile to assume that teachers are so intractible that the only way to assure progress in education is to use schemes that by-pass the teacher's judgment. The flurry toward the development of teacher-proof curricula has subsided; the aftermath has left some noble failures that attest to the folly of trying to alter schooling without altering teachers. Though teachers may well be the factors in the formula least amenable to change, it does not follow that the only alternative is to organize matters so as to minimize any effect the teacher might have. Indeed, the resistance of many teachers to manipulation may well be our best safeguard against ill-conceived or hastily adopted programs. If new curricula are to be implemented, they will be implemented through the teachers in the classroom or not at all, at least as our schools are presently constituted. We would do well, however, to remember that teachers resist manipulation. Significant improvement in the schools will not come about without institutional support and incentive.

SOME ESSENTIAL STEPS

In view of all this it seems to me that there are three essential steps that must be taken. First, we must acknowledge the great importance of teacher in-service education and assign it high priority in the administration of schooling. Second, having acknowledged need and priority, we must design and initiate new organizational procedures with which to pursue teacher improvement. And, third, we must create a new management role—that of a training specialist—to insure that these procedures are carried out efficiently. By elaborating briefly on each of these three steps I can perhaps summarize the reasoning which underlies them.

The notion that teachers must periodically be given an opportunity to update their skills has long been a canon of school administration. By and large, however, the notion has been supported with sporadic gestures rather than with significant activity. The sins of omission and commission, referred to earlier, are testimony to our failure to do what is needed. Moreover, industry's recent decision to enter the field of teacher in-service education—on a profit-making basis—is a further indication of the great void that exists. It suffices to say that although we may have thought the matter important, we have done little to back up our convictions. As things now stand, resultingly, we must become activists or other agencies will fill the void.

Once we determine to respond to the challenge confronting us, and to attack teacher growth with vigor and authenticity, we shall need to create a new kind of organizational machinery. In other words, the existing provisions for in-service education are grossly inadequate. They suffer from three predominant and interrelated weaknesses: (1) time is not available on a regular and systematic basis for teacher retraining; (2) insufficient money is spent on retraining; and (3) an efficient method of retraining has not yet been devised. The challenge, therefore, is to cope with each of these weaknesses in the best way we can. The teacher's workday, for example, must somehow be rearranged so that on-the-job professional improvement actually takes place. We must also take a hard look at the various ways in which we now spend money on the professional development of the teacher and find out if it would be possible to spend the money with greater intelligence and benefit. Then, once we have overcome the problems of time and money, we must utilize what is known about human retraining—within the context of the special conditions imposed by the role of teacher—and attempt to design the best in-service education system possible.

Finally, with respect to the third of the three steps that seem to me to be essential, we must begin to make use of a new role. My argument here stems from a belief that retraining is sufficiently important to warrant its own kind of leadership agent. Despite the school principal's profound influence on teachers' attitudes and work climate, he cannot, for a variety of reasons, and particularly because of the present structure of American education, devote adequate attention to staff development. Unless there would be drastic change in the structure and organization of the American school, the principal cannot fulfill the training agent role I have in mind.

A precise set of specifications regarding this new training specialist's function does not now exist. These specifications, I believe, can only come with trial and error. A few of the characteristics he needs, however, are already obvious. To begin with, he must know learning and teaching. Beyond this, he must be an expert diagnostician, able to assist teachers to assess their strengths and weaknesses. As a specialist in performance assessment, he must have the capacity to assist teachers to find the kind of teaching responsibilities for which they are best suited. For example, in a situation in which a teacher achieves poor results, the specialist would be able either to assist the teacher to overcome his pedagogical deficiencies or to alter the teacher's assignments so that his talents were used more appropriately.

The training specialist would be a bit of a heretic, at least to the extent that he would actively seek ways to unfetter in-service training from the traditions of the past. He would know, moreover, the expectations of students and parents and the pulse of the community in which he worked. And, above all, he would have the leadership to inspire those with whom he worked to teach somewhere near their optimal capacity.

Consider, for example, the fact that the distinguishing characteristic of a great baseball manager is not simply his knowledge of the game but his ability to draw forth the best the players have to give to the game. Similarly, the great ballet master, the effective corporation executive, and the foremost symphony conductor all have the capacity to evoke high achievement in others. This aspect of leadership has never been actively developed in the field of education.

Such a training specialist would have access to all the resources essential to effective retraining and would have a position of line authority. His chief function would be to insure an optimum "fit" between person and task, and to instill a sense of high aspiration and adequacy. I recognize that I am, in these remarks, indeed opting for a rare sort of bird. I am convinced, however, that there is a need for such specialists; that individuals with the necessary talent are available; that money for their support can be found within existing school budgets; and that they would generate dramatic improvements in the quality of teaching that goes on in the nation's schools.

As this volume suggests, in-service programs are a vital component of any plan for introducing and implementing innovative curricula. If such programs have had limited success in reaching their goals, the reason may lie in the narrowness of their vision. As was pointed out earlier, a piecemeal approach is bound to be insufficient. Provisions for teachers' professional growth must be regularized into ongoing programs. While one aim of these programs may well be familiarizing the teacher with new materials and with methods and techniques for handling them, other endeavors must deal with basic pedagogy. Certification does not automatically confer either total or lasting competence; the teacher must continue to develop throughout his professional life. A preoccupation with innovation leaves unanswered the more seminal questions about how something is taught so that learning takes place. It is the consideration of these questions that can provide a school staff with a core of common concern that might serve as a base for a good in-service program.

With respect to "things done which should better have been left undone," one of the most serious flaws in the present system of training can be seen in the fact that we have taken in-service training from the setting and environment in which it is most likely to flourish—from the school. It is a curious example of the perversity which characterizes much of education that, possessed of the finest laboratory available for the development of a good method of teacher retraining, we substitute alternate, and far less suitable, settings. Where better to pursue the skills, knowledges, and attitudes that enhance instruction than in the natural habitat of teaching: the schools. It is in this climate that the teacher must operate; it is in this milieu, with all of its rituals and politics, that he feels most natural in the role of teacher. The place where he must work is the logical one for nurturing his professional development.

All too often, retraining takes teachers away from their schools. At the extreme, through a return to college or university for another round of course work complete with lectures (frequently on the shortcomings of the lecture method), tests, papers, and so forth, a total role reversal is accomplished. One learns to teach, after all, by teaching. Although a bit of this course work may be good for the soul, it probably does not bear in any direct way on what the teacher worries about or does. When all is said and done, it is practice—ordered and directed by sound criticism—that makes the difference. Lack of criticism makes it easy to practice one's errors. Thus the habit of analytical critique, by the teacher himself, by his peers, and even by his students, must be firmly established.

Finally, we have done what people in a technological age have always done. Frustrated by the magnitude of problems that deal with human wants and needs, we have turned to technical questions, engineering questions, that lend themselves to rational solutions: hence our preoccupation with materials over people. Much of our activity is given to developing expertise and technical finesse in our teachers. We roam about in the cognitive domain not because we think it is the more important, although some obviously do hold that view, but because the terrain is much more uncertain in the affective domain.

Yet we know that more than knowledge about subject and method, the teacher needs knowledge about the children he teaches. Methods will change, schools will vary, as will society's expectations. The constant factor will be people (teachers) dealing with people (children). Until our programs of in-service education include an emphasis on humanistic skills, they will remain incomplete. There are already some beginnings. Encounter groups, sensitivity sessions, and interaction analyses all seek to get at the dynamics of interpersonal relationships. The first efforts are spotty and incomplete, and they sometimes become lost in their psychic turbulence—but they do indicate that the interpersonal relationships between pupil and teacher need work.

We erect buildings, train teachers, and create schools toward the end of helping children to learn. If they do not, the empire we have built is counterfeit. It would be tempting to blame teachers for all of our educational shortcomings, but that is not the way it is. Change most often is spawned by those with power, and therefore it is those with power who must overcome the inadequacies that exist.

We need to help teachers develop a wide repertory of skills and competencies. But we must recognize that the key to the kind of teaching we seek lies as much in teachers' attitudes and commitments as in their technical finesse. Those attitudes and commitments are the result of lifelong experiences. They were learned in the classrooms where today's teachers were once children. They were learned in colleges and graduate schools presided over by other teachers. They are daily learned in each teacher's encounters with administrator, colleague, child. And these lessons will be deepened by the manner and matter of the policies we embrace.

The burden upon us is heavy to provide meaningful programs that demonstrate, in their content, in their organization, and in their administration, an awareness and a sensitivity to the needs of the teachers as they facilitate the learning of children. We must learn what to do and what not to do; until there is health in this part of the educational system, we cannot move ahead with the critical and primary goal—helping the young to learn.

■ CLUES TO ACTION

Meade makes it clear that our efforts to perpetuate the continuing education of teachers are hampered by our limited knowledge of teaching itself. Until we have a better understanding of the precise relationship between teaching and learning, so that we can establish direct connections between one and the other, our efforts to improve the quality of teaching will have little effectiveness. Since he regards teaching as a helping act, as activity that should help children to learn, Meade is troubled by our failure to analyze teaching, to distinguish among its many discrete elements, and to construct viable theories of the various processes involved.

Meade concurs with several of the previous writers with respect to the desirability of teacher specialization, and also with respect to the required continuity between pre-service and in-service learning. He suggests, moreover, that the importance of in-service education stems in part from the fact that no pre-service program can produce a thoroughly competent practitioner. In this connection, he believes that not only do we need a larger number of adept college training supervisors, but also these supervisors must play a dominant role in the education that continues after the teacher enters service.

Departing to an extent from several of the views set forth earlier, Meade wants the school system to take a harder line in regard to setting minimally acceptable standards of performance. Although sensitive to the teacher's need for involvement, and mindful of the importance of teacher-determined relevancy, he believes that the school system itself must identify the kind and quality of teaching it wants. In a sense, then, he seems to imply that the system should identify professional growth goals and teachers should be allowed personal prerogatives with respect to the ways in which these goals are achieved. The approach has considerable appeal in that it provides for reasonable consistency in teaching approach and performance standards, and at the same time it allows the individual teacher a modicum of autonomy.

Aware of the restrictions placed upon our present administrators, Meade calls for a new kind of training specialist and for a more comprehensive organization for teacher continuing education: "First, we must acknowledge the great importance of teacher in-service education and assign it high priority in the administration of schooling. Second, having acknowledged need and priority, we must design and initiate new organizational procedures with which to pursue teacher improvement. And, third, we must create a new management role—that of a training specialist—to insure that these procedures are carried out efficiently." Meade's formula, then, requires not only a greater investment of time and money, but also the development of methods for finding and training people for a new kind of leadership role. Such individuals exist, Meade feels; if given money and administrative support, they could very possibly bring about dramatic improvement.

Finally, Meade reinforces the ideas of Thelen and Jackson regarding our need for humane teaching. Technical skills, he says, are important, but no more so than the skills of interacting effectively with children. The impact of a technically skilled teacher is easily weakened by an irresponsible or defective attitude, and by shallow commitment. If we neglect to keep this in mind, we may allow our interest in method and material to overshadow our interest in people.

■ OPERATIONAL IMPLICATIONS

1. The improvement of teaching must go hand-in-hand with the establishment of standards of performance. **Professional growth programs must equip teachers to accurately assess the quality of their performance.**

2. The training of a teacher begins in the training institution and concludes in the public school. **The training supervisors who work with prospective teachers in the training institutions should continue the training relationship after the teacher enters service.**

3. The management of programs of professional growth is a highly specialized aspect of personnel administration. **We would be advised to create and legitimize a new kind of management role—that of a training specialist concerned exclusively with the improvement of teaching.**

4. It is unlikely that any teacher will ever reach his ultimate performance potential. **Continuing education, on a systematic basis, must become a routine aspect of professional life.**

louis fischer

CHAPTER TEN

IN-SERVICE EDUCATION:
An immodest proposal

Allen labelled his suggestions a "modest proposal," although perhaps they are not. In the same way the comprehensive look I have suggested is immodest in one sense, yet quite simple in another. To put it bluntly, and in the simplest of terms, it is nonsense to discuss in-service education independently of pre-service preparation. The very idea of in-service education of teachers presupposes some common foundation, some minimal *professional* preparation that all teachers must have. A hard look at the facts will quickly destroy such a presupposition.

A credential is a legal instrument used to license people in order that we have an "adult in each classroom." It is a delusion to conclude that a credential is an indicium of pre-service teacher preparation. With the host of credentials, emergency certificates, partial fulfillment credentials, and other euphemisms used to lower standards while appearing to keep them, legislatures, boards, and state departments of education have effectively erased any professional common denominators from teacher education. In the state of California, for example, a candidate for an elementary credential may teach for seven years without completing his requirements for a credential. Is he in his "pre-service" period during these years? A more extreme example comes to us from the same state, where a new credential was authorized recently for the teaching of Afro-American studies. Since a candidate is allowed to teach after completing sixty semester units or the equivalent of two years of collegiate studies, and since he needs to continue his studies at the rate of only six semester units per year, he may take up to fifteen years to attain his full credential. Is he in his "pre-service" period during these years?

The above concerns cannot be dismissed lightly. Large numbers of practitioners enter the vocation of teaching without the screening or approval of any accredited college or university. In fact in some states, such as California, a substantial majority enter by direct application, avoiding the need to meet institutional standards. All this, of course, undercuts even minimal common denominators in the professional content of "pre-service" education, rendering the term meaningless. Since pre- and in-service education are necessarily complementary concepts, both have lost their meanings.

The concepts "pre-service" and "in-service" teacher education would make sense if, and only if, there were an agreed-upon, explicit level of preparation before one were allowed to function as a teacher. Such preparation must be necessary and sufficient in law and in practice for one to enter the occupation and insure to the public a certain level of minimal competence in the various professional roles a teacher must perform. Whatever might follow to upgrade a teacher *in his professional roles* would be in-service education.

Until we have some professionally agreed-upon and specified level of preparation, and thus control over entry into teaching, it may well be of benefit to eliminate the pre- and in-service distinction and simply talk about the education of teachers. We may even borrow some titles or slogans used by our professionally more experienced brethren in medicine and law, who speak of "lifelong learning" or the "continuous education of the Bar." In order to explicate the foregoing, I will attempt to outline a set of concepts that, in my opinion, should guide us in the education of teachers.

1. Should a teacher not have a first-rate general or liberal education? Who can rationally urge that the basic education of teachers should be of lower quality than that of lawyers, business executives, physicians, or priests? Current patterns of pre-professional preparation must undergo careful but rigorous scrutiny. While much revision is needed in such programs, teachers as human beings, as general citizens, should be at least as well educated as those who enter our currently high status occupations. Such preparation, although necessary, has nothing to do with the professional education of teachers any more than it can be considered in the professional education of physicians or lawyers.

2. Should a teacher have a sound knowledge of the sequence of human development from birth to maturity? Since he teaches children and youth; since he interprets school decisions to the public; and since he helps create or select curricular materials for schools and school systems, a fair level of understanding of child and adolescent development seems necessary.

3. Should a teacher have a working understanding of how people learn, of competing psychological theories and the evidence offered by them in support of their claims? The answer again seems to be an almost self-evident yes.

4. Should a teacher be sufficiently knowledgeable about the principles and methods of educational research to be at least an intelligent *consumer* of research findings? While it is clearly unreasonable to expect most teachers to carry on research in their already overburdened positions, it does not appear unreasonable to expect professional practitioners to be able to read intelligently publications directly relevant to their work.

5. Should a teacher have a sound understanding of the culture that supports his activities and that, with some selectivity, he is charged to perpetuate? The answer again must be in the affirmative, particularly in a diverse, conflict-ridden, highly pluralistic culture such as that of an urban, postindustrial U.S.A. In the absence of such understandings on the part of the majority of our teachers, it is not surprising that they are ineffective pawns in the midst of giant cultural upheavals and power struggles. A thorough comprehension of our culture conflicts would be required for teachers to understand such recent developments as the Black and Brown Revolutions, student militancy, the challenge of the communications media–industrial combines, the organizational struggles among teachers, state aid to church-related schools, the war on poverty, and a host of others, each having significant bearings on public education.

6. Should a teacher understand the differences between relying on authority, tradition, intuition, common sense, or revelation, and relying on tested experience for knowledge, truth, or values? If he is to avoid an aimless, eclectic borrowing of any passing idea in an expedient manner, he must have examined alternative conceptual schemes and educational philosophies and developed an internally consistent guide to policy and practice.

7. Should the teacher be acquainted with the stream of educational history, the past efforts, successes, and failures in the long, long struggle toward high quality, humane, universal schooling? Since those who don't know the mistakes of the past are more likely to repeat them, and since an appreciation of and pride in a profession are less likely without a sound understanding of its history, strong arguments can be made for including such study in the education of teachers. Clever demagogues, in and out of education, are less likely to mislead the public and the teachers if many teachers stand well informed, to refute misrepresentations, falsehoods, and empty slogans.

8. Should a teacher have an understanding of the total range of the curriculum with particular knowledge of his own area or age level of specialization? Should he understand the principles and processes of curricular change? Would any but a most limited notion of professionalism support a negative answer here?

9. Should a teacher have sound knowledge of the means, methods, and materials with which to teach his children? Should he also know the important research related to such methodology? One criterion of professionalism is having a body of "funded knowledge," which includes tested methods of solving professional problems.

10. Should the preparation of teachers include an opportunity to work with students in a variety of learning situations under the guidance of experienced professionals? This is about the only question with a universal Yes for an answer.

11. Should a teacher learn to work in an effective, cooperative fashion with peers, authority figures, and the lay public as well as with children? Since his success in the field requires such abilities, a good case can be made for its inclusion in professional preparation.

12. Should a teacher be acquainted with the range of journals, newsletters, official publications, and organizations that offer assistance relevant to his work? How can one be a functioning professional without such awareness?

13. Should a teacher have knowledge of ways and means of gaining further knowledge about subject areas, about children and youth, and about his community? In the long run, these skills of inquiry might have more professional pay-off value than any other single item noted. Just as "learning to learn" is recognized as an overarching objective for all our students, is it now per force a key ingredient of professional preparation?

14. Should a teacher have a clear understanding of the ideals of our democracy? Should he not have a *functional* commitment

to them? Should he not have a well-formulated, clearly understood conception of the relevance of the ideals of democracy
to his various roles as a teacher? Without such preparation
will we ever create an intelligent commitment to the ideals of
democracy in the bulk of our population?

The foregoing fourteen items are not presented in a particular sequence. Their chronology does not imply any rank order of
importance or power. I would consider them all necessary to a
conception of a fully functioning professional teacher. At the
same time, it is not suggested here that no one enter a classroom
without meeting each ideal.

To be brutally frank, the professional preparation of
teachers is seriously inadequate. The most highly regarded programs have serious gaps and inadequacies. The post-Sputnik
reappraisal led to widespread buttressing of the general or liberal
education of teachers[1] and to subject matter specialization but, if
anything, weakened professional preparation.

With the overwhelming lay control of teacher education, all
visible current and proposed efforts on the horizon are but efforts
to patch up leaking and crumbling dams. We need new architects
to design and build new dams! Where is the bold vision needed to
conceive a defensible teacher education program? Ideals? Of
course we must have them. The ideals of today will be the
realities of tomorrow. Years ago the visionaries proposed that in
some far-off utopia of the future, even elementary school teachers
would have four years of college education. This ideal we now
take for granted as a minimal requirement. But today we lack
bold and currently relevant ideals. Why not a visionary plan that
would encompass most of the professional maturity attempted in
the previously stated fourteen points?

Whether we label such a preparation pre- or in-service is

---

[1] As noted before, this is not to imply approval of current patterns of so-called
general and liberal education. Sixty semester units do not necessarily provide
a coherent system of ideas, attitudes, and skills, and there is little evidence to
support the implied assumption that "liberal" education liberalizes or liberates
its recipients.

irrelevant. It is a trivial label, yet damaging. It is damaging because the laymen who control entry into teaching have changed and will continue to change minimal standards as supply and demand dictate. They will set minimal standards, which quickly become norms. The norms then become normative. In other words: "If you can become a teacher with such-and-such a minimal preparation, that's how you should become a teacher." By and large, in-service education then becomes a search for how-to-do-it recipes and credit accumulation for salary hurdle purposes. Sound in-service education must build on sound pre-service preparation and is continuous with it!

In the absence of a common, agreed-upon program of teacher education, any effort at in-service education that has surface validity will be useful for some teachers and useless for others. Large-scale, systematic, efficient use of time, energy, and money in such a case is not possible. Programs will continue on a hit and miss basis.

Given an adequate preparatory program, in-service education, more properly referred to as continuing education for teachers, should become completely voluntary and a matter for self-selection. Before this can become a reality, however, certain complicated problems must be faced, having to do with authoritative knowledge in education.

THE NEED FOR AUTHORITY IN EDUCATION

The optimal use of in-service education, whether to carry out the clinical supervision model of Fischler, the performance criteria model of Allen, or any other systematic model, presupposes agreement upon what constitutes reliable knowledge concerning teaching. I submit that such knowledge is nonexistent and the methods whereby it might be created are not yet agreed upon.

Let me briefly develop this point. It is quite clear that conflicting, vague, and ambiguous notions exist concerning the proper place of authority in a democratic social order. It is also clear that, in principle, we can distinguish authoritarian from authoritative behavior. In a democratic social order, in and out of education, authoritarian behavior is illegitimate, whereas authoritative decision making is legitimate and necessary. Realizing the risk of oversimplification, the following capsule distinction might be useful:

Authoritative behavior refers to one based upon a high degree of competence, both substantive and methodological, in an area of knowledge relevant to a task at hand. Authoritative statements are openly examinable and are open to public criticism and revision in light of new evidence. Their purpose is to advance inquiry and thus lead to the further development of the individuals relying upon such statements.

By contrast *authoritarian* refers to persons or manners of behavior that are not publicly examinable and openly revised in light of evidence. The authoritarian position is usually held by virture of force, tradition, birth, or hidden manipulation. It is not crucial that such a person have the knowledge or skill appropriate to the task; his main concern is power, not knowledge or human growth. Authoritarian statements tend to end inquiry, not further it.

If education or teaching is ever to earn the high designation of "profession," it must develop and accept one or more authoritative methods of producing and testing its knowledge claims. When a profession, any profession, refers to its "funded knowledge," its "body of reliable knowledge," or "professional knowledge," the necessary implication is that there exists an open, publicly examinable, and criticizable method for generating and testing ideas, procedures, and generalizations unique to its set of professional problems. Medicine has its main knowledge claims tested in the crucible of observable experience through the methods of the empirical sciences; law produces its body of funded knowledge through the authoritative system of the courts; but where are the accepted, open, publicly testable methods to provide reliable knowledge in education? Don't we still rely from time to time on untested common sense, intuition, tradition, supposedly self-evident principles, authority, and, on occasion, on the results of scientific experimentation? Furthermore, what is to prevent a tenured teacher from rejecting the most carefully tested, research-based conclusion related to his work?

Is it pessimistic to conclude that in the absence of authoritative methods to produce and use reliable knowledge neither pre- nor in-service teacher education will advance beyond the current levels of sub-professional status? It might be more honest to stop massaging our egos by referring to teachers as professionals. Perhaps an honest admission is in order to the effect that current patterns of preparation, even with a full credential, simply produce an emergency level beginner in teaching. Many who thus enter the field become skilled workers or dedicated civil servants. Some, no one knows how many, continue growing toward professional maturity, while an indefinite number "angle through the system" quietly, damaging children while collecting their monthly pay. Unless we develop and agree upon some authoritative knowledge in education, we cannot eliminate this last group, nor help the first group grow into that ill-defined category of the "professional."

As a working ideal for professional status in our field, I would again refer to the earlier fourteen points. Although its full realization could not be expected at the point of entry into teaching, it is offered as a defensible ideal toward which all practitioners should be helped to develop. Clearly, not all who enter the field of teaching will achieve equal mastery in each of the fourteen areas specified. But why should an identical profile be expected or even desirable? We can expect and encourage differential development and still insist upon some common minimums. Although the analogy may be belabored, we could learn from law or medicine in this respect.

Given such minimum, yet higher than what are currently accepted as adequate, pre-service programs, in-service education should develop primarily on a self-selective basis. Such development would be the case particularly when we came closer and closer to accepting what I called authoritative methods of testing educational knowledge.

If I as a lawyer do not voluntarily keep abreast of current

knowledge, an authoritative method supported by the legal profession will force me to do so. If I as a physician do not voluntarily keep abreast of current knowledge, an authoritative method supported by the medical profession will force me to do so. Of course there are obsolete practitioners in each of these fields. However, in *principle* they can be held up to the standards of currently approved, tested knowledge. In *principle* this is not the case in education. This difference, more than the marketplace economics, makes it possible for law and medicine to rely on self-selection and self-discipline for in-service education at a time when so many teachers must be cajoled, bribed, or forced to continue their professional growth.

This immodest proposal accepts a "growth perspective" of teacher education. The pre- and in-service designations serve merely a legal purpose to identify a stage in professional development where agreed-upon minimal competence has been attained. This level of competence would have to be certified by the occupational group and enforced by the legal machinery of the state. Continued professional growth would be expected as a matter of course, with a variety of arrangements available to encourage such growing.

Several writers in this volume, in propounding principles that call for multiple approaches to in-service education, have stressed the need for flexibility and feedback. It is almost self-evident that schools and school systems ought not be rigid and inflexible in the continuing education of their teachers. Although this is a time-honored principle, it appears that schools throughout the nation have been violating it.

Currently, under the influence of system-analytic models, our authors call for flexible approaches with feedback built in to provide for continual self-correction. Tyler predicts, "The training program will build in feedback as teachers work on problems, so that a basis for correction and revision is available." Allen suggests "self-modifying task descriptions" and calls for "a kind of research that will feed back into the program and hence make it self-adjusting to a large extent." Bush, Fischler, Thelen, and others all seem to agree that what is learned from an in-service education activity, either through action-research, through more basic research, or for that matter through any other means, should be used to alter the system itself. This general model is currently referred to as feedback, while earlier analysts spoke of the theory-action-theory-action . . . continuum. A key function of theory is to guide practice, just as one outcome of practice (or application) is the testing and modification of theory.

It should be noted that the principle of feedback, like the theory-application continuum, is eminently defensible. One can go overboard, however, in placing too much faith in the so-called self-regulating method of science. Is any method really self-correcting? Or is the method merely open ended and inviting of criticism for the purposes of continual improvement? The potential of feedback in in-service education is just as dependent on alert, inquiring, mature, objective educators as the supposedly self-correcting methods of the sciences are dependent on similar qualities in the scientists. I believe that both historical and present developments in the sciences would support this conclusion.

There is a danger that educators will substitute new mysticism for old. The danger is that we will shift from what Allen calls the "mysticism currently tied to promotion via time spent and units earned" to a new mysticism based on the *language* of scientism and system analysis. In the absence of specific example, descriptions, field explorations, and experimentation, we are merely offered inspiring and bold statements about objectivity, explicitly differentiated performance criteria, self-modifying task descriptions that begin to sound very much like verbal magic: a new mysticism. This is not a blanket indictment of the rationale of guided change through the systematic utilization of feedback. It is an effort to warn against the magic of words and to call for careful, tedious field testing of ideas in the necessary professional task of grounding our theories in practice and guiding our practices with theories.

Unique and unprecedented opportunities lie before us to realize these ideals of voluntary, self-selective training. Without a doubt, the vast majority of our population values formal schooling and knows that the quality of teachers and teaching is crucial. Without a doubt, the civil rights revolution, the Black and Brown Revolutions, the urban crises, and student militancy, to name but a few of our major current problems, are closely tied to the quality of public education. There is high probability that substantial amounts of money can be diverted in the very near future from war efforts to educational efforts. Finally, a factor that has been broadly overlooked in long-range planning, a significant decline in the national birth rate, will make it possible for us to shift our attention from quantity to quality. Within the near future, school enrollments will decline. The almost twenty-year post–World War II tidal wave of students that inundated our schools will sharply decline, making possible flexible, creative use of teaching personnel. Simultaneously, collegiate enrollments will be at an all time peak. If supply and demand principles operate, we should be able to be more selective than ever before in screening teaching applicants and enforcing professionally defensible standards for entrance into teaching. With such prospects in sight, the fourteen principles offered as realistic ideals could indeed be called modest. When we consider the progress made by more mature professions in the pursuit of their ideals, educators should remember the injunction by a former president of Brandeis University to the effect that anyone who does not have ideals is not a realist.

SOME INTERIM PROPOSALS

To state it once again for the sake of clarity and emphasis, drastic revision of our preconceptions related to in-service education is long overdue. The terms "pre-service" and "in-service" teacher education must be relegated to the archives of history as no longer useful. We must specify standards of *entry* into teaching that are intellectually, morally, and professionally justifiable. Furthermore, we must specify a set of characteristics that will identify a fully functioning, mature member of the teaching profession. Such an effort was indicated in the set of fourteen points briefly stated above. Thus, our concern must be on the continual education of teachers from neophyte status through maturity. The ultimate propellant along the way will be professional self-respect, the desire to know, and the esteem as well as authoritative standards of professional colleagues. Before we reach these ideals, and perhaps as emergency measures and means to assist the hundreds of thousands of ill-prepared practitioners, a list of interim proposals may be offered. Most of these are not original but have already been used successfully in school districts, suggested in journals, or gleaned from discussions with classroom teachers.

Proposal 1: Schools and school systems should provide alternative and even rival systems of in-service education. They should explore and experiment, purposely maximizing the Hawthorne effect.

Proposal 2: Related to the first proposal, stimulation of in-service education should be centralized but the means and methods decentralized. Thus we are more likely to encourage creative variation, and through the cooperation of rival subsystems we all benefit. It is useful to note here that rivalry, not competition, is emphasized throughout. Rivals, as in sport activities, can and do help each other, whereas the objective of a competitor is to eliminate his opponent. A competitor benefits from the poor showing of his opponent, whereas rivals strive in a cooperative manner for each to attain ever higher levels of excellence.

Proposal 3: Significant models or examples of teacher growth should be publicized. This will influence others to engage in the race against obsolescence, will reinforce the efforts through professional recognition, and may lead to the more careful testing of the idea in practice.

Proposal 4: Time for in-service growth should be provided The most widely heard complaint among practicing teachers is aimed at the after-school, evening, Saturday morning, or similarly sandwiched-in efforts at in-service education. Carefully planned programs must be built around the summer months, sabbaticals, and other released-time arrangements. With the increasing flexibility in the use of teachers and schedules, it is quite feasible to make available blocks of time to individuals or groups of teachers to be used for professional growth. Sabbaticals can vary in length; individuals can be released from the classroom one day a week for X number of weeks; the school year can be scheduled on the basis of six weeks of instruction followed by a week for professional growth, and so on. We can all break out of the rigid scheduling practices of the past as some schools already have done.

Proposal 5: Schools should overhire by ten per cent and at any one time have ten per cent of the faculty pursue agreed-upon professional growth activities. Means and results should feed back into the total group to stimulate and encourage others, to maximize the results of successful experiences and to help others avoid blind alleys.

Proposal 6: While the desirability of scientific research is acknowledged, schooling must proceed in the absence of definitive findings. Rely, without apology, on professional judgment, on the carefully considered shared opinions of teachers and administrators. Encourage careful investigation of their recommendations, but professional opinion is to be respected while we await the results of controlled experiments. Every profession uses its "expert opinions" while attempting to ground its knowledge on publicly testable methodology.

Proposal 7: Schools should encourage variety in workshops and study groups: formal course work and independent study related to both substantive and methodological phases of the several roles of a teacher. At the same time, they should reduce or eliminate the connection between in-service activities and the pay check. Schools should introduce other means of progression up the salary ladder, preferably on the basis of performance criteria. Such criteria should be applied by fellow teachers trained to observe, analyze, and evaluate professional behavior.

Proposal 8: The potential of team teaching for professional growth is too often ignored. If properly used, this can be an instrument of amazing versatility, not the least aspect of which is the continual opportunity for team members to learn from each other. It can also be a powerful way of introducing the minimally prepared neophyte into the complexities of teaching and helping him grow toward professional maturity.

Proposal 9: Instead of colleges and other outside agencies offering courses or suggesting workshops and institutes, increasingly the responsibility for professional growth should be shifted to the individual practitioners. They must be involved in assessing their own strengths and shortcomings, as well as in charting their directions of growth. In an occupation like teaching, where groups of people of necessity work together toward common goals, it would be desirable to create some internal machinery within a school system that would help diagnose and assess the functioning of individual or team practitioners in order to suggest directions for continued development. The machinery for this assessment should be separate and distinct from decisions concerning retention or tenure.

Proposal 10: To take the foregoing point one step further, on occasion, outside assessment teams should be brought into the school district. These teams, composed of knowledgeable professionals, act as objective inquirers to provide an independent audit of the needs of the system. Since they would be similar to our accrediting teams, a sympathetic but critical analysis would be made of the in-service needs of the district without the socio-psychological difficulties likely to be encountered by internal assessment teams, principals, and central office personnel.

CONCLUDING REMARKS

The foregoing ten proposals are by no means exhaustive, and most of them are not original. In the current state of anarchy (or is it merely pluralism?) the proposals are offered as useful, since no single pattern could legitimately be applied as relevant to the variety of problems extant. It should also be clear that these proposals and the efforts based on them should not mislead us into thinking that they can substitute for the more challenging long-range task—the adequate professional education of teachers.

■ *CLUES TO ACTION*

Fischer contends, in plain terms, that the professional education of teachers is badly in need of repair. Describing some of the inadequacies in a series of fourteen points, he argues, like the previous writers, that it is folly to attempt to separate pre-service from in-service development. Above all, however, he makes it clear that anything we attempt in the way of improving matters will be hampered by the absence of "authority" in education.

He distinguishes between authoritarian and authoritative behavior, suggesting that the former stems from political power whereas the latter stems from demonstrated competence. Fischer maintains that little good will come from our programs of teacher continuing education until we have authoritative methods of teaching upon which we can rely. Untested common sense may, upon close examination, prove to be nonsense. Thus our fundamental task is to free ourselves from the dictates of our intuition and our traditions and, instead, to base our programs on proved methods and principles. Without authoritative standards, as Fischer indicates, it will continue to be relatively easy for teachers—advertently or inadvertently—"to angle through the system, quietly damaging children."

The development and popularization of authoritative methods, Fischer believes, will eventually serve to professionalize teaching. Acceptability of established methods, in other words, will establish minimal levels of performance. Once these minimal levels are widely supported by the profession, teachers will be compelled either to meet them or to suffer various kinds of censures. "The ultimate propellant," he says, "will be professional self-respect, the desire to know, and the esteem as well as the authoritative standards of professional colleagues."

Pointing out that any correspondence between the possession of a teaching license and professional competence is purely happenstance, Fischer foresees—like Allen—the necessity for routine assessment. In this connection other forces are becoming evident that will make it less and less easy for an inadequate teacher to survive on mediocre teaching. For example, the increasing utilization of technological apparatus will, if nothing else, illuminate a student's learning disabilities and achievement deficit much more clearly. Evidence of this sort will, of course, constitute a strong indictment of teaching ineffectuality. Too, such performance evidence will also be a powerful stimulus to teacher commitment; it is less easy, in short, to be complacent when one's inadequacies are easily ascertained.

The significance of teacher continuing education is explicated most dramatically in Fischer's suggestion that schools overstaff their teaching faculties by ten per cent, thus permitting teachers to engage in professional growth activities during a substantial portion of their work time. In keeping with Meade and Tyler, he sees considerable potential in the opportunity for team learning. He shares also Meade's conviction that while the system should stimulate and insure that professional growth is a routine occurrence, the means of this growth should be a matter of individual prerogative. As with the lawyer and the doctor, Fischer construes professionalism to include a strong personal interest in extending one's ability.

■ OPERATIONAL IMPLICATIONS

1. Teaching competence embodies a number of specific capacities. **Professional growth activities should go beyond the mindless mastery of a teaching technique.**

2. Professional standards stem from a body of reliable, authoritative knowledge. **The perennial training of the teacher in service should relate directly to such authoritative standards.**

3. Time is an essential requirement in acquiring new understanding and skills. **Schools should have a teaching staff of sufficient size to permit individuals to devote some of their time to professional improvement.**

4. Practicing teachers, as a group, constitute powerful research teams for new ideas and practices. **Teachers could well be encouraged to engage in the systematic field testing of new ideas in education, with the support and guidance of training specialists. Such field work could become a significant part of continuing education.**

louis j. rubin

CHAPTER ELEVEN

TEACHER GROWTH IN PERSPECTIVE

I should acknowledge, at the outset, that I concur with most of the arguments presented by my colleagues: In-service education has indeed been virtually a lost cause. Taken *in toto*, the conceptions set forth in the previous chapters lead to three fundamental conclusions: teacher professional growth has not been taken seriously, it lacks a systematic methodology, and it has been managed with astonishing clumsiness. It is not surprising, therefore, that teachers have grown accustomed to its impotence, and that administrators have come to regard it as a routine exercise in futility.

I would like first to comment briefly upon some of the propositions that already have been advanced, mainly to amplify their implications with some of my own research findings, and then to consider several other aspects of teacher growth.

Bush and Allen and Meade and Fischer, it seems to me,

touch upon a point of great significance when they express concern over the lack of continuity between pre-service and in-service learning. Whether one prefers to view teaching as an art or as a science, there is an inescapable need to acquire an integrated set of skills and understandings. Many of these can be learned only after the teacher has left the training institution and is ensconced, foursquare, in the realities of the school scene. The experiments we conducted at the Center for Coordinated Education suggest moreover that time is an indispensable element in the development of craftsmanship. Skillful teaching, in other words, rarely is developed without several years of practice, howsoever good the preliminary training. As Fischer implies, it is therefore logical to conceive of professional growth as an enterprise that may begin in the training institutions but must extend well into the early years of professional service. True competence is nurtured by meaningful experience. We must, therefore, overcome the notion that training is synonymous with ability.

Appropriately, Bush draws attention to the lack of rigor that has accompanied most in-service education endeavors. More often than not, the programs are characterized by a conspicuous lack of precision: that is, a learning objective is not coupled with an efficient means to its attainment. An attempt to improve science teaching, for example, often amounts to no more than a few lectures on inductive learning. Realistically, however, better science teaching will not come about until a teacher has mastered techniques that are superior to those he is using. Such mastery, obviously, almost never is a by-product of listening to a lecture or viewing a demonstration. The development of skill in teaching is no different from the development of skill in cooking, carpentry, or painting. The practitioner must engage in repeated practice, evaluate his progress in some systematic way, and cumulatively increase his adeptness.

Our exploratory programs demonstrated that there is no reason why teachers, day by day, cannot become a bit more proficient. Too often we have succumbed to the mystique that the continuing education of teachers must occur outside the teacher's classroom and away from children who are learning. Much as a surgeon learns, operation by operation, a teacher learns, lesson by lesson. Given a rational system of improvement—one in which the growth objectives are clear and in which there is a suitable fit between means and ends—a teacher in his fifth year of teaching should be infinitely more able than he was in his first year. That this is not always the case is perhaps the severest criticism of our present system.

Tyler's conclusion that we have not made an adequate effort to provide the support essential to the continuing education of teachers is germane in this regard. While, admittedly, it is the teacher who must achieve understanding and acquire skill, we are naive to assume that these are automatic by-products of training. It is, as Meade suggests, necessary for educational leadership to establish an environment that is conducive to growth. Such an environment will necessitate the repair of many of our personnel management practices.

In the present way of things, as a case in point, better performance in the classroom ordinarily does not result in any direct pay-off to the teacher. As a result, teachers frequently do not find it imperative to increase their competence. Most teachers have a genuine desire to teach as well as they can, but their motivation often is dissipated by a variety of organizational adversities. An administrator, for example, may emphasize rigid student control to such an extent that permitting the free play of natural learning is detrimental to a teacher's reputation. Thus, even where the opportunity for professional growth is high, teacher incentive may be low.

It is doubtful, moreover, whether we can get very far without some provision for rewarding superior teaching. Apart from the fact that most humans have a strong interest in recognition, the failure to distinguish—in the average school—teaching that is very good or very bad tends to imply either that we do not know the difference or that we do not care. The nature of the reward, I suspect, is not crucial. Although monetary incentives are often suggested, it may well be that an honorific title like *master teacher*, if it carries sufficient distinction, might do as well.

The expectation of sustained renewal, to cite another instance of faulty organizational management, has never really permeated our professional ethos. Improvement is not the inevitable consequence of experience. The practitioner's failure to mature through seasoning is perhaps more a problem of demand than of lethargy. Like most other workers, teachers tend to function at the prevailing level of expectation. It often is possible to obtain a finer performance simply by raising the going rate. Interestingly enough, higher expectancies, in most cases, do not seem to either threaten or fatigue teachers. Although greater amounts of energy and commitment are called into play, the additional levy usually is offset by the intrinsic satisfaction that comes from contributing significantly to the progress of one's students. It is this reservoir of personal philanthropy—the human benevolence that makes education a helping profession—that we must begin to draw upon more heavily.

In most instances we act, to illustrate still another weakness in our treatment of teachers, as if the pleasure of labor were a natural consequence of employment. As Thelen so aptly points out, the missionary spirit no longer is a reliable impetus to inspired toil. The fact that vast numbers of teachers perform below their potential is familiar testimony to this condition. One of our more conspicuous failures, therefore, has been our seeming unwillingness to explore various ways in which the job satisfaction of teachers can be increased. The joys of productive work come in many shapes and forms, and we perhaps have unwittingly wasted the pleasures of craftsmanship through our method of organizing the relationship between children, teachers, and administrators.

All of these, it seems to me, are secondary implications of Tyler's primary concern about inadequate institutional support. Although other examples could be cited, perhaps it is sufficient to observe that professional improvement cannot flourish in an environment of impoverished morale.

In recent decades, social scientists have learned much about the internal workings of organizational life. These findings for the most part have been ignored in our primitive approach to structuring the school. An ongoing confrontation between two opposing camps serves as a useful illustration. There are those, for example, who are convinced that the salvation of schooling lies in the production of instructional materials that overcome any limitations which may abide in the individual teacher. And there are those who are equally convinced that the teacher must captain his own professional soul and be free to manage his own intellectual pursuits. It is likely, however, that sanity lies somewhere between these two extremes. To ignore the importance of clear teaching objectives, sound methods, and responsible evaluation would be irrational. But it would be equally foolish to assume that teachers are pawns who can be manipulated either through the genius of their administrators or through prescribing inalterable behavior. We are driven to search for ordered regularity, as we should be, but the more we become preoccupied with such ordering, the easier it is to forget the irregularities in human emotion and intellect.

Earlier in this volume, Meade argues for a new kind of training specialist. I could not be more fully in accord with his argument. The capacity to facilitate the growth of others is a very special skill, one that can lead to a fresh conception of teacher development. While I also endorse his belief in the need for external guidance, I am a bit more committed, perhaps, to self-directed growth than he is. However, I suspect the difference is more a matter of balance between internal and external intervention than of outright disagreement. Neither guidance from an expert colleague nor exposure to a useful procedure ought to be allowed to diminish the individual's freedom. To allow teachers to learn good methods is sensible: in so doing, however, to deny them the right to look for an even better plan would be senseless. With teacher and child alike, coercion may bring monetary gains, but its end result is destructive to the spirit.

If there is to be significant improvement in education, the nation's teachers as professionals must participate in their own intellectual growth. They must, in short, have an improvement program that allows them to advance their professional artistry.

The program must first acknowledge that the competence and zeal of the teacher are far and away the two most important factors in quality instruction. Teachers differ tremendously in their strengths and weaknesses, in their intellectual backgrounds, and in their interpersonal responses. Yet we tend in our teacher education efforts to treat them as all of a kind. Thus, the various recommendations on individualization that have been made in the preceding chapters seem to me to have great significance.

Perhaps the greatest argument in favor of a new approach to the continuing education of teachers stems from this pressing need to accommodate teacher differences, a need that arises simultaneously on several fronts. Successful teaching, for example, requires a number of distinct skills. Teachers differ markedly in the degree to which they have mastered these skills. Their professional needs, accordingly, are anything but uniform. As things now stand, there is little if any effort to differentiate individual need in professional improvement programs.

The American system of education being what it is, all our schools are not the same. Parents frequently have different expectations for their children, and even when their aspirations are similar, children do not learn in the same way. Thus an intellectual idea may have more relevance for one group of youth than for another; consequently the teaching of eighth grade history may need to vary from situation to situation. We must therefore devise some system through which we can help teachers acquire the skills with which to accomplish a particular teaching goal, in a particular educational setting, with a particular kind of learner. In short, we must make it possible for the teacher to function effectively in the subculture of the school in which he finds himself. Since teachers are as unique as other humans, and since the appropriateness of a teaching technique varies with the task at hand, the continuing education of teachers will need to be dealt with multilaterally rather than unilaterally. These, I believe, are the ramifications of the references by Allen, Bush, Lippitt, and Fox to instructional alternatives. Hence, one of our crucial problems is to invent procedures through which professional growth can be personalized, allowing teachers to cope with their own idiosyncratic needs, to begin at their own level of sophistication, and to progress at their own optimal rate.

The difference between routine teaching and inspired teaching depends to a large degree upon the teacher's own sense of motivation and commitment. The desire to change, if it is to be consequential, must come from within the individual teacher himself. In-service education should not be, as it has sometimes been, merely another theater for puppets. It should set a stage for growth—but in the tradition of the commedia dell'arte, where actors did not memorize, but improvised their lines.

Good teaching depends upon more than a knowledge of technique alone. Allen, for example, refers to a mastery of subject, instructional adeptness, and "personological" skills. Since these labels encompass most of the behavior we ordinarily conceive of as teaching, they probably are as useful as any others. Underlying such general attributes, however, there may be something more fundamental. The way a teacher perceives of himself and his role, his attitude toward education, his belief in the children he teaches, and his basic commitments all influence the quality of his work. Perceptions are often misperceptions. Our attitudes, values, and beliefs can be distorted by defective experiences. Sharpening one's sense of purpose, too, must be a component of continuing education. Real learning causes the learner to alter his behavior. In-service education, then, must offer a rich opportunity to acquire personal insights that lead to new ways of behaving in the classroom. In view of the enormous influence our beliefs have on our actions, the scant attention we have given to teachers' values is little short of remarkable.

I believe this is what Jackson has in mind when he urges that we give teachers more time to think about the consequences of what they are doing, for it is the teacher's values that will determine what he will consider as appropriate learning behavior in his students. Values are the stuff that thought is made of. How the teacher feels about something, how strongly, and in what order of importance are tightly interwoven with his view of the educational process. Our values, in effect, are the filters through which we interpret our experiences and process the facts we encounter. As the basis of conscious or unconscious choice, they direct our thoughts into arbitrary patterns. They label, as Whitehead said, "matters of importance" as opposed to matters of mere occurrence by providing an orientation toward perception and knowledge. Values determine whether a thought will be thought, whether an experience will be perceived, and whether the perception itself will be valid or invalid. It follows, therefore, that the agenda for the renewal of the teacher ought rightly to include a clarification of values and beliefs.

Once thought through and clarified, these values and beliefs assume new attention and respect. The desire to perform at an optimal level rarely is stimulated when one does not believe in the worth of what he does. There can be little doubt that many teachers look upon some of their assigned teaching functions with less than unreserved favor. Some view what they take to be the "establishment's goals" with outright disdain. Under these circumstances, nothing we organize in the way of continuing teacher education will have very much benefit. Until we initiate the kind of education we can convince teachers is significant, the in-service activities we design will have limited return.

PAST, PRESENT, AND FUTURE

Social change always seems chaotic for two reasons: first, societies change unevenly, so that some elements invariably lag behind others, and, second, the need to abandon old convictions and adopt new ones is not conducive to tranquility. We tend, moreover, to adjust slowly and to become comfortable with a change long after its initial impetus has occurred. As a consequence, man's quest for a stable social scene comes to little more than wishful thinking. The rupture between the generations is in part a manifestation of this endless necessity to readjust; the young, having fewer traditions to yield, find adaptation far easier than their elders. Thus, when societies change very rapidly, as presently is the case, grandfathers, sons, and grandsons are impelled by different philosophies, and conflict becomes inevitable.

Those who are charged with the revision of schooling are therefore faced with a hopeless dilemma, since no conception of education is likely to satisfy everyone. Inasmuch as schools traditionally are most responsive to the particular generation in power, they tend, as they change, to compromise between extremes and to deal with current rather than impending crises. This, of course, forces education to remain in a constant state of social senescence. Whether we could anticipate the future with greater shrewdness and persuade those in power to take the long rather than the short view remains unknown because a potent attempt has never been made.

As we organize for the needed reform of teacher in-service education, it may be possible to take advantage of social forecasting and in so doing to concern ourselves not with the transition from past to present, but with the forthcoming transition between present and future. The movement to innovate has now achieved significant momentum. Major overhauls have been made in most areas of the curriculum. Research and development efforts are so prolific that it literally is impossible to keep pace with all that is going on. If we look ahead, if only with fractional astuteness, and foresee the margin between where we are and where we must go, we might now begin to prepare teachers who will be able to function effectively in the schools of 1984, a date but fourteen short years away.

We know, for example, that it will be possible to harness the computer to monitor learning, child by child. We also know from a growing body of research that given the construction of alternate methods and materials, it will be possible to teach whatever curriculum we wish to all youth—debunking the pervasive notion that many children cannot learn. There are new conceptions of public education that respect the critical importance of early childhood education, and exploratory classrooms designed to overcome our historical predilection for separating the affective and cognitive aspects of learning. Whatever the nature of the innovations, however, their success is inextricably linked to the human teacher who puts them to use in the classroom. The importance of perennially updating the practitioner cannot help but increase in the period ahead.

Beyond these matters, there will be a profound reversal in our cultural ethos. The grandfathers of today were weaned on a belief in orderly and gradual social change. Hence they came to expect the school to serve as an agency for cultural transmission, as an institution that would transfer the accumulated cultural heritage from generation to generation. The grandsons of today do indeed march to the beat of a different drummer. Whereas their grandfathers were motivated by a fear of material want, the young of today are inspired by a fear of unfound identity and by the wish to achieve a sense of personal worth. Turner describes the coming metamorphosis as follows:

Another indication of the changes that are taking place can be found in the new way of viewing the concept of guilt. It is instructive to compare the earlier writings of Margaret Mead with the more recent writings of Helen Merrill Lynd. Margaret Mead distinguished guilt, as a highly internalized sense of right and wrong, from shame, that involved a more external sense. In societies dominated by shame one does not feel upset about doing wrong, but only about being discovered or exposed in the act of doing wrong. In societies dominated by guilt one feels bad about the very idea of doing wrong. Whether he is exposed or not. In this view of course, guilt represents a higher dedication to one's ideals and values, and under some circumstances it may be a good thing that people do experience guilt. Helen Lynd, on the other hand, seems to extend the implication of Freud's views more fully, and guilt becomes an unqualified evil thing. It becomes the impediment to individual autonomy and to an individual sense of worth. Guilt is the invasion of the self by arbitrary and external standards. We have the impression that Lynd's usage has been gaining currency at the expense of Margaret Mead's.[1]

One hears of newspaper reporters who refuse to perpetuate the editorial policy of their papers, of bureaucrats who are unwilling to implement decisions with which they disagree, and of bus drivers who alter company-established routes to better meet the needs of their passengers. Everywhere there seems to be a rising expectation that one's work allow for more than a mere acceptance of external dictation. Similarly, teacher militancy is more than a cant phrase. In the time to come, teachers are likely

[1] Ralph H. Turner, "The Theme of Contemporary Social Movements," *British Journal of Sociology* 20 (December 1969): 402.

to be swept along not only by their own desires for independent action but by a growing societal concern for individualism. The teacher's regular contact with youth, heightened by a wish to understand the workings of their emotional interest, makes the teacher highly susceptible to the values that motivate the young. And the young will in all probability continue to reject mass tradition and to eulogize a kind of personal determinism. All of this leads to the conclusion that, if we can, it would be wise to cast an eye to the future and to begin the cultivation of teachers who will be at home with the ethos of the next generation.

RADICAL REFORM

A number of theorists—if one judges their aggregate impact—are calling for a radical reform of the educational system itself. Indeed, several of the chapters in this volume press not for isolated tinkering but for major revolutions. Here, too, the innuendoes for teacher professional growth are obvious. The classic "curricular lag," in which a substantial period of time elapses between the development of a practice and its widespread adoption, is to a considerable extent attributable to our ineffectuality in updating teaching methodology. If the movement for radical reform gains momentum, the "lag" time will, of course, increase unless compensatory measures are taken.

Three other projections also reinforce the importance of teacher improvement. One has to do with the possibility of teacher specialization, to which Allen and Bush have already alluded, another with job accountability, and still another with what might be called precision teaching.

Management specialists have for years argued that the range of tasks performed by the typical teacher was far too great to permit uniformly high proficiency. Once regarded as impractical, the possibility of a rational division of labor among the teachers in a school is now viewed with considerably more optimism. If the staffing pattern permitted teachers to do the things at which they were best and to avoid the things at which they were poorest, consistently better teaching would take place. Such specialization would also reduce the complexities of professional growth, since as the range of teaching responsibilities is decreased, it is easier to develop strong competency. Greater specialization, admittedly, would necessitate a massive reorganization of the teaching system and could lead to excessive fragmentation and disjointedness. All things considered, however, the advantages would seem to outweigh the disadvantages, particularly if the division of labor were attacked with prudence.

As a consequence of our growing understanding of the way children learn, new instructional methodologies are far more precise than their precursors. Usually, less is left to chance and more is prescribed. Thus teacher training itself can become much more precise. Theoretically, at least, the possibility of guaranteeing pedagogical effectiveness will increase. If this is the case, the possibility of insisting upon demonstrable performance will increase correspondingly. In the absence of methods that under specified conditions brought predictable results, in-service education activities understandably were vague and nebulous. With the development of more systematic procedures, however, the retraining activities themselves can become equally systematic.

The issues that immediately arise in this connection are those of accountability. Rising educational costs and a mounting dissatisfaction (both rational and irrational) with the output of the schools have increased the clamor for assessment. Despite various forms of counterresistance, the odds are that the demand for rigorous evaluation will grow. The potential of measuring incremental gains in a child's learning, together with the possibility of linking these to the specific instruction he has received, will almost certainly lead to a greater emphasis on assessment. Concomitantly, there will be a greater effort to fix accountability upon the individual teacher. One may reasonably assume, as a consequence, that the teacher's desire to pass evaluative scrutiny will increase proportionately. And one may further assume that teachers themselves will solicit professional improvement activities that hold up under the same kind of assessment—activities that, in effect, guarantee greater teaching proficiency.

It seems to me that an additional aspect of professional improvement, related to group communication, has been overlooked:

the observation of skilled performance. In view of the amount of time and energy that most professions give to the analysis of technique, teaching's limited concern for artistic style seems extraordinary. It is not uncommon, for example, to find that in the whole of a career a teacher has spent less than a dozen hours watching a colleague perform. What little opportunity there is usually occurs at the time of student teaching, when inexperience can easily deprive the observation of meaning.

The benefits of analyzing expert performance go beyond a perception of what can be accomplished by a skilled practitioner. Not only can the observer study learners' reactions to various instructional tactics, but also he will find it almost impossible to avoid comparing his own maneuvers with what he sees someone else do. These comparisons obviously help to illuminate alternatives. In an earlier chapter, Meade refers to the benefits of collaborative criticism. Observation feeds such criticism both directly and indirectly. Of even greater consequence, however, it nurtures a sense of identity with a fine art, a pride in workmanship, and a deeper appreciation of style and technique. It serves, in short, to elevate teaching from an artless chore to an opportunity for imaginative virtuosity.

Before turning to the unfinished business of leadership, it might be well to summarize the underlying arguments that I have tried to outline. A teacher prepares to teach by spending four or five years at a training institution. There, in the present way of things, he learns a sampling of man's accumulated knowledge, something about the theory of education, and a few prescriptions regarding the art and science of teaching. Even if this preparation were adequate, and clearly it is not, his skills would become old-fashioned in the space of a very short time. Yet, after this brief apprenticeship, the usual teacher will labor at his craft for the next thirty to forty years. Thus, at the moment he leaves the professional school, the teacher is en route to a state of obsolescence. It has been said, with good reason, that the teacher who has not studied, say, chemistry during the past five years no longer is master of his subject and well may fill his students with misconceptions.

The need for perennial teacher education that counteracts

outdated and defective techniques is hardly unknown. In-service education has been a standard educational artifact for most of the twentieth century. That its benefits have been recognized, however, has not been of much consequence. Men tend to survive whatever does not bother them greatly, and the futility of most professional growth activities has not been much of a bother. Our prolonged complacency must be interrupted for several reasons. First, bad situations ought not go unremedied. Second, since a burgeoning program of research and development has greatly enlarged the possibilities for revitalizing education, teachers are likely to be reduced to using stale procedures more quickly than in the past. Third, the availability of new technology makes it possible to attack professional growth with greater efficiency and precision. And, fourth, there is much to suggest that teachers are best developed *after* they are in service rather than before.

THE TASKS OF LEADERSHIP

In view of all this, the dimensions of the needed reforms are obvious. To begin with, we must have a sharp reversal in our policies regarding the ongoing education of the practicing teacher. The veneration of professional growth must have its place among other educational priorities. The movement will require time, money, energy, and commitment. If we acknowledge that our schools can be no better than the teachers who serve them—and there seems to be no way to avoid this circumstance—an obsession with the continual betterment of teaching is essential. If we fail to overcome our deficiencies, we may well waste all the other efforts that have been invested in the educational enterprise.

Given a set of policies that reflect a serious concern for teacher improvement, other practical matters remain. We must, for example, develop effective models of successful growth programs. Teaching is a complex business, and one practitioner may be weakened by poor teaching methods, another by an inadequate knowledge supply, another by a faulty perception of his role, and still another by a predisposition to sociological prejudice. It therefore will be necessary to find activities through which various kinds of teaching difficulties can be rectified. We still know far too little about attitudinal change, about the best way to enhance instructional effectiveness, and about procedures that refurbish the teacher's sense of purpose. In addition, all these solutions must be integrated with a set of theoretical principles— principles, incidentally, that have not yet been adequately synthesized from the data of the social sciences. The unfinished business confronting school leadership is thus self-evident.

Finally, despite our incomplete grasp, we must nonetheless energize ourselves. I recently conducted teacher retraining experiments in some forty-five school districts throughout the nation. The results demonstrated that professional improvement can go hand in hand with professional service. Among other things, we were able to transfer successful teaching strategies from one teacher to another; to achieve measurable growth through programs that went on during the teaching day; and, perhaps of greatest importance, to make continuing education a conscious part of professional life. The modest success of these experiments suggests that the frontier is farther ahead than most of us suspect. If we were to do no more than capitalize upon the potentials now available, enormous improvements would take place. We must begin, perhaps, by recognizing that it is time to begin.

■ CLUES TO ACTION

I have devoted a part of my chapter to reiterating many of the major points that have been made throughout the book. Like many of the other writers, I contend that much of the finesse teachers need can be acquired only after they enter professional service. To repeat my earlier point, time is an indispensable element in the development of craftsmanship. The practitioner must engage in repeated practice, evaluate his progress in some systematic way, and cumulatively increase his adeptness.

I also cite the profession's failure to attend adequately to achievement motivation. I am concerned not only because the existing system tends to destroy much natural motivation, but also because we do not in any tangible way acknowledge either superior effort or superior performance. I believe that our failure to distinguish either very good or very bad teaching is debilitating to teacher morale, and I suggest that we re-examine the need to make greater use of both intrinsic and extrinsic reinforcement. And, in the same connection, I think that in-service education classically has suffered from the profession's inability to establish in teachers the expectation of continual growth. I suggest, in short, that a new conception of personnel management is sorely needed.

I also believe that there would be much profit in drawing more fully upon recent research dealing with the change of human behavior; the present approach to staff development, in view of these findings, is primitive. For example, since teachers obviously are influenced by their own attitudes, values, and beliefs, faulty perceptions may distort the effectiveness of teachers' technical skills. I therefore underscore Jackson's notion that teachers must have more time to think about the consequences of what they are doing. Our unwillingness to give due respect to teachers' attitudes and beliefs, moreover, has forced many teachers to strive toward teaching objectives with which they basically disagree. Under these circumstances, nothing we organize in the way of continuing teacher education will have much benefit.

I think it is unlikely that teachers will settle for a minor role in determining instructional policy. Rather, they will expect reasonable autonomy with respect to both their teaching and their own efforts to improve. If breakthroughs in the research on teaching make it possible to develop instructional programs that *guarantee* student learning, it will be possible to hold teachers more accountable for their results. Teachers, in turn, may then demand that their own professional growth programs *guarantee* the mastery of new knowledge and skill. If, in other words, it becomes possible to accurately rate teaching performance, it also will become possible to rate the usefulness of learning programs that the teachers themselves undergo.

I believe that much of the responsibility for improving the learning provisions for teachers in service will fall on educational leadership. Not only must school leaders explore new potentials in research and development, but also, of even greater importance, they must formulate a rational theory of teacher professional growth. In so doing, I suggest that leadership concern itself not only with effective ways of facilitating the acquisition of new capabilities, but with efforts to increase teachers' desire to perform somewhere near their optimal capacity. The wish to excel, I think, is not widely characteristic of the profession.

Thus we must so arrange matters that teachers develop a greater faith in the worth of their work. Along with many of the previous writers, I bet heavily on the useful by-products of teacher interaction. The opportunity to observe others, I think, often kindles an awareness of new alternatives. And the opportunity to observe and interact with the truly gifted practitioner leads to an authentic sense of professionalism.

■ OPERATIONAL IMPLICATIONS

1. Many teaching competencies can be acquired only after the teacher has become familiar with schools and with children. **Once he enters service, the teacher must work toward the mastery of specific skills through repeated practice and regular evaluation.**

2. An interest in fine teaching does not occur as a matter of course, and even when it exists, it may be dissipated by excessive organizational constraints or by weak morale. **We must make greater use of both intrinsic and extrinsic incentives to high achievement.**

3. The trained teacher's potential often is undermined by his fundamental disagreement with the instructional goals he is asked to accomplish. **In our programs of professional growth, we must give far more attention to the attitudes, values, and beliefs that influence the individual teacher's behavior.**

4. The responsibility for revitalizing the professional growth of teachers lies with educational leadership. **The principal, the supervisor, and the superintendent all must begin to regard the arrangement of procedures for improvement of teaching as one of their primary obligations.**

5. The observation of skilled teaching is a significant stimulation to professional growth. **The regular observation of master teachers should be a routine aspect of professional life.**

louis j. rubin

CHAPTER TWELVE

THE SELF-EVOLVING TEACHER

The eleven chapters that have preceded, and the fifty-five operational implications which they yielded, are hardly a blueprint for a revolution in teacher in-service education. Nonetheless, taken collectively, they do suggest that a revolution of some kind is sorely needed. Many of the deficiencies have been identified and a number of solutions prescribed. As editor, it would be presumptuous of me to pass judgment on the notions set forth by my colleagues, and to do no more than summarize their ideas would be useless redundancy. Accordingly, what follows is the exercise of an editor's privilege to have his "last word" and to opt for his own prejudices.

In expressing my point of view, I am inclined, early on, to note that while the volume deals with the perennial education of teachers, it also carries a powerful, if implicit, argument for the self-evolving administrator. Reduced to its essence, the argument implies that educational leaders must in the foreseeable future concern themselves with two critical matters: the acquisition of new insights regarding what has been called "people knowledge"—a knowledge of self and of others—and the search for formulas with which to manage systematic school reform.

In such a social organization as the school, the gifted leader most often is distinguished by the values he embraces, by the depth of his commitments, by his trust in those with whom he works, and by his fundamental humaneness. He must, in short, find the delicate balance between finesse and feeling. A knowledge of systems theory, as a case in point, is undoubtedly of advantage to a superintendent. The man who lacks it would do well to overcome his ignorance. Yet the administrator who allows his theoretical knowledge to weaken his human interactions, or the one who abdicates responsibility because of counterfeit kindness, also fails his charge. Followers prize leaders who demonstrate both strength and altruism; alone, neither seems to suffice. When our creative abilities are blunted by tyrannical manipulation, we are as disillusioned as we are when—out of either blindness or default—our leaders fail to provide us with needed guidance. We wish both to act upon our own judgment and to be protected from its inadequacies. Thus, it is the capacity to help others reach their fullest potential that is perhaps the greatest virtue of leadership.

In the management of an effective organization, the equilibrium between freedom and control is exceedingly fragile. For this reason, I suspect that, as the reader pursues the recommendations of the writers the largest danger is tilting too far on the side of authoritarianism. Not only is the power of office seductive, but the slowness of human change breeds impatience, and it often is difficult to avoid imposing one's personal convictions on others. The aim, therefore, is to acquire an administrative style in which there is a strong emphasis on shared decision making and on the exploitation of individuality. It is this kind of leadership that best nurtures the human capacity for self-directed growth.

In all likelihood, the greatest utility of the chapter implications is that of prompting imaginative action on the part of school leaders. While many of the points have been set in theory, the operational clues that they spawn are sufficiently practical that, in most cases, they can immediately be put to use. Some, of course, are open to dispute. However, in view of our limited knowledge of the subject, this is inevitable and perhaps even desirable. The administrator who wishes to test their worth not only can adapt them to his situation; he can modify them according to the dictates of his own experience and wisdom. If the results are disappointing, he at least will have demonstrated that some promising ideas fail the hard test of reality. And if others prove valuable, so much the better.

CONCEPT OF THE SELF-EVOLVING TEACHER

Because the concept of a self-evolving teacher has only recently become a matter of serious study, there is much that is unclear. As in any speculation that tries to clarify the unknown, when more is understood it will be necessary to discard some assumptions and formulate new ones. Much of this sorting out of good and bad ideas is best done by the practitioner in the field. Only the user really knows the true value of a tool. In a sense, then, the volume is an invitation to practical action.

If there is any one central controversy in the writing that has preceded, it is the long-standing conflict between utilitarianism and humanism. Whenever the question of changing human behavior arises, the morality and the efficacy of manipulation soon become dominant issues. Since maturation is the transition between a supporting environment and self-sufficiency, are we to trust in the sanative benefits of healthy experience, or are we to place our faith in the methodology of science and assume that human behavior—because it is predictable—can be shaped and controlled by calculated intervention? Precisely the same issue, of course, is at stake in the current debates regarding the ways teachers ought to work with children.

There are no sure answers, save for the fact that there are obvious advantages (and disadvantages) to each position. It would seem reasonable, therefore, to avoid an improvident dichotomy and, instead, to clarify the disparities and seek a solution to the dilemma.

Human behavior *is* lawful. No action is without its cause. Moreover, the causes—the forces that govern our conduct—are rarely simplistic. They constitute a complicated mix of perception, attitude, belief, value, and identity. All of these, however, are alterable, either by accident or design. An honest man, threatened with disaster, may lie, and a lazy teacher, facing dismissal, may suddenly become energetic. Reward and punishment are powerful incentives and they can indeed be used to control human action. Hence it must be acknowledged that conditioned reflex therapy, operant conditioning, and other forms of behavioral influence do work. Thus, if we wish, we can domesticate the spirit of teachers, ministers, and surgeons as effectively as we do dogs and parrots. What remains, then, is the question of whether such training is ethical or permanent, and whether it destroys something that is peculiarly human.

Sanative experience, in contrast, builds on the psychodynamics of self-evolution. Experience that increases insight, deepens awareness, enlarges one's sense of options, or that reduces the anxiety of change, is sanative. Such experience is the seminal element of growth. In authentic growth, each man directs his own evolution because, when the incidental trappings of circumstance are shorn away, each man is responsible only to himself. Our actions may be rational or irrational, constructive or destructive, self-aggrandizing or self-destroying, but, always, they are actions we choose for ourselves. Confronted with the same situation, a coward may choose flight and a hero, death, but each will choose. Since this is so, we do not mature if, for one reason or another, we persist in making choices that restrict our intellectual or emotional evolution. The teacher who cannot bear the risk of something new will choose the security of something old. A sanative experience, by reducing unnecessary constraints, facilitates the making of wise choices. And wise choices, in turn, nurture self-evolution.

Nonetheless, to facilitate is not to guarantee. A healthy experience can provide new insight or heightened awareness, but these are both essential and insufficient when the object is permanent change in behavior. They must be coupled with other requirements: with desire, with persistence, perhaps with courage, and, above all, with an efficient method of some kind. It is here that we can most easily distinguish between outer manipulation and inner self-determinism. One may *decide* to alter his behavior, as in self-evolution, or one may be *coerced* into changing, as in behavioral conditioning. But in either instance a pattern must occur: the desired behavior must be repeated over a period of time and the tendency to regress, to slip back into old habits, must be counteracted. The critical difference is that in self-evolution the driving forces are will and desire, whereas in manipulative conditioning they are reward and punishment. In the former the mechanism is self-imposed impulse; in the latter it is the compulsion of the conditioning system.

Consider, for example, a teacher who is inclined to lecture excessively in the classroom. If we measure the amount of teacher-talk each day, assign the teacher to extra after-school duty when it does not decrease, and allow him to go home early when it does, we may, over time, succeed in changing the teacher's behavior. It is not necessary that the teacher even understand why or how the conditioning operates. Thus we alter behavior but inhibit freedom. In effect, we convert the teacher into a machine whose output and function can be modified as required. If, in contrast, we arrange a series of experiences that enable him to perceive the benefits of limited lecturing—if we allow him to observe his own and his students' behavior on film, to visit the room of a teacher who is a gifted discussion leader, and to grasp the contrast between passive and active learning—we may also, over time, find that his behavior has changed. Insight, desire, and self-imposed effort serve as substitutes for manipulation. Crucially, however, the person's sense of freedom is strengthened rather than weakened. To be sure, self-directed growth may be somewhat less expedient and less certain, but in the long run it is likely to prove a far better investment: a machine must be readjusted over and over, whereas a liberated person sees to his own evolution.

All of this notwithstanding, whether the teacher is impelled by the threat of electric shock, or by the inner urge to make a greater contribution to the lives of his students, the quality of his work hangs on his technical skills. And technical skill comes only from painstaking and systematic attention. Put another way, deftness is developed through the correction of flaws. It is possible, after all, to be well intentioned, compassionate, free spirited—and yet clumsy. So, once we go beyond the matter of motivation and incentive, the mechanics of skill learning are the same. The teacher who wishes to master a new skill to better help his students and the one who wishes to master the skill to gain an extrinsic reward must both follow the fundamental principle of skill development: systematic practice and correction. There is no other way.

Among all that is unclear, consequently, four propositions seem reasonable. First, as educational reform occurs, teachers will need to acquire new skills; second, these skills can be mastered only through methodical and intelligent training; third, it is possible to determine whether or not such mastery has been attained; and, fourth, given a legitimate opportunity and a supporting environment, teachers will strive to improve without artificial manipulation.

MEANS AND ENDS

When all is said and done, the measure of a teacher's ability lies in what the students have learned. In working to increase the competence of his staff, therefore, the administrator ought to encourage teachers to aim for a precisely defined outcome. To the extent possible, the aim probably should be defined behaviorally. The more accurately the goal is perceived, the easier it is to determine whether or not it has been reached. The objective may be learning to solve quadratic equations or learning to identify the beliefs that separate political conservatism and radicalism, or it may have to do with helping a child increase his feeling of self-worth. Unless the teaching task is this explicit, it is difficult for teachers to assess their own effectiveness. The proposition that there be reasonable precision in defining teaching goals and in determining the extent to which they have been reached ought, however, to carry a qualifying note. Teaching objectives can be good or bad. And even when they are good, there normally are a variety of procedures through which they can be pursued. Moreover, administrative insistence upon precision and rigor does not mean that teachers cannot determine their own objectives; nor does it mean that these objectives should not deal with children's feelings as well as their intellects; and it does not free the administrator from his obligation to support teachers who have aims with which he may not wholly agree.

From this it follows logically that teachers should be continuously encouraged to assess the variance between their intent and their result. Any disparity between the two is an indicator of trouble. The search for such disparity serves a dual purpose: first, it permits the teacher to recognize a technical weakness; second, this recognition, in itself, is a strong inducement to improve.

My own studies lead me to believe that many teaching habits are difficult to alter. When a teacher is working with familiar instructional material—with a unit, say, that has been in use for several years—testing for disparity between aim and outcome can be noxious and spiritless. As a consequence, we have found it preferable to use a new, or at least different, instructional task for the purpose of developing a technical skill, and to work on one particular skill at a time. The object, to repeat, is not to prove that the teacher is good or bad, but to analyze form and style with a view toward planned reconstruction.

If it is apparent that a teacher is not accomplishing his goal, there obviously is something flawed about either his means or his ends. If, upon careful examination, the objectives seem reasonable, the next step is to diagnose the method and discover what is wrong. Many devices can be used for this kind of diagnostic analysis. Several systems have been devised, for example, which make it possible to examine the interaction between teacher and child. Often an otherwise skillful teacher will overemphasize a particular kind of learning, pursue objectives that are relatively insignificant, or inadvertently overlook opportunities to go beyond the lesson plan. To deal with these problems it is necessary to obtain an accurate record of the teacher's work so that clues to improvement can be obtained.

Whether or not a teacher can judge his own technical weaknesses accurately is thus far unclear. Some experimental programs now under development provide the teacher with a sort of structured guide for self-analysis; others make use of a trained collaborator who assists in the diagnosis. The video camera, as several of the earlier chapters suggest, is a powerful aid in analyzing performance. Once recorded on tape, the teacher's behavior can be dissected step by step. Although the analysis of a teaching episode seems complicated and cumbersome, in reality it is not. A number of experiments, carried on while I directed the Center for Coordinated Education, demonstrated rather conclusively that regular diagnosis can be made a routine part of professional life. The ways, both formal and informal, of appraising teaching effectiveness are virtually limitless. Whatever the means of diagnosis and whatever the conditions under which it occurs, the critical objective is to locate pedagogical weaknesses, whether they have to do with a faulty conceptual orientation, poor methodology, or an inadequate teaching environment.

Finally, of course, there is the need to initiate activities that will overcome the problems which have been noted. Some errors in form are relatively widespread (for example, many teachers do not stimulate sufficient learning excitement) and some are unique (a particular teacher will favor certain children during classroom discussions). Similarly, some errors, once recognized, are easy to remedy and others require repeated corrective treatment. In the main, teaching skills—like all other categories of skills—are the product of controlled practice. It is important to observe, in this connection, that the remediation of teaching errors and the mastery of new technical skills are greatly expedited when teachers perceive that their administrators genuinely value—and reward—improved performance. The extent of the administrator's interest in professional growth is reflected in the time and resources he makes available, in his acknowledgment of the improvement that has occurred, and, generally, in the importance he attaches to a continuous struggle for teaching artistry.

Apart from the diagnosis and correction of individual teaching errors, much can be done to assist an entire faculty to master a new technique. If, illustratively, a school decides to individualize instruction, it then becomes essential for the staff to develop a number of new skills. Teachers frequently learn more efficiently as a group than as individuals. The adept administrator, consequently, can engage his faculty, simultaneously, in the controlled practice of a new method. The advantages, particularly those of peer involvement and group reinforcement, are sizeable. These benefits notwithstanding, since there is considerable individual variation in the rate and degree of skill mastery, there is no way to avoid the systematic diagnosis and correction of errors.

The willingness to use a technique is inseparable from attitude and belief. For example, the teacher who has little faith in heuristic learning will not readily strive for the mastery of a teaching method based on student inquiry. Consequently, attitudinal change must sometimes precede the introduction of a technique. In this connection also, as social psychologists have long shown, the group can have a powerful influence upon the individual's belief system. To push the point a step further, not only is a teacher's faith in a particular method linked to his attitudes toward students and the educational process, but the use of a new technique often demands a corresponding increase in knowledge. As a case in point, the teacher who undertakes to lead an open discussion on a controversial issue must be better informed than the one who merely asks his students to answer the questions at the end of the chapter. All these factors must be taken into account in designing a program of teacher professional growth. I have stressed technique not because it is all that should be considered but because it is the culmination of teaching virtuosity. It suffices to say, therefore, that the mere possession of a skill is not enough; its potential also must be valued. In teaching, as elsewhere in life, we are likely to do whatever we think it is important to do.

The problems are difficult but they are far from insurmountable. When things go right, that is, when a school faculty is given good reason to value change, when the worth of a different technique is demonstrated effectively, when the conditions that underlie its use are made clear, and when teachers have a reasonable opportunity to become self-evolving, it is possible to make a dramatic improvement in the quality of teaching that goes on in a school.

Admittedly, the systematic introduction of a new teaching method involves a latent risk. No teaching method will work with every child or be used productively by every teacher. There is an abiding danger, therefore, that the mandatory use of a particular method will impose a massive rigidity on the school, inhibit imaginative teaching, quench creativity, and work to the harm of some children. The antidote, logically, lies in conceiving of staff development as a program that increases rather than decreases the number of teaching options available to the teacher. When a teacher commands several alternative ways of accomplishing a specified objective, the efficacy of classroom instruction rises markedly. Unhappily, this is rarely the case: more often than not, teachers have but one way of doing what they wish to do.

TRICKS OF THE TRADE

The concept of individual difference in learning has by now been widely accepted. The failure to learn in the vast majority of cases can be counteracted by altering the instructional method, the amount of reinforcement, or both. As more and more research evidence comes in, it is becoming apparent that with the next generation of teachers, the bench mark of master performance will lie in an extensive repertory of technique. Because the individualization of instruction cannot be divorced from a broad range of teaching methods, when a teacher is reduced to one way, individualization clearly is impossible. Facilitating the acquisition of diverse teaching methods, therefore, ought properly to be a major administrative concern. And, since precise behavioral targets are as applicable to the principal and superintendent as to the teacher, the administrator would be well advised to fix his sights and assess his results accordingly. In a typical faculty, the odds are that different teachers will use dissimilar procedures to pursue the same curricular goals. There are tricks to the teaching trade, and an effort to encourage teachers to share these tricks, opening themselves to new ways, will produce striking benefits.

One other aspect of individualizing teacher growth is of great significance. Normally, a teacher brings a unique personality and a particular set of role prejudices to his work. Together, these exert a profound influence on his classroom conduct. What the teacher feels, to put the problem another way, cannot be separated from what he does. Beliefs, however, are not immutable. When the crucial ingredients of growth—opportunity and incentive—are present, teachers will frequently alter their convictions, even long-standing ones. Thus, any experience that extends the teacher's perception of his role is exceedingly valuable. Whereas a teaching skill is developed through sustained classroom practice, the ability to make a lesson relevant to a learner depends upon a sensitivity to the student's nature and interests. Thus an important facet of professional growth lies in familiarizing teachers with the private lives of the youngsters with whom they work. Through a grasp of the kind of teaching actions that increase the connective tissue between what goes on in the classroom and what goes on outside, teachers can reformulate their sense of purpose and begin to see that subject matter can be used as a bridge between classroom and life. New insights arise—insights that set the stage for a better mix between formal lessons and the real problems of existence. In sum, the principal who makes it possible for his teachers to become more aware of the unmet needs of their students and, out of this awareness, to arrive at new commitments does much to defeat the dreariness that so often characterizes schooling. Given a legitimate chance—and the establishment's blessing—even the average teacher is capable of a striking change for the better.

Independence and inventiveness have virtually become lost arts in teaching. The fault, moreover, lies not with teachers but with the system. Inflexible courses of study, prescriptive teaching manuals, and an exaggerated reliance on expert opinion have caused teachers to doubt their own intuitiveness, to follow fashionable dogma mindlessly, and to become heavily dependent upon the recommendations of others —recommendations that, even when they are basically sound, often do not fit the atypical situation. Helping teachers to unfetter their own creativity would help matters a great deal. It is true that creative endeavor will produce more failures than successes. However, if the criteria for a successful solution are clear and there is a steadfast willingness to test against these criteria, it is easy to recognize and discard failures. Not only is experimentation an essential ingredient in self-growth; it also makes a monumental contribution to job satisfaction, to commitment, and to the gradual development of an individual style that is congruent with the teacher's nature and takes advantage of his unique attributes.

Order and organization are indispensable in the school. If one teaching method is clearly better than another, its widespread use ought to be encouraged. Within these provisions, however, there is abundant room for exception. Perhaps our obsessive dedication to rule and regulation, to bureaucratic routine and procedure, has contributed most to the defeat of individuality in teaching. It should not be so; instead of neutralizing difference, the sensible administrator exaggerates it; rather than encourage homogeneity, he seeks diversity.

Deciding when to hold to the pattern and when to deviate is admittedly a delicate administrative decision. Assume, for example, that a teacher does not do well at teaching fractions. There are at least three alternatives. One is to make the teacher more adept by providing training in a good method; another is to arrange for experiences which enable him to fashion a better method for himself; and still another is to free him from the need to teach fractions. Which choice is best depends upon circumstance. What is significant, however, is that a range of options does exist. We need not assume, in other words, that all teachers must be good at teaching fractions, or that they must teach in the same way. Even in the regimented world of industry, those who speak of "hired hands" eventually learn that different hands are better suited to different purposes.

A CURRICULUM-PROOF TEACHER

Good teaching is not likely to come about accidentally. As things now stand, there is a pervasive belief that professional growth is something to be "done and gotten over with." Precisely the opposite attitude should prevail; teachers should aspire toward sustained improvement, and policy makers should (1) make possible and (2) expect that the extension of competence be endless. There is an unfortunate tendency to assume that the possession of a license or credential and teaching ability are synonymous. What is worse, there is an even greater tendency to assume that teachers, once trained, can automatically adjust to whatever new teaching programs are invented. At a time when massive efforts to change instruction are under way, when new approaches to learning are being installed at an unprecedented pace, these assumptions constitute a great handicap. In point of fact, a carefully designed educational innovation is more likely to fail because of scant teacher preparation than because of any other inadequacy.

There is some validity to the traditional complaint of teachers that administrators have a penchant for in-service programs that lack practicality. It is relatively easy to offer an after-school lecture, but it is a good deal more difficult to arrange for the systematic mastery of a pedagogical skill. Administrators, too, have a justifiable grievance: for the most part, research and development specialists have not yet devised growth experiences that are practical and efficient. In the recent past, happily, there has been fresh interest in the problem and several developmental activities are under way. In the main, these deal with generic teaching skills that have wide utility throughout the curriculum. Little has been done, however, with respect to the special requirements posed by many of the new innovations, or with respect to methods for coping with such long-standing problems as the alienated learner, classroom management, the use of technological apparatus, and the like. Hence, a good many of the pragmatic concerns of the teachers are still ignored.

If we can turn the policy corner so that professional growth is regarded not as something the system does to the individual but rather as something the individual does to himself, the possibilities for nurturing a self-evolving teacher become more viable. To accomplish this transition we will need a realignment of some of our basic conceptions regarding the teacher's place in the educational hierarchy. For example, we will need to grant teachers greater independence of mind and spirit, and to parallel this freedom with increased responsibility for the quality of their work. As any seasoned administrator knows, poor teachers get unimpressive results with the best of methods, and gifted teachers get spectacular results with virtually any method. Instead of going after a teacher-proof curriculum, we would do better to work toward a curriculum-proof teacher. It will be necessary, also, to rid ourselves of the defensiveness that has become so characteristic of the teaching profession. Just as it is rare to find a professor who is willing to criticize the teaching of a colleague (and even more rare to find one who will acknowledge his own pedagogical shortcomings), it is difficult to find situations in which teachers have not been taught by the system to camouflage their difficulties. In a curious misinterpretation of the meaning of professional ethics, it generally is regarded as poor form to question the procedures of another teacher—however helpfully— or to admit a weakness to a co-worker. In our experiments we found that professional defensiveness can be eliminated when the leadership is not authoritarian and when candor is not treated punitively. The principal who inspires trust, who has the ego strength to concede his own mistakes, and who facilitates the cooperative invention of solutions to common teaching problems generally is able to establish an unrepressed working climate in his school. By and large, teachers are a highly committed lot; they are willing to do away with fraudulent ethics and deliberate deception almost as soon as the situation permits openness to be nonthreatening.

The independent teacher, accountable for the consequences of his teaching and profoundly interested in developing his expertness, will not be content with a script that programs his actions. What this means, of course, is that the demand for more professionalism must be matched with a larger participation in the control of the enterprise. The authentic professional finds it important to involve himself in the formulation of policy, the setting of priorities, the selection of objectives, and so on, since professionalism, by its very nature, is based upon conscientious self-discipline and deep involvement. If we expect teachers to become masters of their craft, to quest continually for greater proficiency, and to be aroused by their own imagination, we cannot at the same time expect that they willingly will submit to managerial domination. The fact that so many teachers function well below their potential suggests that their desire to excel is feeble because they have been deprived of a just partnership in the endeavor. Where there is a rational division of responsibility and both teacher and administrator are true professionals, neither is diminished by shared authority.

The use of evaluative procedures to measure instructional efficiency has, over the past decade or so, sponsored considerable dispute. While ratings are generally threatening to workers, it is my belief that a properly managed effort to assess performance need neither contribute to demoralization nor put the teacher at any disadvantage. By proper management I mean to imply a deliberate attempt to respect the limitations of assessment, to avoid a distortion of its usefulness, and to guard against the many ways in which it can be abused. The point in evaluating performance is not to create a basis for reward or punishment but to map desirable improvements. Beyond this, given clear criteria and respectable assessment instruments, there is no reason why teachers should not evaluate and analyze their own performance. The chief difficulties with analyzing performance are (a) that the evaluation devices may deal with a part rather than the whole of the teaching objectives (a teacher may teach children good reading skills and at the same time destroy their joy in reading) and (b) that the evaluation may rate achievement without illuminating specific strengths and weaknesses, thus depriving the teacher of corrective clues.

Independent action, professionalism, and accountability must, of course, go hand in hand. Performance standards have bedeviled school leaders since the first teacher gave a test to the first student. Insofar as the purpose of schooling is the education of the student, the yardstick for measuring the quality of instruction must lie in the amount and kind of learning that have taken place. It is common to assume that teachers are resistant to performance standards, but, in point of fact, student achievement tests are an accepted fixture in the classroom. Too, all teachers are rated by their administrators, at least during the early stages of their careers, and hence teaching performance routinely is assessed on one basis or another. The criteria used in the rating may or may not be significant, and the rater may use objective or subjective evidence, but assessment nevertheless does go on. It is not, after all, impossible to distinguish between good and bad work. Good lawyers win most of their cases, good physicians cure most of their patients, and good football coaches win most of their games. Similarly, first-rate teachers enable their students to learn more than second-rate ones. The real issues, consequently, have to do with the appropriateness of the standards, the effectiveness of the evaluative devices, and the use that is made of the results.

It is at once apparent that the extent of a child's learning will depend upon his own aptitude, his teacher's adeptness, and the richness of the environment. Able students often learn despite the impediment of a poor teacher, and children with limited ability can learn a great deal when they are guided by a skilled teacher. It is also obvious that performance cannot be assessed without reference to some objective. The objective may be predetermined (finding kindling for a fire) or it may be open-minded (combing the beach to see what turns up). If, in short, the target is to teach the student algebra, the amount of algebra learned is a valid test of the teacher's effectiveness. The teacher's empathy may help the student over an emotional hurdle; but if the learner does not master his algebra, at least part of the teaching performance must be regarded as ineffectual. On the other hand, if the objective is to help the student cope with an emotional disability, a different kind of assessment must be made. It is clear, therefore, that since we hold teachers accountable for many different kinds of objectives, we must judge their effectiveness on an equally large number of scales. This complexity notwithstanding, wherever we set an objective we can establish some form of criterion, and wherever we have a criterion we can make judgments about the quality of performance. Admittedly, it is simpler to measure knowledge of algebra than to determine emotional stability; nonetheless, there are indicators of a sort for both, and these can be used to at least estimate the teacher's impact upon the child. Do not mistake me here: to say that we can specify objectives and assess the extent to which they have been achieved does not imply that we can, or should, predetermine everything that happens in a learning encounter.

It is highly doubtful whether at the present time we could invoke a comprehensive system of teacher evaluation. Much developmental work stands between our present half-understanding and this goal. There is, however, much that an administrator can do to extend teachers' concern for quality performance. Toward this end, self-appraisal is perhaps more useful than external ratings. The attitude of mind that begets an interest in excellence also leads to pride in workmanship. For example, one gardener cuts grass and waters plants, whereas another aspires toward a lovely garden. In the same spirit, one teacher places lessons before the child and another makes a genuine effort to teach. If school leaders were to exaggerate the teacher's preoccupation with quality of performance, playing upon the human desire to do well, it is likely that there would be a profound difference in the classroom.

If the foregoing notions have merit, we do not have to look far to discover what must be done. New modes of behavior develop when particular actions are rehearsed again and again until they become an organic part of the individual. Accordingly, in-service education must begin with perception, kindle the freedom and the lust to change, then provide a method and support, and end in the confirmation of newborn habits. In this form, professional growth becomes self-transcendence.

Where the desired change is a matter of ritual, the difficulties are minor. Where it is a matter of value, or belief, or master craftsmanship, there is no easy way. The individual must fend for himself, negotiating among the available choices and anticipating that good intent must be conjoined with determination, that the chief rewards will come in the shape of intrinsic satisfaction, that success is not inevitable and the goal not permanent, that change is never free from stress, that skills enlarge with practice and atrophy with neglect, and that despite his best efforts he may fall short with some of his students. Even in the face of these risks, however, the vast majority of teachers will accept the odds if there is a reasonable opportunity to grow. They will accept them because the alternative is to be deprived of satisfying labor and to remain inert.

INDEX